feather
craft

feather
craft

The Amazing Birds and Feathers Used in Classic Salmon Flies

KEVIN W. ERICKSON

STACKPOLE
BOOKS

Lanham • Boulder • New York • London

Published by Stackpole Books
An imprint of Globe Pequot
Trade Division of The Rowman & Littlefield Publishing Group, Inc.
4501 Forbes Boulevard, Suite 200, Lanham, Maryland 20706

Distributed by NATIONAL BOOK NETWORK
800-462-6420

All photographs and illustrations by the author
Bird illustrations by Allison McClay

British Library Cataloguing in Publication Information available
Library of Congress Cataloging-in-Publication Data available

ISBN 978-0-8117-1779-3 (hardcover)
ISBN 978-0-8117-6545-9 (e-book)

♾™ The paper used in this publication meets the minimum requirements of American
National Standard for Information Sciences—Permanence of Paper for Printed Library
Materials, ANSI/NISO Z39.48-1992.

Printed in the United States of America

Dedicated to my family:
My mother Martha, father Leo, sister Linda, brothers Mark and Joel.
All supported, encouraged, and put up with me when the fly-fishing and fly-tying
bug bit hard and never let go. Miss you, Mom, Dad, and Mark.

And dedicated to Betty Jo, for whom Jo's Jewel was designed and named.
My better half, best friend, love of my life. She likewise always encourages and supports all
of my many endeavors—especially if they involve an outing to the Oregon Coast.

Contents

Acknowledgments

Many thanks are due to many people for their help in bringing this work to life.

First to thank is William Chinn Jr., who is recognized as one of the best classic salmon fly tiers of any era. I was fortunate that Bill lived close enough to the fly shops I worked at and would come by and share his latest creations with me. His trademark small wooden fly boxes lined with sheepskin were always a great showcase for his amazing flies. Dave McNeese put it best when he told me that "seeing Bill's flies was like getting to see Marilyn Monroe in the nude." His flies are works of art, and his style of tying always made the fly look as though it were flowing through the current even when standing still. I credit Bill with inspiring me to try tying the classics, and while I still have a long way to go to rise to his level, I appreciate his sharing his flies and tips and tricks. Some images of Bill's inspirational works appear on this page.

The Champion

The Captain

The Jock Scott

Also a *big* thanks to Bill Bakke for his wonderful foreword.

Thanks to Don Nelson, owner of River City Fly Shop in Beaverton, Oregon. His selection of materials rivals any shop anywhere. Thanks for letting me hang around the shop so much that you finally put me to work teaching classes—which I have always enjoyed.

Thanks to the Kaufmanns—Randall, Mary, Lance, Tresa, and Oda—for many years of fun working together; all of the trips and adventures at Christmas Island, Casa Blanca, Montana, Idaho, and elsewhere; and for sharing your knowledge, expertise, and above all friendship over the years.

Thanks to Doug Millsap, owner of Featherfreak .com, for his excellent materials, many of which were used in the making of the flies herein. I always appreciated his critiques, input, and encouragement in this project. Find his offerings at www .featherfreak.com.

Thanks to David and Elizabeth Johnson. Dave has shared many insights on fly fishing and tying over the years, including his amazing fish-catching creation called the Medusa. See the Medusa and more at www.flytyking.com. And thanks Elizabeth, for being so special and sharing Dave with us all.

Thanks to John and Amy Hazel, owners of Deschutes Angler in Maupin, Oregon, on the web at www.deschutesangler.com. Thanks, John, for the many trips to "The Feeders" on the East Fork for sea-run cutts. Lots of good memories of when the March Browns were popping and the big fish were sipping. John and Amy have always been great friends, plus they're expert anglers and have a nice fly shop with a good selection of conventional and classic tying materials.

Thanks Brian O'Keefe, a fabulous photographer who inspired me to strive to learn how to get photos as dramatic in form and color as his. I'm still trying to get there, and it's been a fun trip.

Thanks also to longtime best friends Gregory Smith and Shawn MacFarlane, fishing buddies who always encouraged me to "go out and field test" my latest patterns of any type with them. Thanks for the great trips on the Deschutes, Nunnally and Lenice Lakes, Davis Lake, the East Fork Lewis, Washougal, Kalama (especially the infamous "Raisin Bagel Run"), and so many other places too numerous to mention. Our trips were always fun and educational as we compared various patterns each had tied and shared time on the water and at the campsite. Our tying sessions helped get me to where I am today.

Introduction

Whom is this book for, and what is it all about? This book is for anyone who likes birds, feathers, fishing flies, vivid colors and patterns, photography, and beautiful art—in other words, just about everyone! The focus is on the birds and their feathers and how the feathers are utilized to make classic salmon flies for fishing.

Classic salmon flies—or classic full-dressed Atlantic salmon flies, as they are also more formally known—are considered the "high art" of fly tying, often combining a mix of exotic furs, yarns, flosses, feathers, and other materials in a formal design intended to catch the eye of the angler as much or more than the eye of the fish. Tied in hand, by hand, from the 17th century to today, some classic salmon flies contain up to 30 or more materials in one fly. The finished flies are a combination of incredible natural beauty and inspired human design and craftsmanship, often bordering on fine art as much as or more than a fishing lure.

In this book, complete step-by-step, start-to-finish instructions and photos of how to tie each classic salmon fly are included. They show how the flies are made for those who've never seen the process before and aid those tiers wanting to duplicate the flies shown herein. The method of wrapping thread around the hook and the materials to make the fly have remained the same over the last five centuries (yes, since around the year 1500) regardless of the type of fly you are creating, whether for salmon, trout, bass, or any other species in fresh or salt water. Just vary the materials used and the sequence in which they are attached to the hook, and you have an infinite number of combinations limited only by the imagination.

Whether you are an avid fly tier or have never before seen how a fishing fly is made, there is something here for you. You will see many examples of what is often considered the "art and science" of fly tying, spotlighting the beauty of nature and the various ways the feathers are used.

The birds and their feathers come in an incredible array of sizes, shapes, textures, and colors. You would never know so many different birds exist and wouldn't normally encounter them unless you were active in tying classic salmon flies or were an avid bird enthusiast dedicated to searching out the most exotic species imaginable. Evolution has produced a huge diversity of species and subspecies with amazing differences and yet similarities in all. After 40 years of tying flies, I still find it fascinating that the structure of the feathers where fibers from totally different birds can be joined or "married" together as if the combination came from one single bird.

As many of these exotic materials are both difficult and expensive to obtain today, I'll provide a list of fair to great substitutes and where to get them. This will encourage you to tie and even fish these flies and many others. A good number of the substitutes are even better than the originals, having better marrying qualities and better coloration and feather/fiber length than the originally used genuine feathers.

Those interested in photography will learn what equipment was used, how the photos were set up, and how they were taken. Anyone wanting to take sharp, clear photos with good color and depth of field will find details (see "About the Photography," page 263) to help them in their efforts. You will also see some top-notch artwork provided by Portland, Oregon–area artist Allison McClay. I wanted an Old World look and feel for the images: an accurate representation of the bird and feathers, yet an artistic rendering of a live bird to show what the source of the feathers looks like. She exceeded my hopes and expectations and produced outstanding images.

Foreword: Conservation of the Birds and Fisheries

Conservation is important in fly tying as well as fishing. I learned about that connection from Roderick Haig-Brown's books where rivers, their unique character and fish, shaped how one fishes and the patterns of flies that seem to make sense. At the fly tier's bench one encounters conservation through materials like feathers used to dress a certain pattern. It can even be extended to hooks and tinsel. I have been looking for a Hardy salmon hook for years because I like the shape and gape, and for fine flat French silver tinsel. But these are manufactured items, products of a time and purpose, while the feathers are of living Nature. Many birds that had the feathers called for in a dressing are now rare and off-limits to the tier, or worse, extinct.

There are conservation efforts to save the kori bustard population and replenish their abundance in the wild. This work is the concern and purpose of the Kori Species Survival Plan mentioned in this book. There are also conservation efforts to save and prevent the extinction of the salmonids so that these animals are once again resilient and productive in a constantly changing environment. I founded the Native Fish Society to address those issues and what seem to be intractable problems of native fish management. These concerns can come together at the fly tier's bench. The conservation of birds and salmonids have common problems related to overuse and loss of habitats that sustain them. They each have an evolutionary history that extends back in time millions of years. The salmon swam in rivers where saber-toothed tigers and mastodons drank, and it is possible to trace the feathers in your treasured collection to the age of dinosaurs.

There is a lot to be said about keeping the problems of conservation separate from one's time tying flies and fishing favorite water. They are certainly connected, but not all the time. When I am tying a new pattern for summer steelhead, I am thinking of that time when I saw a strong fish move in the deep emerald current. It helps to know the preferences of the moment for trout, steelhead, Pacific salmon, and Atlantic salmon when on the water so that it is possible to address the variables and hope for success. What I do not comprehend is not moving from the fascination of fishing and the catch to caring about the future of a river and its fish so that there is a future, even if it is not for you but for others.

When I walked into Chuck Campbell's office at the Oregon Game Commission in the 1960s and asked him why the Wind River steelhead are larger than those in the Deschutes, he pointed me to the library in his office and I began to read the scientific literature for the answer. I did not realize it at the time, but my fishing experience had introduced me to a life's work: Life-history diversity of fish in their home rivers is important. If we would only protect and appreciate what we have, the fish and experience can be maintained beyond our time.

Like Haig-Brown I started out with the worm, and in the case of the invasive carp, the dough ball. I eventually learned that carp take a dry fly, and fishing a fly for trout and steelhead is more interesting. Having a fish take a fly is perhaps less mechanical, for one works with the flow of the water and must learn how to use the line to fish effectively. I learned that a Thor or a Skykomish Sunrise is not necessary to catch a steelhead. Certainly the trout are selective for size, color, and presentation, if they are interested at all. Steelhead are more likely to take a wee fly than a large one when the water is warmer. Having a steelhead take a size 12 or even one dressed on a 16 hook is not only interesting, but can be more productive.

A local, long-standing fly-fishing club has a remarkable collection of books, rods, flies, and art with considerable historical importance. It is truly a treasure in a safe place. Looking through it, it occurred to me that the rivers and their fish that this collection bring to mind are not safe or well protected, even though they are a treasure and the source for all this memorabilia. We can fish, invent flies, re-create the historic patterns, and enjoy the creation of flies for art's sake, but we have not been able to hold on to the rivers and fish that inspire it all. That thought caused me to organize for the fish and rely on anglers and many who do not fish to help protect what remains of our wild native fish and their rivers.

Because salmonids are locally adapting to the rivers of their birth, they are tuned to the ecological and historic conditions of their home rivers. They are constantly perfecting themselves as they cope with changes in their landscape to remain productive and resilient. Therefore, it makes sense to accept the truth of salmonids and their story of survival over millions of years by focusing conservation on each watershed and its fish. But that is not how government managers view these animals. For them it is easier and less expensive to manage clusters of rivers and salmonids as if they were the same, something called aggregate management. That approach simply means that native wild populations disappear. But no problem! When the wild fish decline, they can be replaced with hatchery fish. Managers even say that we can recover wild fish with hatchery fish, ignoring the fact that human selection is different from that of Nature.

In 1875 the first Fish Commissioner for the United States, Spencer Baird, said that regulation of harvest and protection of habitat is no longer necessary because the supply of salmon can be maintained through artificial production—hatcheries. Development interests and politicians breathed a significant sigh of relief, for now watersheds and the entire landscape can be exploited and the vast salmon runs will flourish. Even though Mr. Baird had not a shred of proof to support his conviction, it became the cultural motive of an entire country to cut the forests, graze the watersheds, build the dams, and irrigate the farms without consequence. Now with most wild native salmon and steelhead protected by the Endangered Species Act, one would expect a change in our cultural obsession to manufacture salmon like we do cars and brown shoes.

In 1805 Lewis and Clark encountered the Columbia River watershed when they came over the Bitterroots into the Clearwater. While they were constantly hungry, they soon learned that bear meat was not pleasant, for it had the taste of old salmon. They opened the way for settlement and the fur trade. The first to go were the beavers and the salmon habitat they created. Even the border between Canada and the United States was decided because the British were unable to catch a salmon on the fly, even though the rivers were filled with them.

Since 1805 at least 40 percent of the historic salmon and steelhead habitat in the Columbia basin is no longer accessible to them. The Columbia River once supported an estimated 16 million wild salmon, an estimate that probably falls well short of the actual truth. Since the late 1970s more than $14 billion has been spent to rebuild the salmon runs, but the modest rebuilding goal of 5 million fish has eluded those spending these public funds. We have continued to replace the wild salmon with hatcheries and to invest in habitat restoration that cannot keep pace with its degradation.

A wake-up bell rang a few years ago on the Connecticut River, the focus of Atlantic salmon restoration, when the US Fish and Wildlife Service concluded that the expense was just too much; the cost-to-benefit ratio was no longer worth it. The Connecticut experience provides an important lesson: Once you lose the wild salmon, recovery is not possible. The Penobscot salmon didn't work in the Connecticut nor did fish from other rivers.

In the Northwest we have learned through research in genetics and evaluation of hatchery fish impacts on wild salmonids, that hatcheries have a fatal flaw and are not a reliable recovery option for wild salmonids. The problem is that the government fish managers are still trying to make the hatcheries work based on the 1875 false premise offered by Commissioner Baird.

So why does hatchery technology have such a strong hold on government agencies and the public? Why are they immune to scientific information? There are a few obvious impediments to proper wild salmonid management:

1. The agencies came online under the influence of the Baird premise, bolstered by organized hatchery advocates such as the American Fisheries Society promoting a hatchery solution to declining salmon runs exploited by commercial fisheries and corporate canneries. The first Columbia River hatchery was built in Oregon on the Clackamas River in 1877 at the insistence of the cannery owners.

2. Political support from state and federal lawmakers are more interested in mitigating damage than protecting salmon habitat, a continuing commitment by politicians. This approach leaves the door open to exploit watersheds for commercial development sustained by the myth that damaged salmon runs can be replaced with hatchery fish.

3. Fishery management agencies have secured huge subsidies from pubic funds distributed by politicians.

4. The fishery agencies are organized to produce a product for public and commercial consumption rather than focused on conservation so that wild salmonids and the future of the fishery is sustainable.

The fishery managers escape public accountability for hatcheries because the cost to produce a hatchery fish that is harvested is never displayed or discussed. The agencies justify the hatchery program based on the benefits it provides, not the cost to provide them. In 2002 the Independent Economic Advisory Board (IEAB), for the first time, evaluated how much it cost to produce a harvested salmon, and in some cases that cost exceeded over $100,000. That news caused a ripple of panic in the fishery agencies, and when the IEAB proposed to do a complete economic evaluation of Columbia River hatcheries, the funding for it vanished.

To change how we manage salmonids requires social change in a culture that defines natural resources as products for commercial markets. As John Livingston said, "Once a thing is perceived as having some utility—any utility—and is thus perceived as a 'resource,' its depletion is only a matter of time."

Salmon conservation is of national importance because at least on the West Coast, there are still wild native salmonids and productive rivers from which it is possible make a stand and create an outcome that is not extinction. It will require a shift in our perspective where we respect wild salmonids and protect their home rivers. The public, through political initiatives, has persistently forced fishery managers to protect wild salmon. These actions go back to the 1940s and recently through petitioning the government to protect wild salmonids as endangered species.

I have my favorite rivers and have developed flies that seem to be wonderfully effective on them. I have learned from those rivers the habits of the fish, even which rock they like to hold by. I have been taught by the river and its fish about how to be successful some of the time. My affection and knowledge is place-based, attached to certain rivers. I fish other places and use what I have learned in those places, but I always return to my home streams. Place-based experiences and management go hand in hand. It makes sense because we become emotionally attached to rivers and the special experiences they give us, just as the salmon are adapting continuously to their home rivers. With the extinction of a salmon or steelhead run, there is an extinction of experience, commitment, and respect for rivers and their fish. Our job is to stop that erosion, for it is not inevitable.

Willis Rich's tagging experiments on Pacific salmon beginning in 1916 resulted in the concept of the Home Stream Theory for salmon, saying, "The results have shown beyond any reasonable doubt that the marked fish return in overwhelming proportions to the stream and even to the tributary in which they spent the early part of their existence. In the conservation of any natural biological resource it may, I believe, be considered self-evident that the population must be the unit to be treated. Diverse evidence points so clearly to the existence of local, self-perpetuating populations in the Pacific salmon that any hypotheses that do not conform must be subject to considerable doubt."

Contemporary fishery management has accepted Rich's premise: Salmon do return to their natal stream to spawn and rear their young. What is lacking is attention to conservation of populations by species in each watershed. This is called river-specific management. Canadian and European salmon managers have adopted conservation objectives by river and stock, and in some cases hatchery salmon releases have been terminated for the purpose of protecting the natural wild salmon.

Management of Pacific salmon and steelhead will have to be focused on local populations if they are to be recovered and sustained. To avoid extinction due to inappropriate management, changes need to be made. These include (1) setting a wild spawner abundance objective by species in each watershed, (2) establishing a nutrient enrichment target from carcasses of naturally spawning wild fish, (3) establishing land and water management agreements in each watershed to protect and improve the life cycle rearing requirements of wild salmonids, (4) controlling hatchery fish genetic and ecological impacts on wild salmonids, (5) establishing quantifiable criteria to monitor and evaluate conservation actions, (6) stopping kill fisheries on juveniles, (7) eliminating transfers of fish and eggs among watersheds, and (8) maintaining the life-history diversity of locally adapting populations of salmonids.

Restoring wild birds such as the kori bustard and wild salmon have a lot in common—maintaining the diversity of locally adapting populations and the habitats that sustain them—and that requires holding those in charge of management accountable.

—Bill Bakke
December 29, 2015

Author's Note: Bill Bakke is Director of Science and Conservation and the founder of the Native Fish Society. Their mission statement is simple: "Guided by the best available science, Native Fish Society advocates for the recovery of wild, native fish and promotes the stewardship of the habitats that sustain them." The society's goal has been to advance the recovery and protection of self-sustaining wild, native fish populations in the Pacific Northwest by working to enact fish-friendly policies and promote stewardship of their habitats in their home waters.

Bill is also an avid fly angler and has a well-deserved reputation as an expert in the sport. His take on the fisheries and the interrelationship of all things wild, from fish to birds and the environment both need to thrive, provides a great perspective for the birds discussed herein. Please visit and support the Native Fish Society at www.nativefishsociety.org.

The Birds
and Their Feathers

This is a celebration of the amazing way nature has evolved and diversified the birds of the world. Species with elaborate and yet intricate colors. Feathers of many varied sizes, shapes, and structures, all used for day-to-day life and a means to survival.

Birds are indeed amazing in both their differences and at the same time their similarities. Even in the same species, the difference between male and female birds is dramatic. Males are often more colorful or ornamented than females in most, but not all, bird species. The term for this difference is "sexual dimorphism," where the two sexes of the same species exhibit different characteristics. This occurs in many animals, insects, birds, and some plants. Differences may include secondary characteristics such as size, color, and markings and may also include behavioral differences.

Charles Darwin developed much of the theory that helps explain this. Sexual selection is responsible for many of the features unique to one sex in a given species. These features include those acting as ornaments that attract the attention of females, such as long tails on birds. Darwin concluded that color differences between sexes in birds (also known as sexual dichromatism) result largely from female preference for bright colors in males. Color can also aid individuals in recognizing members of their own species. And in species that are not good

to eat, colors can provide a warning to potential predators. Color is also used in contests between males over mates or resources such as territory. Conspicuous colors can help show that an area is already occupied and that the occupant is in good condition and prepared to fight. One example of this difference is the Lady Amherst pheasant.

The male is a mix of bright colors with orange, green, red, and vivid black-and-white feathers throughout. These colors both attract a mate and dissuade potential rivals from competing for a mate or even attempting to enter his territory.

Meanwhile, the female is a very drab tan-and-brown-striped bird. Incubating and raising the young often exposes female birds to more predators, so a subdued coloration provides much-needed camouflage in exposed nesting areas.

Mature birds are an impressive example of evolutionary development. As all evolved from the same early ancestors and have a common lineage, they share characteristics in their physical makeup, including the feathers. This commonality is such that even vastly different birds half a world apart have the same feather structure. See "Anatomy of a Feather and a Fly," chapter 2, for more detail.

With this being the case, fibers from the tail of an African bustard can be joined, or "married," to fibers from the same side of a wing feather from an Indian peacock, and these can then be joined

Male Lady Amherst pheasant back

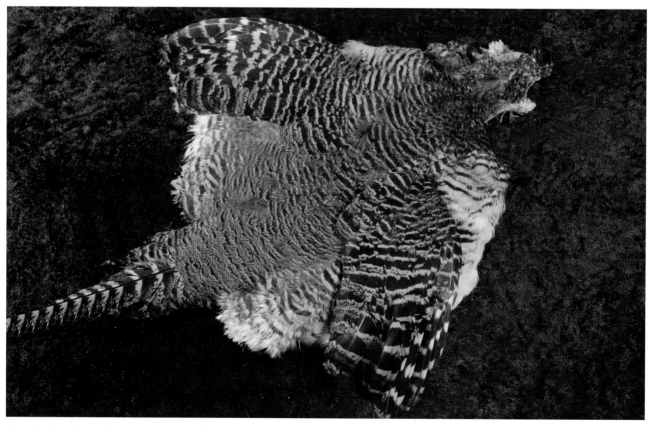

Female Lady Amherst pheasant skin

to the tail of an American turkey, and these can all be joined to fibers from a Chinese pheasant's tail, and so on. When all are joined together, it is as if the single strip came off of one strange bird with a wild pattern and color scheme. And yet many feathers from various birds are radically different in makeup and texture from one another.

While the feathers used in classic salmon flies are amazing, in some cases the birds they are found on are rare and becoming more limited in availability. Deforestation and other habitat loss is a big contributor. Back in the 1700s and 1800s, the millinery (women's head apparel) trade expanded with devastating results. Many species from the incredible birds of paradise to common crows declined, with whole birds sometimes mounted and displayed on a hat as the haute couture of the times. Overhunting and the feather trade also contributed to declining populations in the wild. All of these factors together pushed many species to the brink of extinction.

So while the feathers used herein are authentic, the intent is to show what the actual, traditional materials look like in size, shape, and color. That being the case, a big emphasis I hope to share and encourage you to undertake is the pursuit of readily available feathers, natural or dyed, as substitutes. The classics are challenging enough to tie, but you won't even want to try if you can't find the correct material or a suitable alternative. Excellent substitutes are now available in several forms for those wanting to try their hand at tying a quality fly suitable for framing as the art form they are.

But even beyond that, what about adding a few "fancy feathers" to your fly box for your next steelhead or salmon outing? For example, my "feather sandwich" substitute for the wings, along with some dyed pheasant, can have you tying several Black Argus flies for pennies apiece to actually fish with on your next outing. What an idea! And you won't even try to dive in and retrieve one if you lose it.

I have gradually collected materials over the last 40-plus years and have always tried to confirm their source as legal, such as from bird breeders, historical taxidermy mounts, or ethical resellers with a known reputation for helping with preservation. At times, I had my reservations and wouldn't buy materials from a suspect source. You can somewhat tell what smells right and what doesn't. Use your best judgment on sources and if in doubt, pass. There are several good, reputable sources for materials to get you started and keep you going. Don't expect genuine or substitute materials to be cheap, but many can provide a near-lifetime supply unless you are tying a lot of patterns repeatedly or wasting a lot of materials. Try to be conservative—even the substitute birds can be limited as a source of just the right type of feather.

An example of a quality dealer of genuine and substitute materials is Featherfreak.com, which is run by Doug Millsap. Doug sources materials from known suppliers and scours estate sales and other historical precedent sources for his materials. See his site at www.featherfreak.com. Another great supplier is FeathersMC (www.feathersmc.com). John McLain founded FeathersMC in July 2004 and has been a strong contributor and advocate for the Kori SSP (Species Survival Plan). John actively distributes free kori bustard feathers and encourages donations to the program in return. It's a great win-win situation. The birds need our help, and you may get some feathers out of the deal. Be sure to see the "Organizations to Support" section at the back of the book and give our feathered friends a helping hand.

African Emerald Cuckoo

(*Chrysococcyx cupreus*)

Natural ranges	Sub-Saharan Africa
Habitat	Lowland forest areas throughout West Africa
Size	Averages 8.3 to 9.1 inches (21–23 cm) in length
Weight	Around 1.2 ounces (35 g)
Foods	Insects, such as butterflies, caterpillars, locusts, and ants

The African emerald cuckoo is an Old World cuckoo. It is a vividly colored bird with males having an overall brilliant metallic green plumage with a bright yellow lower breast and abdomen. The tail feathers are tipped with white. It has a short, slim bill and brown-orange eyes. The green plumage makes it blend in and remain well hidden in its surroundings and so it is heard more often than seen.

The feathers are varied in sizes from ¼ inch to 5 or 6 inches in the wings and tails. The amazing metallic green plumage is used in classic salmon flies as wings, veilings, shoulders, sides, and cheeks.

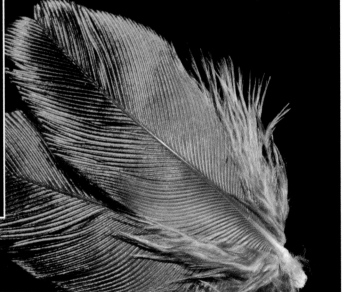

Left: African emerald cuckoo wing feathers

Right: African emerald cuckoo pair of body feathers

African Gray Crowned Crane

(*Balearica regulorum*)

Natural ranges	Equatorial Africa
Habitat	Wetlands including croplands, grasslands and open savannahs
Size	3 feet 4 inches (1 m) tall with a wingspan of 6 feet 6 inches (2 m)
Weight	7.7 pounds (3.5 kg)
Foods	Seeds, grasses, crops, insects, small fish, amphibians, and reptiles

African crowned cranes are considered "living fossils" among cranes. They have existed since the Eocene period from around 54 million years ago through the ice ages to present day.

These cranes are gregarious birds, spending time together and among grazing cattle, catching insects the cattle stir up while feeding and moving. When foraging alone, they stamp their feet when walking to scare up any available food items. Marshes and swamps are favorite areas to feed around for fish and amphibians. Unusual among cranes, African crowned cranes roost in trees. Large flocks gather and roost overnight in open trees.

They use their long legs for wading through the grasses and marshes. The feet are large, yet slender for balance. They live up to 20-plus years in the wild and twice as long in captivity.

Coloration varies slightly by species. Body plumage is mainly gray. The wings are also predominantly white, but contain feathers with a range of colors including the higly sought-after cinnamon primary quills. The head has a crown of stiff spiky barred feathers reminiscent of porcupine quills. The crown feathers are used in classic salmon and other flies for horns, wings, and throats. The body feathers are used for hackles and winging, and the cinnamon-colored wing quills are used in underwings and main wings—either simple strip or in married wings.

Crowned crane body feathers

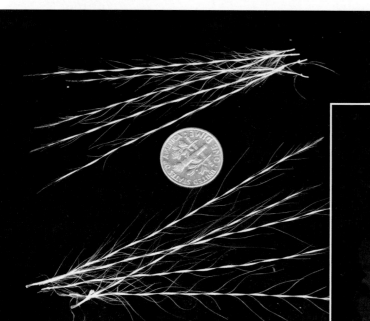

Above: Crowned crane body feather tips

Left: Crowned crane crest feathers

Right: Crowned crane cinnamon wing feather

THE BIRDS AND THEIR FEATHERS ▪ 7

Asian Kingfisher

(Halcyon smyrnensis)

Natural ranges	Asia from Turkey east through India to the Philippines
Habitat	Clean, clear waterways with trees and/or shrubs along the banks
Size	11 inches (28 cm) in length, with a wingspan of 12.5 inches (32 cm)
Weight	1.2 to 1.6 oz (34–46 g)
Foods	Small fish, reptiles, amphibians, crabs, small rodents

The Asian kingfisher, also known as the White-Breasted kingfisher or Smyrna kingfisher, is a tree-living kingfisher. Mainly living around waterways, it is often seen perched on a branch watching intently for a passing fish or other food item for which it can swiftly fly down and pluck out of the water. It can often be found well away from water, as well, when in search of food. The adult male is a large kingfisher, with a bright blue back, wings, and tail. Its head, shoulders, flanks, and lower body are chestnut dark cinnamon brown and the throat and breast are white. The large bill and legs are bright red, making a strikingly colored bird wherever seen. All kingfishers are important indicators of their freshwater environments' health. The highest densities of breeding birds are found in habitats with the highest water quality, so the presence of this bird indicates a healthy habitat area.

The bright blue flank and tail feathers are prized by fly tiers. The body and back feathers are often used as a substitute for the hard-to-find cotinga (blue chatterer) feathers.

Left: Asian kingfisher
Below: Asian kingfisher feather

Black Cockatoo, Red-Tailed

(*Calyptorhynchus banksii*)

Natural ranges	Australia
Habitat	Arid environments
Size	Around 24 inches (60 cm) in length
Weight	Males weigh between 1½ and 2 pounds (670–920 g) Females weigh slightly less at 1.25 to 1.75 pounds (615–870 g)
Foods	Eucalyptus seed and grains as well as larger gum fruits

The red-tailed black cockatoo is a large cockatoo native to Australia. Adult males have a unique pair of bright red sections on the tail that give the species its descriptive name. The species was first described in 1790 as *Psittacus banksii*, and named for English botanist Sir Joseph Banks. Other common names include Banksian black cockatoo or Banks' black cockatoo.

The red-tailed black cockatoo can live in captivity for up to fifty years. The male's plumage is overall black with a distinctive crest made up of long slender feathers from the forehead and extending back over the crown. The tail is also black with two bright red sections. Females are black with yellow-orange stripes in the tail and chest.

Salmon fly patterns calling for black cockatoo (referring to the female) are the Penpergwm Pet, the Cockatoo, the Highland Gem, and the Silver Spectre, among others. Used as sections in wings or singly as horns, the feather is unmistakable and a special addition to any fly. Also of note is the yellow-tailed black cockatoo (*Calyptorhynchus funereus*), used in married wing patterns as well.

Feathers from this bird were not used in the flies in this book, but are used in several other classic patterns.

Red-tailed black cockatoo
female tail with close-up

Red-tailed black cockatoo
male tail with close-up

Yellow-tailed black cockatoo
tail with close-up

Black Francolin

(*Francolinus francolinus*)

Natural ranges	Eastern Turkey through Iran and northeast India. They have been introduced to the Caucasus, Guam, and Hawaiian Islands.
Habitat	Thick vegetation, usually near water. Also croplands with cover, as well as higher brush, forest edges, and deeper grasslands.
Size	13 to 14½ inches (33–36 cm)
Weight	Up to 16 ounces (453 g)
Foods	Grain, grass seeds, berries, shoots, termites, ants, and other insects

The black francolin, also known formerly as the black partridge, is a gamebird in the pheasant family Phasianidae of the order Galliformes. It is a ground-dwelling bird similar to the chukars in habits. Black francolin have many varied feathers. Some are black with white spots. They graduate from matched pairs of feathers on the body with one white spot per feather to two, three, and, finally, four spots per feather. Some have two matched stripes over the length per feather and others on the flanks have white (or is it black?) striping. All are sought after for wings, cheeks, and veiling in varied patterns.

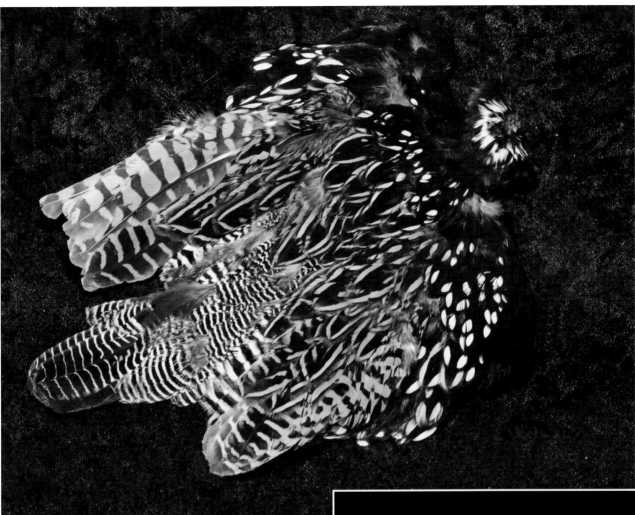

Black francolin skin

Above: Black francolin striped back feather
Top right: Black francolin four-spot feather
Bottom right: Black francolin barred flank feather

Blue Eared Pheasant (*Crossoptilon auritum*)

Natural ranges	Central and western China, northern Sichuan, Tibet, and northward into Gansu in China
Habitat	Coniferous forests at up to 11,500 feet elevation (approximately 3,500 m)
Size	Up to 3 feet 2 inches (96 cm) long
Weight	3 pounds, 10 ounces up to 5 pound 7 ounces (1650–2475 g)
Foods	Insects, bulbs, roots, seeds, and leaves

The blue eared pheasant is a large monotypic species (a genus consisting of only one single species). The blue eared pheasant is not endangered or threatened at this time.

These birds get their name from their overall color "blue" referring to the dark blue-gray body, wings, and tail. The head is topped with a soft black crown and long white ear coverts (feathers covering the ears) behind the eyes. One of the most common and numerous eared pheasants, they are a popular bird for hobbyists and bird fanciers to breed and raise.

For fly tiers, the long-fibered body, flank, and tail feathers make a good substitute for the gray heron used in the past in Spey flies. Spey flies are characterized by the long, flowing "hackle"—a feather wrapped around the hook. The fibers move well in the water, enticing fish to see the fly as a living food item.

Blue eared pheasant skin

Blue eared pheasant tail close-up

Cock of the Rock

Andean (*Rupicola peruviana*)
Guianan (*Rupicola rupicola*)

Natural ranges	Venezuela, Colombia, Ecuador, Peru, and Bolivia
Habitat	Forests, ravines, and near streams at up to 7,900 feet (2,400 m) elevation
Size	Average size 13 inches (32 cm)
Weight	8.3 ounces (235 g)
Foods	Fruits, insects, small reptiles, and frogs

The cock of the rock is a medium-size passerine bird of the cotinga family. It lives in a large natural range of about 100,000 square miles (260,000 km²) across. It typically stays in the lower and middle forest levels, but will range higher in fruiting trees and will sometimes enter and cross clearings.

The Andean cock of the rock is a medium-sized bird with a bright, vivid orange plumage. The Guianan cock of the rock is a close relative with slightly darker-colored plumage. It is this richly-colored plumage that draws the eye of the fly tier and the fish. Used in many patterns for wings, veilings, sides, and cheeks. The cock of the rock adds a bright touch to any fly it is used in.

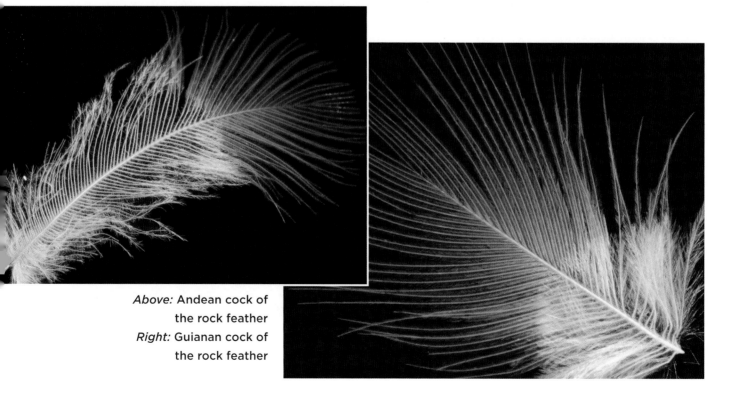

Above: Andean cock of the rock feather
Right: Guianan cock of the rock feather

Cotinga (Blue Chatterer)

Purple-breasted cotinga (*Cotinga cotinga*)
Spangled cotinga (*Cotinga cayana*)
Banded cotinga (*Cotinga maculate*)
Lovely cotinga (*Cotinga amabilis*)
Plum-throated cotinga (*Cotinga maynana*)
Turquoise cotinga (*Cotinga ridgwayi*)
Blue cotinga (*Cotinga nattererii*)

Natural ranges	Southern Mexico to southeastern Brazil
Habitat	Tropical rain forests
Size	7 to 9 inches (18–22 cm)
Weight	2.7 ounces (76 g)
Foods	Fruit and berries and, occasionally, small insects

Cotingas are among the most beautiful and brilliantly colored birds in nature. The males have bright blue plumage with areas of purple. The feathers physical structure refracts the light to give the blue color. See chapter 2, "The Anatomy of a Feather and a Fly," for details.

Blue chatterer is the common name used to describe a blue or sometimes purple feather found in many classic salmon fly patterns. They are often called for on the cheeks of the fly and sometimes as a veiling on the tail or body. A pattern called the Chatterer originated by Major John Traherne in the 1890s calls for this feather for the full length of the hook shank. In order to achieve the "furry" appearance, a lot of feathers are needed—sometimes as many as twenty per side.

Left: A pair of cotinga feathers close-up
Below: A pair of cotinga feathers with a dime

Crawford Kalij Pheasant

(*Lophura leucomelanos crawfurdi*)

Natural ranges	Nepal to western Thailand and introduced to Hawaii
Habitat	Forests and thickets
Size	Males 25 to 29 inches (63–74 cm) long
Weight	1 pound, 8 ounces to nearly 2 pounds (675–850 g)
Foods	Invertebrates, fruits, and berries

The Crawford Kalij pheasant is a beautifully marked bird with barred black and white feathers throughout. While the silver pheasant is colored white with thin black barring and the Lewis's pheasant is the opposite with black feathers with thin white barring, the Crawford is an even mix of white and black and is a perfect blend of the two colors. It has become a bird some breeders and hobbyists appreciate and find a striking addition to their flocks. Every feather is usable on classic salmon flies and other styles as well for tails, veilings, wings, shoulders, throats, and sides. Be sure to see Jon LeBretton's example using Crawford feathers, the Austie's Special on pages 106–7.

Crawford Kalij pheasant skin

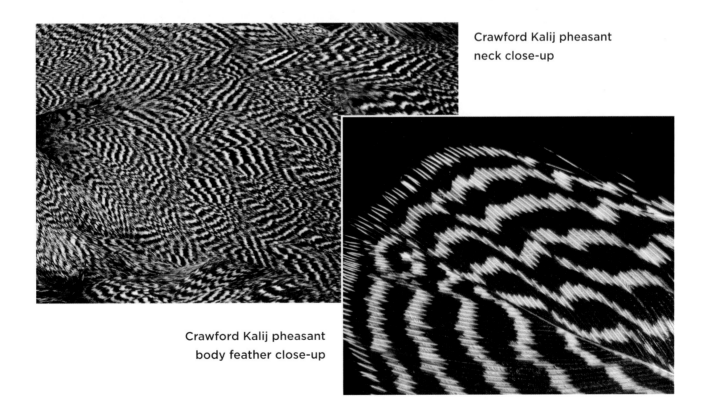

Crawford Kalij pheasant
neck close-up

Crawford Kalij pheasant
body feather close-up

Eastern Wild Turkey

(Meleagris gallopavo silvestris)

Natural ranges	Eastern United States from Maine in the north to northern Florida in the south and west as far as Michigan, Illinois, and Missouri. In Canada from southeastern Manitoba, Ontario, southwestern Quebec (including Pontiac and the lower half of the Western Quebec Seismic Zone), and the Maritime Provinces.
Habitat	Hardwood and mixed conifer-hardwood forests. They also like pastures, fields, orchards, and seasonal marshes.
Size	39 to 49 inches (100–125 cm) in length and with a full wingspan from 4 feet, 1 inch to 4 feet, 9 inches (1.25 to 1.44 m)
Weight	From 11 to 24 pounds (5–11 kg)
Foods	Acorns, beechnuts; fruits of dogwood, grape, black gum, wild cherry, blackberry, and huckleberrys; also ferns, greenbriar, and honeysuckle

This was the first turkey species Europeans encountered in the New World. Its range is one of the largest of all subspecies. As such, they are prolific, with populations ranging from 5.1 to 5.3 million birds. They were first named "forest turkey" in 1817. The wings of the adult male (or "tom" as it is called) are relatively small which leads to a lot of time spent on the ground, flying in short bursts when needed. While domesticated birds are the mainstay for Thanksgiving holiday, many still hunt these wild birds for the table. For fly tiers, virtually all feathers are used—especially the wings and tails. The white-tipped tail is used in the Jock Scott for the underwing. The remaining fibers are used in many simple strip patterns as underwings and married into main wings either as part of the original pattern or as a substitute for other birds. The domesticated white hen tails are highly sought after to dye in solid colors as alternatives to the shorter-fibered goose and swan. They can also be dyed in a special manner to become outstanding substitutes for other exotic birds; see chapter 4, "Substitute Feathers," at the back of the book.

Eastern wild turkey tail fan
Left: Eastern wild turkey tail tip
Bottom left: Eastern wild turkey bronze-tipped tail fan

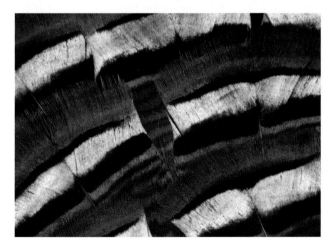

Domestic hen turkey tail dyed and natural tan tails

Emu (*Dromaius novaehollandiae*)

Natural ranges	Australia
Habitat	Sclerophyll forest, savannah woodlands, and grasslands
Size	6 feet 3 inches (1.9 m) in height
Weight	40 to 132 pounds (18 to 60 kg)
Foods	Plants and insects, including grasshoppers, crickets, beetles, and cockroaches

The emu is the second-largest living bird in the world by height, after its relative, the ostrich. Emus are soft-feathered, brown, flightless birds with long necks and legs. They can travel great distances, and can sprint at 30 mph (50 km/h) when necessary. Small stones are swallowed with their food to assist in the grinding up and digestion of their diet. They may have as much as 1.6 pounds (745 g) in their gizzards at one time.

A unique feature of the emu feather is the double rachis emerging from a single shaft. Both of the rachises have the same length. Feathers of emus are most often dyed for fly-tying use as hackles (feathers wrapped around the hook) or as wings on classic salmon flies.

Emu feathers

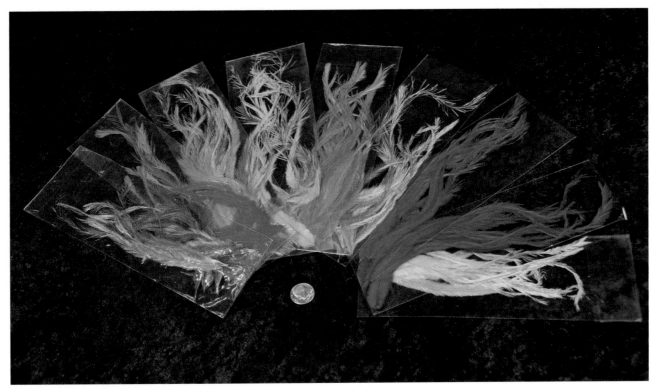

Emu feathers dyed in various colors

Eurasian Bittern (*Botaurus stellaris*)

Natural ranges	Europe, Asia, and Africa
Habitat	Reed beds and thick vegetation near water bodies
Size	27 to 32 inches (69–81 cm) in length with a wingspan of 39 to 51 inches (100–130 cm)
Weight	1 pound, 12 ounces to 4 pounds, 5 ounces (0.87–1.94 kg)
Foods	Fish, small mammals, amphibians, crustaceans, and insects

The Eurasian bittern, or great bittern, is a wading bird in the bittern subfamily Botaurinae of the heron family Ardeidae. It is a secretive bird, preferring to hide, and is seldom seen in the open. The loud call of the male during the breeding season can be heard as it announces its presence while in search of a potential mate. Bitterns have tannish brown plumage covered with dark streaks and bars. As one of its names suggests, this species is the largest of the bitterns. It typically inhabits reed beds and swamps, as well as lakes, lagoons, and sluggish rivers fringed by rank vegetation. It sometimes nests by ponds in agricultural areas, even quite near habitations where suitable habitat exists, but prefers large reed beds of at least 49 acres (20 ha) in which to breed.

Feathers are beautifully mottled brown and tan and are used for winging, shoulders, sides, and hackling. Feathers from this bird were not used in the flies in this book, but are used in several other classic patterns.

Eurasian bittern feather set

Eurasian bittern feather close-up

Eurasian Jay (*Garrulus glandarius*)

Natural ranges	Western Europe and northwestern Africa to the Indian Subcontinent
Habitat	Mixed woodland, particularly with oaks, and urban areas
Size	13 to 14 inches (33–36 cm)
Weight	5.3 to 6.7 ounces (150–190 g)
Foods	Insects, acorns, seeds, berries, bird eggs, and small rodents.

The Eurasian jay is a species of bird found over a vast region and was first called "jay" by English speakers in Great Britain and Ireland. It is the original "jay" after which all others are named.

Coloration overall is tan to brown with blackish wings and tails. The highlight is the wing coverts—small feathers near the body on the front edge of the wings, which are colored a vivid light blue with fine black barring. These are the fly tier's prize. Used in wings and as sides, cheeks, and hackle throats on several patterns including the Nelly Bly shown in detailed steps in chapter 3 starting on page 198.

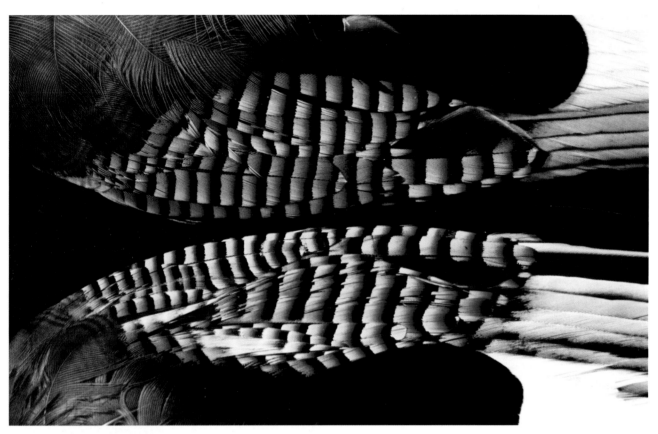

Eurasian jay wing covert close-up

Eurasian jay covert pair close-up

Fairy Bluebird

Asian Fairy Bluebird (*Irena puella*)
Philippine Fairy Bluebird (*Irena cyanogaster*)

Natural ranges	Southern Asia and the Philippines
Habitat	Forests and plantations
Size	9.4 to 10.6 inches (24–27 cm)
Weight	1.8 to 2.7 ounces (56–75 g)
Foods	Fruit, especially figs, and some insects

The two fairy bluebirds are small bird species and, as the names suggest, occur across southern Asia and the Philippines, respectively. They are the sole members of the genus *Irena* and family Irenidae.

They need fruit-bearing forested areas and are generally found in the canopy or thornscrub outside the forested areas. Agile flyers, they are able to pick off fruit and insects while on the wing and then take their prize to a comfortable perch to enjoy at their leisure.

The brilliant crown, back, wing coverlets, and rump are the body's blue parts, while the rest of the feathers are black. The blue feathers make an excellent alternative for the cotinga and are used in wings, veilings, and cheeks on classic salmon flies.

Above: Fairy bluebird feathers with dime
Right: Fairy bluebird feathers ring with dime

Golden-Breasted Starling

(*Lamprotornis regius / Cosmopsarus regius*)

Natural ranges	East Africa, from Somalia, Ethiopia, and Kenya to northern Tanzania
Habitat	Grassland, savannah, and shrubland
Size	12 inches (30 cm)
Weight	1.6 to 2.2 ounces (46–63 g)
Foods	Insects and some fruit

The golden-breasted starling, also known as the royal starling, is a medium-size bird in the starling family. Adult birds catch insects in flight and dig up termite mounds to find prey. The adult has a metallic green head and upper back, bright golden yellow breast and belly, and metallic violet-blue on its wings, back, neck, and long tail feathers. The vivid blue and yellow body and flank feathers are a striking addition to any fly, especially classic salmon patterns. They can be used for tailing, veilings, wings, sides, cheeks, and throats.

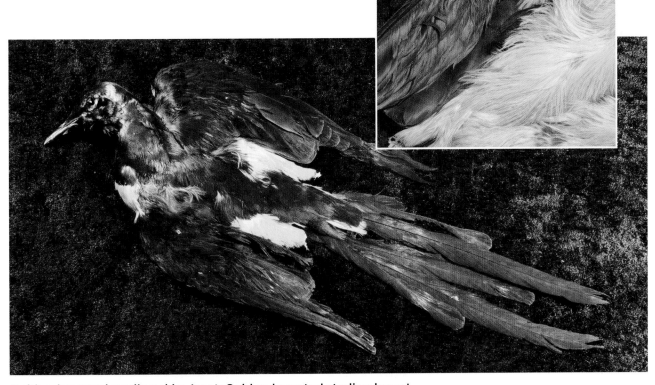

Golden-breasted starling skin; *Inset:* Golden-breasted starling breast

Golden Pheasant (*Chrysolophus pictus*)

Natural ranges	Western China
Habitat	Forests in mountainous areas
Size	35 to 41 inches (90–105 cm)
Weight	2 pounds, 8 ounces to 3 pounds, 8 ounces (1133 to 1587 g)
Foods	Grains, berries, seeds, leaves, and invertebrates

The golden pheasant, or Chinese pheasant, is originally from China, but feral populations have been established in the United Kingdom, Canada, United States, Mexico, Central and South America, some parts of Europe, Australia, and New Zealand. In England they may be found in East Anglia in the dense forests. The adult male is a beautiful and colorful bird, with its tail accounting for fully two-thirds of the total length. A golden pheasant's golden crest and rump and bright red body make it easy to identify. It can spread its deep orange neck "cape" in display, appearing as an alternating black-and-orange fan that covers all of its face except the bright yellow eyes with black pupils. Males have a golden-yellow crest with a hint of red at the tip. The body cape is light orange. The upper back is green, and the rest of the back and rump is golden yellow. The male also has a scarlet breast, flanks, and underbody. A most colorful bird indeed!

The female (hen) is much more subdued, as is typical of most birds, with a mottled brown and tan plumage much like females of the more common pheasants. Despite the male's showy appearance, these birds are very elusive in their normal habitat within the forests. They do roost in trees at night. While they can fly, they prefer to run.

Literally every feather on a golden pheasant is used in one type of fly or another. The golden head crests are used for tails and toppings on classic salmon flies. The orange and black cape feathers, called "tippets," are used in strands for tails and in whole pairs for underwings and main wings. The deep wine-colored breast feathers are used for underwings and throats. A vital bird for any classic salmon fly tier.

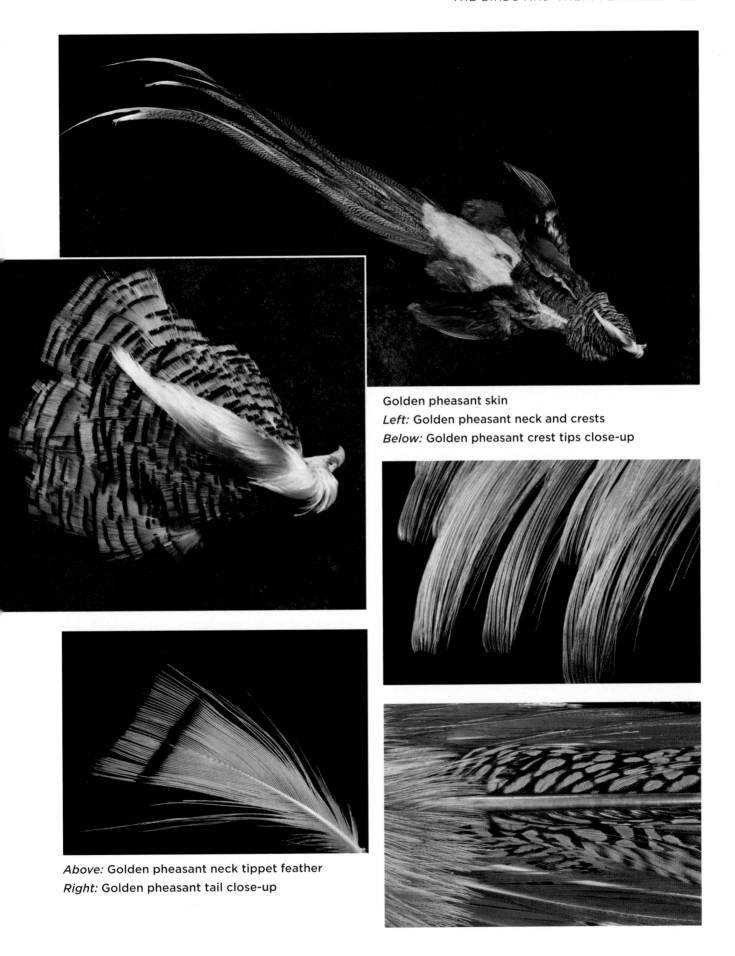

Golden pheasant skin
Left: Golden pheasant neck and crests
Below: Golden pheasant crest tips close-up

Above: Golden pheasant neck tippet feather
Right: Golden pheasant tail close-up

Gray Junglefowl (Jungle Cock) (*Gallus sonneratii*)

Natural ranges	India
Habitat	Thickets, on the forest floor, and in open scrub
Size	25.6 to 30 inches (65 to 75 cm)
Weight	1 pound, 8 ounces to 2 pounds, 8 ounces (680–1133 g)
Foods	Grains, bamboo seeds, berries, insects, and termites

The gray junglefowl, commonly referred to as the jungle cock, is one of the wild ancestors of domestic chickens, together with the red junglefowl and other junglefowls. Mostly ground-dwellers, they will fly up in trees to escape predators and to roost. They have been bred domestically in England since 1862, and their feathers have been commercially supplied from domestic UK stocks for fly tying since 1978.

The male has a black neck cape with elongated feathers, which are dark and end in a small, hard, orange-yellowish end with a white tip. These jungle cock "nails" are used extensively in classic salmon flies as sides. They give a traditional look to the fly and are thought to suggest eyes of baitfish with their light/dark/light coloration. The jungle cock feather has also been used in traditional trout flies: It was tied on the top of a hook in a flat, horizontal position to suggest the body of a small beetle in the fly pattern called the Jassid. Vince Marinaro wrote about it in his classic book *A Modern Dry Fly Code*. Quoting Dick Surrette as to the importance of this fly, "Tied to copy small forms of food just under the surface film, as fish will rise and take this form of food awash, and not on the surface as suspected. A very good fly for late season angling when the trout are selective."

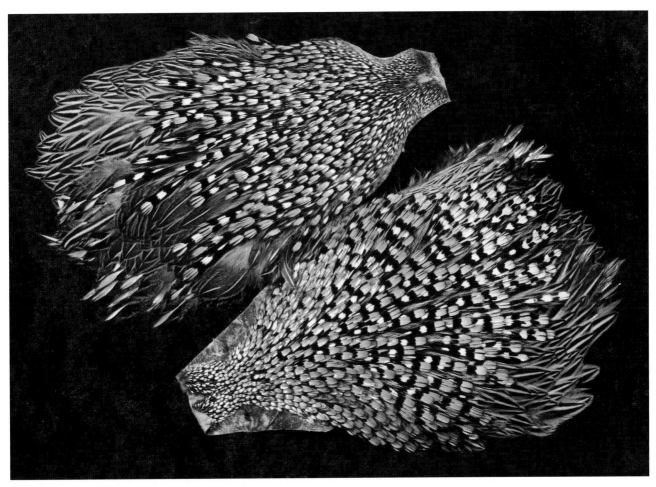

Jungle cock necks

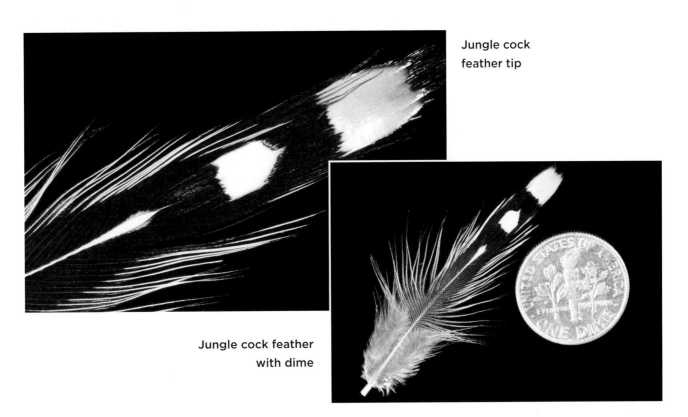

Jungle cock
feather tip

Jungle cock feather
with dime

Great Argus (*Argusianus argus*)

Natural ranges	Borneo, Sumatra, and the Malay Peninsula in Southeast Asia
Habitat	Jungles
Size	63 to 79 inches (160–200 cm) in total length, including a tail of 41 to 56 inches (105–143 cm)
Weight	4.5 to 6 pounds (2–2.7 kg)
Foods	Fruits, seeds, and insects

The great argus is a large species of pheasant. Its scientific name, *Argusianus argus*, is in reference to Argus—a hundred-eyed giant in Greek mythology—for the many eyelike patterns on its wings. The male is among the largest pheasants in both length and weight. It has very long tail feathers raised high when displaying to a potential mate. The male's most spectacular display features are its huge, broad, and greatly elongated secondary wing feathers complete with large "eye spots" (called "ocelli").

As it feeds on the forest floor in early morning and late evening, the great argus blue heads are constantly probing with their yellow beaks as they walk around on their red legs—quite a colorful sight.

The eyed wing quills, center and side tails, and all body feathers are used in one form or another on classic salmon flies. The secondary wings are dyed a rich golden reddish brown as an alternative to the golden pheasant for larger flies.

Great argus wing and tails

Great argus "leopard spot"
body feather

Great argus wing with one yard measure

Great argus tail with yardstick measure

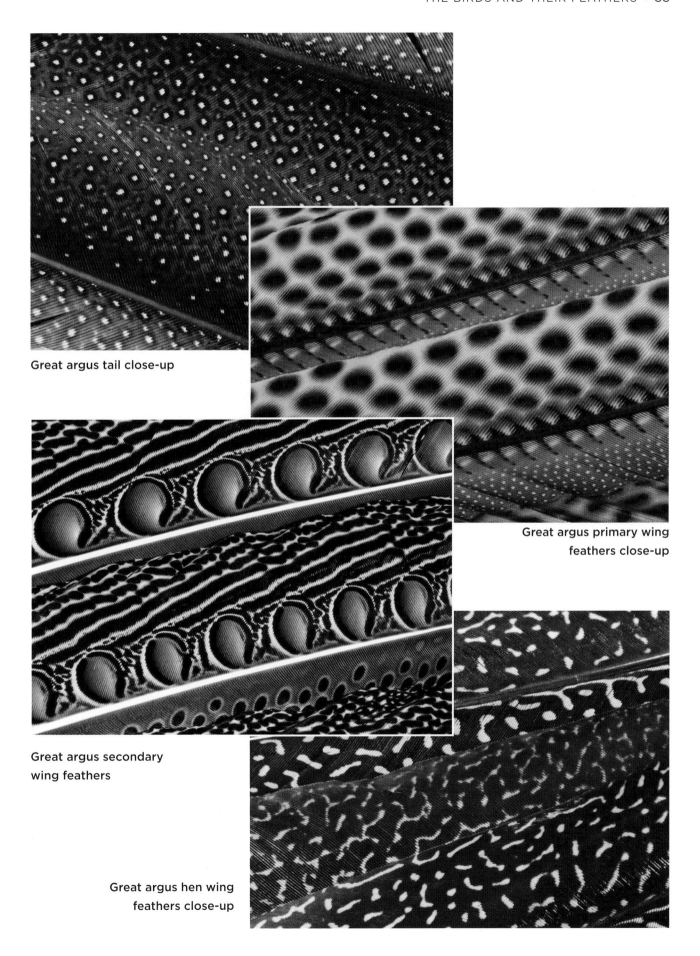

Great argus tail close-up

Great argus primary wing
feathers close-up

Great argus secondary
wing feathers

Great argus hen wing
feathers close-up

Great Bustard (Florican Bustard) (*Otis tarda*)

Natural ranges	Southern and central Europe and across temperate Asia
Habitat	Grassland or open flats or low rolling hills and croplands
Size	2 feet, 11 inches to 3 feet, 5 inches (90–105 cm) tall and a wingspan of 6 feet, 11 inches to 8 feet, 10 inches (2.1–2.7 m)
Weight	13 to 40 pounds (5.8–18 kg)
Foods	Green plant matter, seeds, insects, small rodents, frogs, lizards, and chicks of other birds

The great bustard is the only member of the genus *Otis*. The huge adult is possibly the heaviest living flying animal. The big wingspan gives much-needed lift for takeoffs and the ability to glide without expending great deals of energy.

The commonly used term in classic salmon fly tying is "florican" bustard, but the true name of the bird that the feathers come from is the "great" bustard. The tan-and-chocolate-striped body, wing, and tail feathers are a mainstay in many classic salmon fly married wings along with kori bustard. The large size and unique coloring make great bustard feathers an easily recognizable part of the married wing fly. See the Jock Scott for a pattern using florican (great) bustard in chapter 3, "The Flies."

Florican bustard feather group

Florican bustard feather pairs

Greater Bird of Paradise

(*Paradisaea apoda*)

Natural ranges	Southwest New Guinea, Aru Islands, Indonesia
Habitat	Forests found in lowlands and hills
Size	Up to 17 inches (43 cm) long (excluding the long twin tail wires) with wingspan averaging about 18 inches (46.4 cm)
Weight	7.9 ounces (224 g)
Foods	Fruits, berries, and insects, as well as spiders and worms

The greater bird of paradise is one of thirty-nine recognized species in the Paradisaeidae family. Carolus Linnaeus named the species "legless bird-of-paradise" because early traders sent skins to Europe that were prepared without wings or feet by natives. This led to the misconception that these birds were beautiful visitors from paradise that were kept aloft by their plumes and never touched the earth until death. The greater bird of paradise is the largest member in the genus *Paradisaea* and averages about the size of a crow. The long, flowing display feathers emanating from the male's flanks are the true highlight of the bird's appearance and display. On a full-grown male, they can be up to 25 inches (63.7 cm) long.

The male has an iridescent green face and a yellow-glossed-with-silver-iridescence crown, head, and nape. The rest of the body plumage is maroon-brown. The flank plumes, used in displays, are yellow at the base, turning white and streaked with maroon. When in a courtship dance, the male raises these display feathers as high as possible over its back and quivers to make them sway back and forth in a mesmerizing dance to entice the female. For fly tiers, the magnificent flank display feathers make both full and distinctive hackles and very fine, almost fish-bone-appearing wings. The light color of the feathers lends them to overdyeing in many colors.

Greater bird of paradise head and display feathers

Greater bird of paradise head and display feathers

Guinea Fowl, Helmeted (*Numida meleagris*)

Natural ranges	Africa
Habitat	Savannah or semi-deserts, though some live mainly in forests
Size	16 to 28 inches (40–71 cm)
Weight	1 pound, 8 ounces to 3 pounds, 8 ounces (700–1,600 g)
Foods	Seeds, fruits, snails, spiders, worms, insects, frogs, lizards, small snakes, and small mammals

Guinea fowl (sometimes called "original fowl" or guinea hen) are birds in the Galliformes order. Guinea fowl species are found across sub-Saharan Africa, some almost in the entire range, others more localized, such as the plumed guinea fowl in west-central Africa and the vulturine guinea fowl in Northeast Africa. For this book, we are focusing on the common helmeted guinea fowl. It has been introduced in East Africa, the West Indies, the United States, Britain, and India, where it is raised for food or as pets. Guinea fowl travel behind cattle and herd animals where they forage for food kicked up by the moving animals. They have strong legs and claws and dig in the soil like chickens for food. The dark feathers with white spots or speckling are widely used in classic salmon flies for wings, sides, cheeks, and hackling.

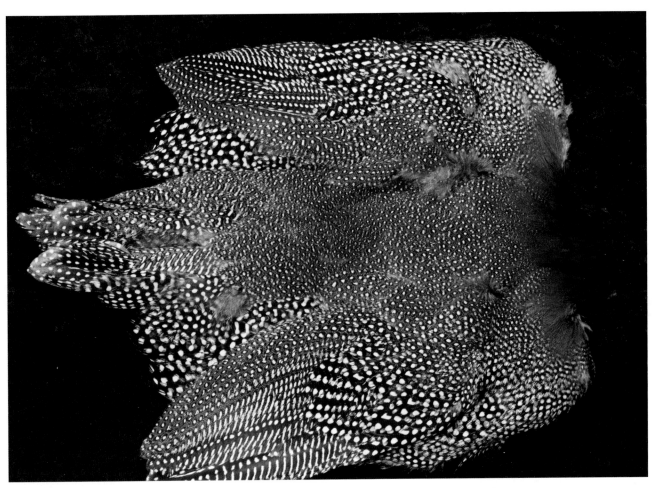

Guinea fowl skin

Guinea fowl back
and wing

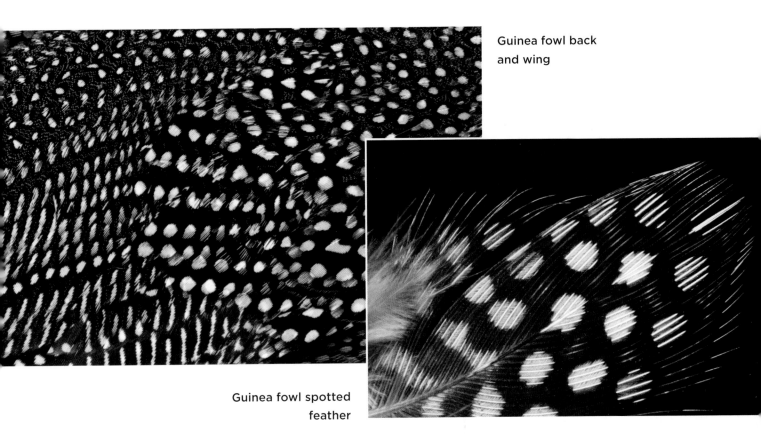

Guinea fowl spotted
feather

Hoopoe (*Upupa epops*)

Natural ranges	Europe, Asia, North Africa, sub-Saharan Africa, and Madagascar
Habitat	Savannahs, grasslands, and forest glades
Size	9.8 to 12.6 inches (25–32 cm) long, with a 17- to 19-inch (44–48 cm) wingspan
Weight	1.6 to 3.1 ounces (46–89 g)
Foods	Insects, small reptiles, frogs, seeds, and berries

The hoopoe is a colorful bird with a distinctive "crown" of long tan feathers with dark spotted tips. It is the only species in the family Upupidae. A possible explanation of the English and scientific names is that they are derived from the French name for the bird, *huppée*, which means "crested." They are very distinctive, with a long, thin, tapering bill. The hoopoe has broad rounded wings and is a strong flyer, capable of picking off flying insects as part of its diet.

Hoopoes have become common in olive groves, orchards, vineyards, parkland, and farmland. Hoopoes typically feed on the ground. They search for insect larvae, pupae, and mole crickets with their long bill and either grab their meal with their strong bill or dig out their find with their strong feet. The wings, tails, and especially the unique crest feathers are all used in classic salmon fly patterns. The crests can be used as tailing, main wings, shoulders, sides, or long cheeks.

Hoopoe mount—head view
Left: Hoopoe mount—back view
Below: Hoopoe head feathers close-up

Impeyan Pheasant

(*Lophophorus impejanus*)

Natural ranges	Himalayas, Bhutan, Pakistan, India, Nepal, and southern Tibet
Habitat	Cool oak and/or conifer forests with open grassy slopes, cliffs, and alpine meadows at 9,000- to 10,000-foot elevations (2,743–3,048 m)
Size	2.3 feet (70 cm) in length
Weight	4 pounds, 5 ounces to 5 pounds, 3 ounces (1,980–2,380 g)
Foods	Tubers and subterranean insects

The Impeyan pheasant, or Himalayan monal, was named after Lady Impey, who first kept them in captivity in Great Britain. They move seasonally down as low as 6,500 feet in winter and up to 16,000 feet in the summer. These pheasants seem to like snow, often seen digging in it for food. They are well equipped for digging with strong legs and sharp bills to root out their food. This pheasant is a large bird, about the size of a smaller goose.

Impeyan pheasants are one of the most beautiful pheasants known. Their plumage is strikingly colored with rich blues, greens, purples, reds, and coppers, and the glossy iridescence gives the impression of highly polished metal. The adult male has a long, metallic-green-tipped crest, much like a peacock; changeable reddish copper on the back and sides of the neck; and a prominent white back and rump. The tail feathers are uniformly dark cinnamon / reddish brown in color, and darker toward the tips.

For the fly tier, every feather is of potential use in classic salmon flies. From the tail and wing to all of the incredible metallic body and head feathers, every single feather is an amazing addition to any fly. The Bronze Pirate (see chapter 3, "The Flies") utilizes the bronze-toned neck feathers. The body feathers are good for full wings, shoulders, sides, and cheeks, as well as veilings and tails. The crests are used in the Bronze Pirate as the wing and also make unique horns as a finishing touch on classic flies.

Impeyan pheasant skin

Impeyan pheasant
bronze neck feathers

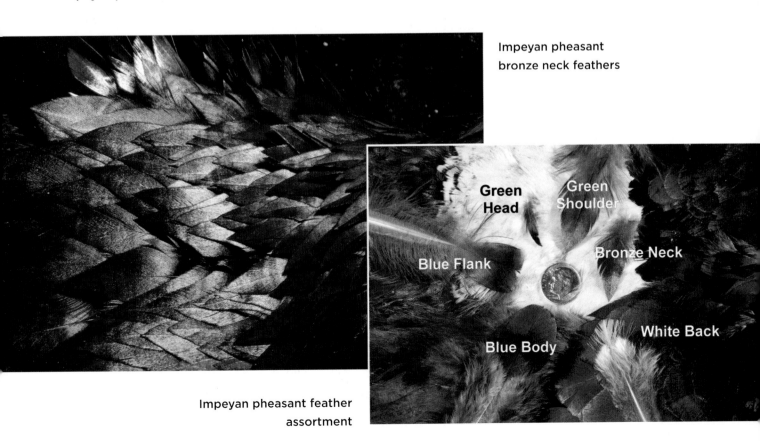

Impeyan pheasant feather
assortment

Green
Head

Green
Shoulder

Blue Flank

Bronze Neck

Blue Body

White Back

Kori Bustard (Speckled Bustard) (*Ardeotis kori*)

Natural ranges	Africa to India to Australia
Habitat	Grassy plains, arid plateaus, scrub, lightly wooded savannah, open dry bushland, and semi-desert all with available cover
Size	3 feet, 11 inches to 4 feet, 11 inches (120–150 cm) long; 2 feet, 4 inches to 3 feet, 11 inches (71–120 cm) tall; and wingspan of around 7 feet, 7 inches to 9 feet (230–275 cm)
Weight	15 to 40 pounds (7–18 kg)
Foods	Grasses, seeds, berries, roots, bulbs, flowers, wild melons, leaves, insects (including locusts, caterpillars, bush crickets, and termites), scorpions, lizards, chameleons, snakes, small mammals, bird eggs, and nestlings

The kori bustard is the largest flying bird native to Africa. It is one of the the large-bodied *Ardeotis* genus. In fact, the male kori bustard may be the heaviest flying animal.

Kori bustards are ground-dwelling birds spending up to 70 percent of their time on foot searching for food. Walking slowly and quietly, they search with their bills for their next meal. They follow large animals to catch insects that are exposed by them.

What kori feathers lack in varied colors they make up for in richly marked fine patterns of buff and brown. Commonly referred to as "speckled" in the fly tying realm, the pattern of light and dark markings makes a unique addition by itself or when incorporated into a "married" wing of any classic fly.

Kori bustard large tail quill

Kori bustard feather close-up

Kori bustard neck
feather pair

Lady Amherst's Pheasant

(*Chrysolophus amherstiae*)

Natural ranges	China and Burma
Habitat	Dense, dark forests with thick undergrowth
Size	39.4 to 47.2 inches (100–120 cm) long with the tail being 31.5 inches (80 cm) of the total length
Weight	1 pound, 8 ounces to almost 2 pounds (675–850 g)
Foods	Grain, seeds, leaves, and invertebrates

The Lady Amherst's pheasant name is in honor of Sarah, Countess of Amherst, wife of William Pitt Amherst, governor general of Bengal, who was responsible for sending the first specimen of the bird to London in 1828. As time went by, a feral population of the birds developed in England. This species is closely related to the golden pheasant, and they are known to have interbred.

It is an easily identifiable bird with its black and white head; long white with black barring tail; orange flanks; and red, blue, white, and yellow body. The "cape" around the neck can be raised in display. Despite the male's showy appearance, these birds are very difficult to see in the wild. They feed on the ground during the day but roost in trees at night. They prefer to walk or run, but if startled they can suddenly burst upwards with great quickness.

For fly tying, every feather is used from head to tail. The white-and-black-barred tippets from the neck cape are used in the Lady Amherst fly. Crests and tippet strands are used in tails. The body feathers are used in wings. The amazing tails are used in strips alone as underwings or main wings, and are often part of a married wing.

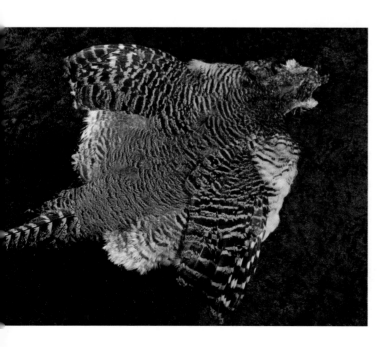

Lady Amherst's pheasant hen skin

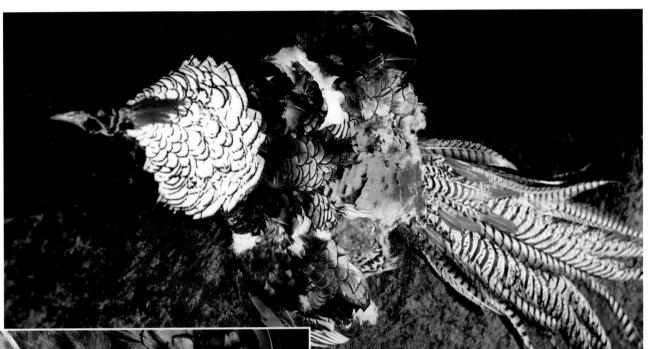

Lady Amherst's pheasant skin
Left: Lady Amherst's pheasant back

Above: Lady Amherst's pheasant tippet feather
Top right: Lady Amherst's pheasant back feather
Bottom right: Lady Amherst's pheasant crest and tippets close-up

Lewis's Silver Pheasant (*Lophura nycthemera lewisi*)

Natural ranges	Cambodia and Thailand
Habitat	Grassy scrub and forests
Size	Average 28 inches (70 cm), including tail of 12 inches (30 cm)
Weight	1 pound, 8 ounces to 2 pounds, 8 ounces (680 to 1134 g)
Foods	Seeds, grains, and fruit, especially berries

The Lewis's silver pheasant is one of fourteen subspecies of silver pheasants. Smaller than the true silver, they are almost an exact negative in color with black feathers with thin white barring. For fly tying, every feather is usable in tails and wings and as hackling. The Noir et Blanc (see chapter 3, "The Flies") has Lewis's silver pheasant in the pattern mix.

Lewis's silver pheasant skin

Lewis's silver pheasant body feather close-up

Macaw, Blue-and-Gold

(Ara ararauna)

Natural ranges	Venezuela and south to Peru, Brazil, Bolivia, and Paraguay
Habitat	Forests and woodlands
Size	30 to 34 inches (76–86 cm)
Weight	2 to 3 pounds (0.9–1.5 kg)
Foods	Nuts, seeds, and fruits

The blue-and-gold macaw is a large parrot of tropical South America. It is one of the larger members of its family. The range extends slightly into Central America, where it is restricted to Panama. A small breeding population has developed in Miami-Dade County, Florida, since the mid-1980s.

These birds use their powerful beaks for breaking nutshells and for climbing up and hanging from trees. They are able to vocalize well, including mimicry of human speech. They are popular in aviculture because of their striking color, ability to talk, ready availability in the marketplace, and close bonding to humans.

Blue-and-gold macaws are vivid in appearance, with blue wings and tail, a dark blue chin, golden breast and abdomen, and a green forehead. Their beaks are black. The naked face is white, turning pink when excited. They are long-lived, surviving thirty to thirty-five years in the wild. The colorful feathers of these macaws are well utilized by fly tiers. The body feathers are used for wings, sides, and cheeks, and single fibers with blue on one side and golden-yellow on the other from the center tails are used for "horns" in many classic salmon patterns.

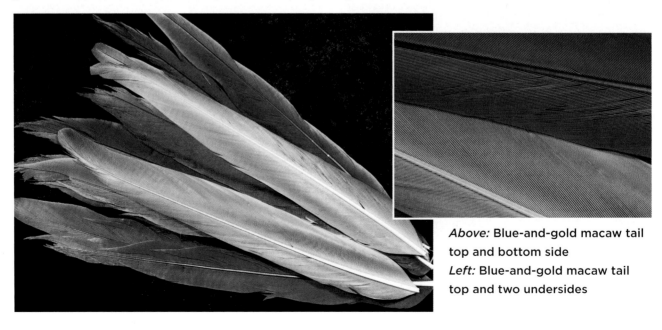

Above: Blue-and-gold macaw tail top and bottom side
Left: Blue-and-gold macaw tail top and two undersides

Macaw, Scarlet

(*Ara macao*)

Natural ranges	Tropical southeastern Mexico to Amazonian Peru, Colombia, Bolivia, Venezuela, Brazil, Panama, Guatemala, and Belize
Habitat	Humid lowland rainforests, woodlands, river edges, and savannahs
Size	32 inches (81 cm) with the tail being about half the overall length
Weight	2 pounds, 3 ounces (1 kg)
Foods	Fruits, nuts, and seeds, including large hard seeds

The scarlet macaw is another large South American parrot, a member of a group of neotropical parrots called macaws. As with others of the species, the scarlet macaw is long-lived. Ages of forty to fifty years are common and some can live up to seventy-five years in captivity. Like the blue and gold cousin, they coexist with humans well. The body feathers are mostly scarlet, and the rump and tail-covert feathers are light blue. The upper wing coverts are yellow with some having green tips, and the upper sides of the flight feathers of the wings are dark blue. The undersides of the wing and tail flight feathers are dark red. For fly tying, the center tail fibers are used for "horns" on many flies and the body and wing feathers are used for wings on flies such as the Shannon, May Queen, and Nelly Bly.

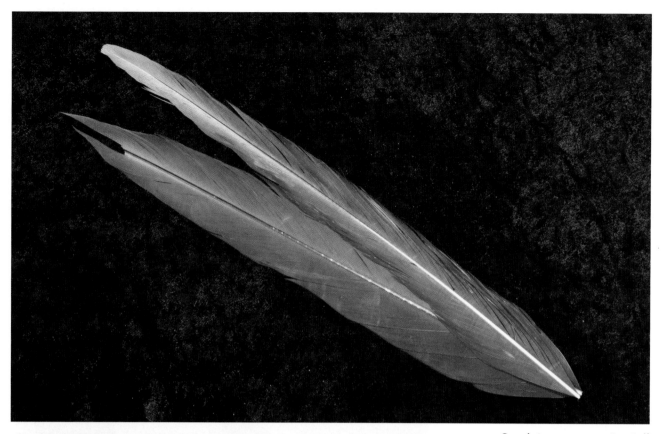

Scarlet macaw center tail

Scarlet macaw ring of
body feathers

Right: Scarlet macaw body
feather close-up

Magnificent Riflebird

(Ptiloris magnificus)

Natural ranges	New Guinea and far northeastern Australia
Habitat	Lowland rain forests
Size	Up to 13.4 inches (34 cm) long
Weight	5.0 to 8.2 ounces
Foods	Fruits and arthropods

The magnificent riflebird is widely distributed and a relatively common species throughout its range. It is of medium size and similar in size to a crow. It has a curved black bill, blackish feet, and a dark brown iris. Males perform special courtship displays on a "dancing perch." During these displays, the male fully extends his wings and raises his tail; he hops upward while swinging his head from side to side, showing off his metallic blue-green triangle-shaped breast shield. The male is an all-black member of the Bird-of-Paradise group and the breast shield is a feature unique to the species. Hundreds of small oval-shaped feathers produce the metallic-like appearance of the iridescent blue-green breast shield. Overall subdued colors make the colorful breastpiece stand out even more when displaying.

The breastshield feathers are used in classic salmon flies in tails, veilings, sides, and cheeks. They add a unique flash of color to any fly adorned with them.

Above: Magnificent riflebird breast feathers with a dime
Left: Magnificent riflebird breast feather pair

Malayan Crested Fireback Pheasant (*Lophura ignita rufa*)

Natural ranges	Thai Malay Peninsula, Borneo, and Sumatra
Habitat	Lowland forests
Size	25.6 to 27.6 inches (65–70 cm)
Weight	4 pounds to 5 pounds, 9 ounces (1810–2605 g)
Foods	Plants, fruits, and small animals

The Malayan crested fireback pheasant is a darkly colored pheasant overall with a dark crest, bluish black plumage, reddish brown rump, and black outer tail feathers. One would consider this bird a great mix of color as is, but add the vivid orange-colored back patch the species shares with the other birds named "fireback" and now you have a very unusual and visually stunning bird.

For the fly tier, the rusty-orange back feathers and all of the blue, purple, and maroon body feathers are perfect for wings on classic salmon flies. See an example (in chapter 3, "The Flies") of the Firebird fly I created.

Malayan crested fireback pheasant skin
Left: Malayan crested fireback pheasant fireback back patch

Above: Malayan crested fireback pheasant tail with dime
Left: Malayan crested fireback pheasant single flank feather with dime

Nicobar Pigeon (*Caloenas nicobarica*)

Natural ranges	Nicobar Islands, east through the Malay Archipelago, to the Solomons and Palau
Habitat	Small islands and in coastal regions
Size	12.7 to 16 inches (32–40 cm)
Weight	1 to 1 pounds, 2 ounces (460–525 g)
Foods	Grains, hard seeds, fruits, insects, and corn

The Nicobar pigeon—also known as the hackled pigeon, white-tailed pigeon, or vulturine pigeon—is one of the most beautiful of the pigeon/dove species. It is the only extant member of the genus *Caloenas* and the closest living relative of the extinct dodo.

The Nicobar pigeons travel in flocks from island to island in search of food and water. They feed on the ground, searching through vegetation and digging with claws and bill. A gizzard stone helps to grind up hard-to-digest food items.

The Nicobar pigeon's head is gray, like the upper neck plumage, which turns into richly colored green and copper hackles. The tail is very short and pure white. The rest of its plumage is metallic green. These metallic green feathers are a special addition to the classic salmon fly as an underwing, main wing, shoulder, side, or cheek. They are used in my creation, the Emerald Isle (in chapter 3, "The Flies").

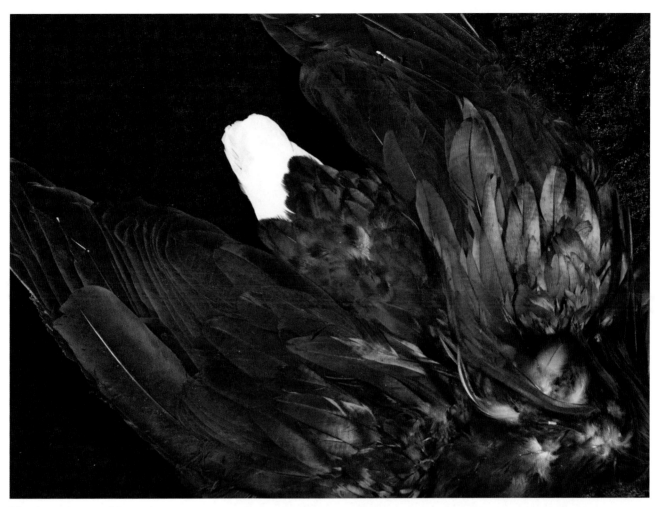

Nicobar pigeon skin

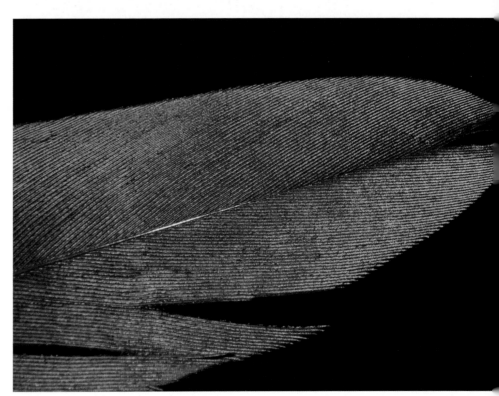

Nicobar pigeon wing
feather tip close-up

Ocellated Turkey (*Meleagris ocellata*)

Natural ranges	Yucatán Peninsula of Mexico, northern parts of Belize, and Guatemala
Habitat	Tropical lowland forests, clearings, and abandoned farm plots
Size	28 to 48 inches (70–122 cm)
Weight	11 to 13 pounds (5–6 kg)
Foods	Seeds, berries, insects, and leaves

The ocellated turkey lives mainly in a 50,000-square-mile (130,000 km²) area that includes all or part of the states of Quintana Roo, Campeche, Yucatán, Tabasco, and Chiapas. Ocellated turkeys spend most of the time on the ground. They prefer to run to escape danger but they can fly for short distances when needed. They usually roost high in trees away from night-hunting predators such as jaguars, and often are together in a family group.

The body feathers of both sexes are an iridescent bronze and green color. Tail feathers are speckled and mottled tan and brown with an eye-shaped, blue-bronze spot near the end with a bright gold tip. These spots, located on the tail, are called "ocelli" and are the basis for the ocellated turkey's name. They have been compared to the "eyes" or ocelli found on peacocks. The upper secondary wing coverts are rich iridescent copper.

The tail, wing, and body feathers are all utilized in classic salmon flies. Tail and wing fibers can be used in strips as underwings or in strands in married wings. The body and flank feathers make nice underwings. See the fly I created, called the Ocellation, as an example (in chapter 3, "The Flies").

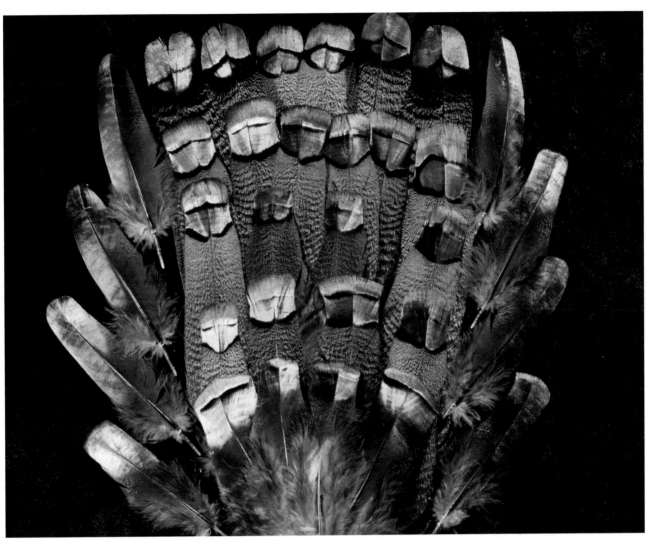

Ocellated turkey tail and wing covert set

Ocellated turkey tails and
flank feathers

Ostrich

(Struthio camelus)

Natural ranges	Africa
Habitat	Savannahs and open grasslands
Size	6 feet, 11 inches to 9 feet, 2 inches (2.1–2.8 m) in height
Weight	139 to 320 pounds (63–145 kg)
Foods	Seeds, shrubs, grass, fruit, flowers, and insects

The ostrich is a large flightless bird. It is the largest living species of bird and lays the biggest eggs. Native to Africa, farm-raised ostriches in Australia, Israel, and New Mexico have established feral populations.

They can weigh as much as two adult humans. An ostrich's lifespan is up to forty-five years. With a long neck and strong legs, the ostrich can run up to 43 mph (70 km/h), the fastest land speed of any bird. Talk about feathers flying! The ostrich is farmed around the world, particularly for its feathers, which are decorative and are also used in feather dusters. Its meat is marketed commercially, with its leanness a common selling point. The feathers of adult males are mostly black, with white primaries and a white tail. Females and young males are grayish brown and white. The feathers lack the tiny hooklets that lock barbs together. They are soft and fluffy and serve as insulation.

The feathers of the ostrich are used extensively in classic salmon flies, mainly as "butts" or "joints" between body sections. Their unique structure allows them to be wrapped around the hook as if it were a miniature hackle. The fibers spring out and provide a spiky appearance.

Ostrich feathers

Ostrich feather close-up

Palawan Peacock Pheasant

(*Polyplectron napoleonis*)

Natural ranges	Palawan Island in the southern part of the Philippine archipelago
Habitat	Humid forests
Size	19.7 to 23.8 inches (50–60 cm)
Weight	Average around 21 ounces (595 g)
Foods	Insect larvae and adults, mollusks, centipedes, and termites. Also small frogs, seeds, and berries in the wild, as well as mealworms, crickets, and grasshoppers in captivity.

The Palawan peacock pheasant populations are, unfortunately, small in their natural ranges, but breeders around the world (such as Allandoo Pheasantry in Scotland at www.allandoopheasantry .com) are helping maintain and even increase populations.

The Palawan peacock pheasant is a medium-size bird. It is considered one of the most beautiful members of the pheasant family, with highly iridescent electric blue-violet and metallic green-turquoise tipped feathers on its back and breast, and an underbody that is dark black. Each tail plume and upper-tail covert is marked with highly iridescent, reflective ocelli or "eye," singly or in pairs. The body feathers are a special addition to any classic salmon fly as a main wing, shoulder, side, or cheek. See the Ocellation, Glimpse of Paradise, and Jo's Jewel for examples of their uses (in chapter 3, "The Flies").

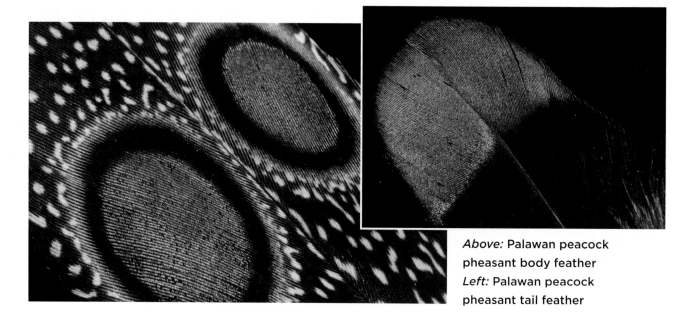

Above: Palawan peacock pheasant body feather
Left: Palawan peacock pheasant tail feather

Peacock, India Blue and Java Green

INDIA BLUE PEACOCK

(*Pavo cristatus*)

Natural ranges	Indian subcontinent
Habitat	Open forest or cultivated land
Size	Bill to tail of 39 to 45 inches (100–115 cm); length to the end of a fully grown train measures as much as 77 to 89 inches (195–225 cm).
Weight	8 pounds, 10 ounces to 13 pounds, 3 ounces (4–6 kg)
Foods	Berries, grains, snakes, lizards, and small rodents

JAVA GREEN PEACOCK

(*Pavo muticus*)

Natural ranges	Eastern and northeastern India, northern Myanmar, southern China, Laos, Thailand, Vietnam, Cambodia, Peninsular Malaysia, and Java
Habitat	Tropical and subtropical, as well as evergreen and deciduous forests
Size	5 feet, 11 inches to 9 feet, 10 inches (1.8–3 m) including its "train," which measures 4 feet, 7 inches to 5 feet, 3 inches (1.4–1.6 m); wingspan averages around 3 feet, 11 inches (1.2 m) and can reach 5 feet, 3 inches (1.6 m) in big males.
Weight	8 pounds, 10 ounces to 13 pounds, 3 ounces (4–6 kg)
Foods	Fruits, invertebrates, reptiles, frogs, insects, snakes, and rodents

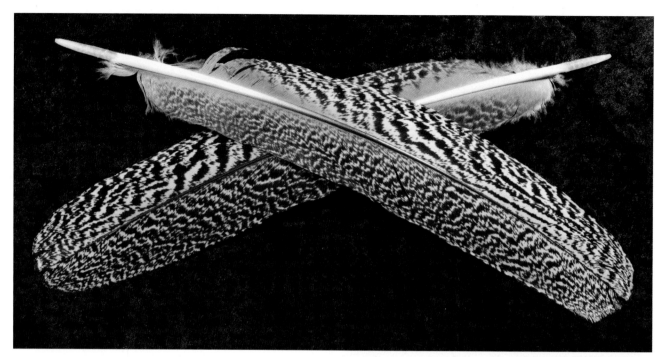

India blue peacock secondary
mottled wing quill pair

The **India blue peacock** is a large, brightly colored species of peafowl and is a prolific bird that provides a source of natural beauty wherever it is found. It has been introduced to many parts of the world and has become feral in some areas. Alexander the Great is generally credited with introducing it into Europe. Some say it arrived in Athens by 450 BC. It lives in small nomadic groups and will try to escape predators on foot, though it can take wing to escape if needed and fly into tall trees to roost.

India blue peacocks are recognized for the male's large, colorful "tail" with large "eyes" (called "ocelli") used as display feathers to attract a female. These feathers actually grow from their back. The "train" is made up of these display feathers. Colors are not from green or blue pigments but from the microstructure of the feathers that refract and reflect light. This gives these feathers, and many on the rest of the bird, a glossy "metallic" appearance.

The **Java green peacock** (Green peafowl) is the closest relative of the India blue peacock (*Pavo cristatus*), which is found mainly on the Indian subcontinent. Green peafowl are large birds with strong flight muscles and a sizable wingspan. This combination enables the Java green peacock to fly well and over long distances; it is often observed in flight.

India blue peacock green flank feather

India blue peacock "eyed" tail feather close-up

Top right: India blue peacock "sword"
flank feathers close-up
Bottom right: India blue peacock
crest feathers with dime

Green peafowl are found in a wide range of habitats, a factor enabling them to survive in a large area and sustain their populations. They are mainly ground-dwellers unless disturbed. In the evenings they do fly up to roost in family units in the trees.

Both peacocks have amazing feathers of all sizes, shapes, and colors. Starting at the top, the crests are the crown jewels of the peacock—long rachises topped with a small jewel of fibers. Then down the neck and body to the richly colored blue and green contour feathers. Next the wings—shoulder, primary, and secondary all valuable for underwings and main wings in whole-feather or married strip-wing flies. Then the flank and tail feathers, and the amazing eyed tails and shorter richly colored sword feathers. All are useful for wings, toppings, and strands wrapped around the hook for bodies. The peacock's use in fly tying is limitless—it is truly an important source of amazing feathers.

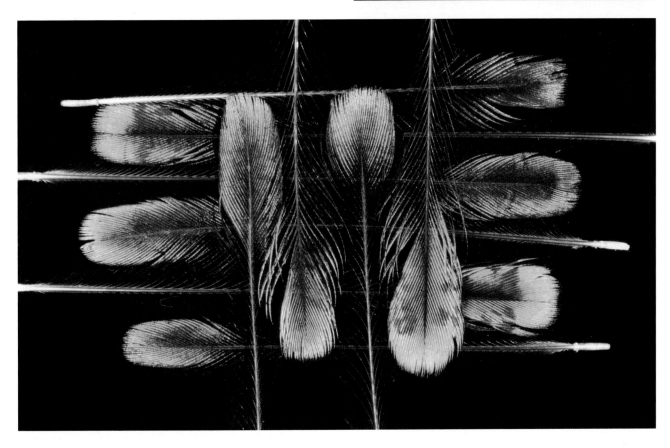

Java green peacock male crests

Peacock Pheasants

Peacock pheasants are a bird genus, *Polyplectron*, of the family Phasianidae, consisting of eight species. Here we will focus on four. All wild populations are in Southeast Asia, but breeders have been raising these birds domestically for many years and have helped provide a limited source of feathers. Here are brief descriptions of each of the four birds whose feathers are utilized herein:

GERMAIN'S PEACOCK PHEASANT

(*Polyplectron germaini*)

Natural ranges	Indochina, southern Vietnam, and eastern Cambodia
Habitat	Jungles, damp and semi-evergreen forests
Size	Average 23.6 inches (60 cm)
Weight	Around 25 to 30 ounces (700–850 g)
Foods	Insects, grubs, fruits, and plant matter

The name of Germain's peacock pheasant commemorates the French Colonial army's veterinary surgeon Louis Rodolphe Germain. The bird is medium-size and has richly colored brown with fine tan mottling feathers, many with dark metallic blue-green rounded ends.

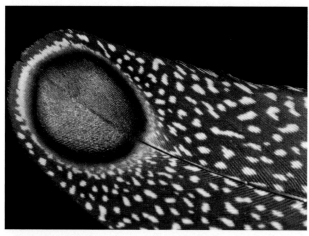

Germain's peacock pheasant feather close-up

GRAY PEACOCK PHEASANT

(*Polyplectron bicalcaratum*)

Natural ranges	Northeast India and Southeast Asia
Habitat	Lowland and hill forests
Size	30 inches (76 cm)
Weight	26.5 to 33.5 ounces (750–950 g)
Foods	Seeds, termites, and invertebrates

The gray peacock pheasant is a large pheasant, often found on the ground sifting through leaves and underbrush in search of food. It is covered with mottled brown and gray feathers with rounded ends similar to the Germain's but with lighter coloration and more purple and green in the rounded ends of the feathers.

Gray peacock pheasant skin
Right: Gray peacock pheasant feather close-up

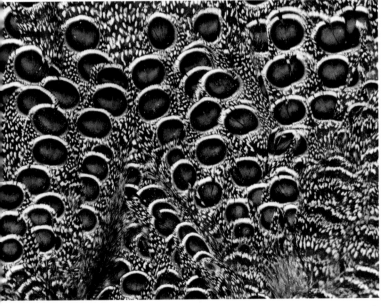

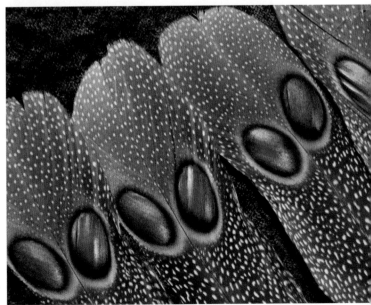

Above: Gray peacock pheasant back
Right: Gray peacock pheasant tail pairs

MALAYAN PEACOCK PHEASANT

(Polyplectron malacense)

Natural ranges	Central Malaysia, Thailand
Habitat	Lowland forests
Size	19.7 inches (50 cm)
Weight	21 to 25 ounces (600–700 g)
Foods	Insects, mollusks, isopods, seeds, fruits, and small arthropods

The Malayan peacock pheasant is also known as the crested peacock pheasant or Malaysian peacock pheasant. This is a medium-size pheasant that spends most of its time on the ground in search of food. It forages utilizing its feet and bill to uncover morsels from underneath forest debris. Its feathers are a rich amber-tan with brown spots, again having the large rounded ends with a metallic black ringed greenish "eye" or ocelli.

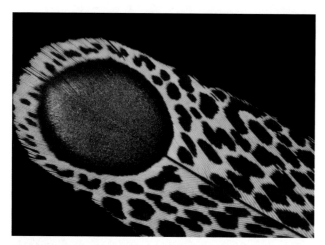

Malayan peacock pheasant feather close-up

MOUNTAIN PEACOCK PHEASANT

(Polyplectron inopinatum)

Natural ranges	Central Malay Peninsula
Habitat	Mountain forests
Size	21.7 to 25.6 inches (55–65 cm)
Weight	23 to 28 ounces (650–800 g)
Foods	Berries and insects, including beetles and ants

The mountain peacock pheasant, also known as Rothschild's peacock pheasant or mirror pheasant, is a medium-size pheasant, similar to the domestic North American Ringneck pheasant in size. The feathers are a rich rusty-amber color wth light oval-shaped ends with black ringed metallic dark-green spots. Of any of the peacock pheasants, the mountain pheasant feathers look most like a real "eye" with the light, oval background and dark "pupil-like" eye spot.

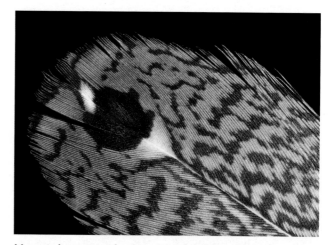

Mountain peacock pheasant feather close-up

All of the peacock pheasant body and wing feathers are a truly unique addition to any classic salmon fly. They can be used as full main wings in patterns such as the Leopard and Emerald Isle (see chapter 3, "The Flies"). They are also excellent additions as small pairs for tails, sides or cheeks. While it may be difficult to find authentic feathers, don't let this limit tying these patterns or other patterns. Try my new "feather sandwich" approach to creating substitutes shown on page 256 and have fun creating your next classic!

Peacock pheasant feather pairs, labeled

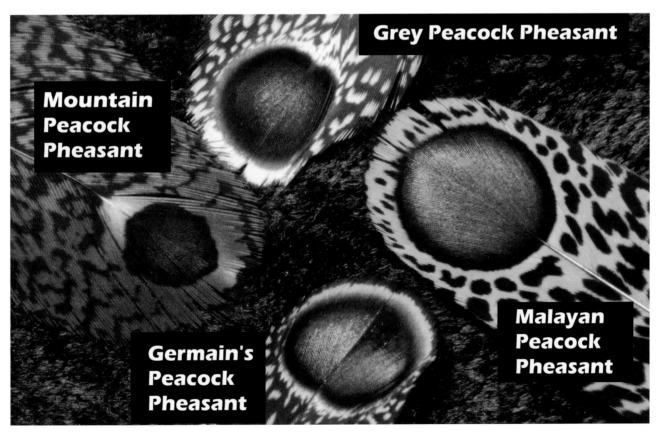

Peacock pheasant feathers close-up, labeled

Red-Ruffed Fruitcrow (Indian Crow) *(Pyroderus scutatus)*

Natural ranges	Venezuela, Guyana, east Andean slopes in Peru, Andean slopes in northwestern Ecuador, Colombia, western Venezuela, Venezuelan Coastal Range, southeastern Brazil, eastern Paraguay, northeastern Argentina
Habitat	Humid forest, especially in highlands
Size	16 to 18 inches (43–46 cm)
Weight	14.5 to 14.7 ounces (413–419 g)
Foods	Fruits and large insects

The red-ruffed fruitcrow, or Indian crow as it is commonly called in fly-tying circles, is a species of bird in the monotypic genus *Pyroderus*, in the cotinga family. The Indian crow is similar in appearance to the common American crow (*Corvus brachyrhynchos*) with the plumage primarily black, but with one major exception: a bright orange-crimson patch on the throat. It is this patch of colorful feathers that the fly tier seeks out. The vividly colored breast feathers are used in many flies and in many parts. The Black Prince is the only fly that uses the black feathers from the nape of the Indian crow as body veilings. Classic salmon flies that use the red breast feathers from the Indian crow include the Blue Goldfinch (tail, wing, and cheeks), Carnegie (body veilings), Red Sandy (tail and wing), Chatterer (wing), Widgeon (tail and cheeks), and Wilson (cheeks). In this book they are used in the Jock Scott, Black Argus, Firebird, Nelly Bly, and Ocellation (chapter 3, "The Flies").

Indian crow feather ring

Below: Indian crow
feather close-up

Resplendent Quetzal

(*Pharomachrus mocinno*)

Natural ranges	Chiapas, Mexico, to western Panama
Habitat	Mountain cloud forests
Size	14 to 16 inches (36–40 cm) plus up to 26 inches (65 cm) of tail streamer on the male
Weight	Average 7.4 ounces (210 g)
Foods	Fruits, insects, frogs, and lizards. Particularly important are wild avocados and other fruit of the laurel family.

The resplendent quetzal is well-known for its colorful plumage and plays an important role in Mesoamerican mythologies. The resplendent quetzal is pictured on Guatemala's flag and coat of arms since it is the national bird. Resplendent quetzals are weak fliers and have many predators, including eagles, hawks, owls, emerald toucanets, brown jays, long-tailed weasels, squirrels, and the kinkajou.

Resplendent quetzals have an iridescent metallic-green body and vivid red breast. Their long tails are far longer than the rest of the body and flutter when trailing behind in flight. The primary wing coverts are also unusually long and give a fringed appearance. The male also has a distinctive crest. All of these magical feathers are very vivid in color. The dyed emu substitute used to imitate the long tail does an admirable job simulating the rich color and texture of the real feathers. Quetzal feathers can be used in classic salmon flies for tails, veilings, wings, shoulders, sides, and cheeks.

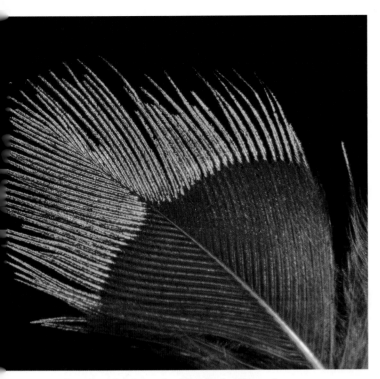

Resplendent quetzal body feather close-up

Resplendent quetzal breast feather close-up

Resplendent quetzal tail feather substitute of dyed emu

Satyr Tragopan

(*Tragopan satyra*)

Natural ranges	Himalayan reaches of India, Tibet, Nepal, and Bhutan
Habitat	Oak and rhododendron forests with dense undergrowth and bamboo clumps, along the edge of the forest or deep in the undergrowth. They range from 8,000 to 14,000 feet (2,438–4,267 m) elevation in summer and around 6,000 feet (1,828 m) in winter.
Size	2 feet 4 inches (70 cm)
Weight	4 pounds (1.8 kg)
Foods	Insects; green plant matter; berries; fruits; petals, buds, and leaves of plants, such as paper laurel, rhododendron, ferns, and daphne; bastard cinnamon; bamboo shoots; rhododendron seeds; and bulbs

The satyr tragopan, also known as the crimson horned pheasant, is a colorful bird with unique feathers found only on tragopans. The feathers are bright crimson-orange on the neck and breast of the males and each has a black ring with a white center on the tip of the feather. The other tragopans have slightly different configurations, but all follow a similar makeup.

These are used for main wings, sides, and cheeks in classic salmon flies. See the Spotted Tiger for an example, which I created (see chapter 3, "The Flies") to showcase both the satyr and Temminck's tragopan feathers (p. 87) in the wing and cheeks.

Satyr tragopan pheasant skin

Left: Satyr tragopan pheasant breast
Below: Satyr tragopan pheasant feather close-up

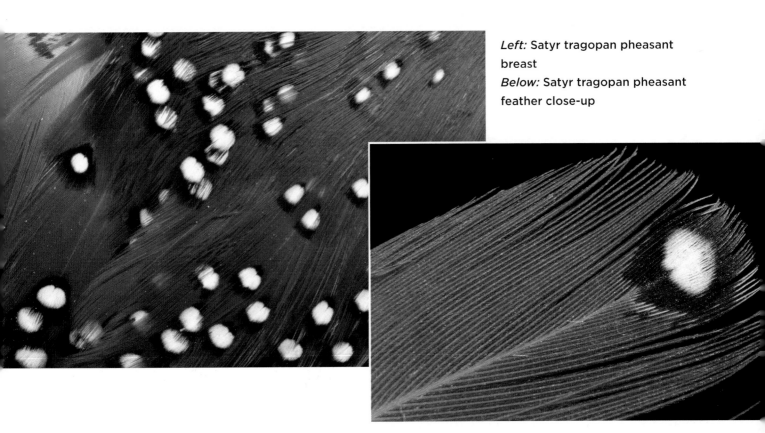

Sebright Chickens, Roosters and Hens (*Gallus gallus domesticus*)

Natural ranges	Developed in England, but raised anywhere
Habitat	Domestic farms
Size	13 to 15 inches (33–38 cm)
Weight	Average 22 ounces (625 g)
Foods	Seeds, grains

Named after its developer, Sir John Saunders Sebright (1767–1846), the 7th Sebright Baronet and a member of Parliament for Hertfordshire, a county in southern England, the Sebright is one of the oldest recorded British "true" bantam chickens. It was developed in the 19th century through a selective breeding program to produce an ornamental breed. All Sebrights have feathers "laced" (ringed) around the edges with black, on a base of either dark gold or whitish silver. Sebrights are one of only a few chicken breeds in which the roosters are "hen-feathered," meaning they have none of the long, sickle-shaped feathers common in most roosters that appear in the tail, neck, and saddle. Sebright feathers are used in all manner of classic salmon fly tying, such as hackles wrapped around the hook and winging as either supportive underwings or as layered main wings with multiple colors overlapping. The possibilities are endless.

Sebright chicken necks in a row

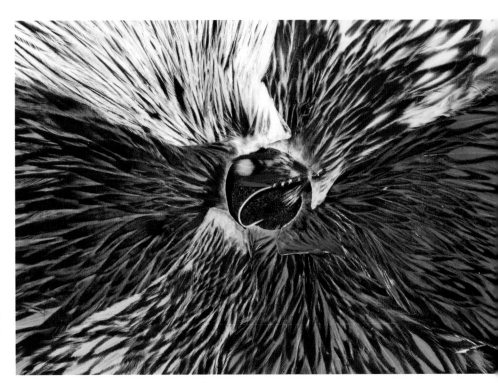

Sebright chicken necks
in a circle

Siamese Fireback Pheasant (*Lophura diardi*)

Natural ranges	Cambodia, Laos, Thailand, and Vietnam
Habitat	Lowland and evergreen forests, bamboo forest, secondary growth, and scrub in the plains and foothills up to 2,600 feet (800 m)
Size	31.5 inches (80 cm) with the tail being 13 to 14 inches (33–36 cm) of that overall length
Weight	3 pounds, 2 ounces (1,420 g)
Foods	Invertebrates, fruits, and berries

The Siamese fireback pheasant is also known as Diard's fireback, commemorating French naturalist Pierre-Médard Diard. The Siamese fireback male is a visually attractive bird with bright red wattles and legs, dark curved tail, and finely marked subdued gray feathered body. It also has the golden yellowish orange back that gives the bird its name and shades of dark red and blue on the flanks. Add to this the ornamental black crest feathers, and you have a striking bird that is subtle overall but shows flashes of color at any time.

For the fly tier, the crests make great horns and tails. The gray body feathers, especially the black-tipped shoulder feathers, make nice shoulders and sides. The prizes are the fireback feathers for brilliantly colored wings, sides, and cheeks. See some used in the Firebird fly I created (chapter 3, "The Flies").

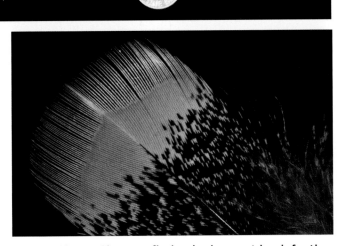

Siamese fireback pheasant skin
Left: Siamese fireback pheasant shoulder, flank, and back feathers with dime

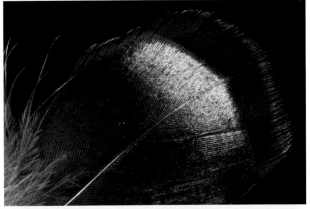

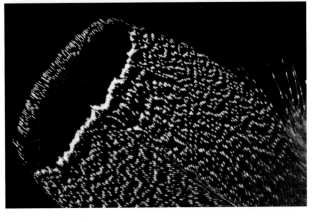

Above: Siamese fireback pheasant back feather close-up. *Top right:* Siamese fireback pheasant flank feather close-up. *Bottom right:* Siamese fireback pheasant black-tipped shoulder feather close-up

Silver Pheasant (*Lophura nycthemera*)

Natural ranges	Mainland Southeast Asia and eastern and southern China; also introduced populations in Hawaii and the US mainland
Habitat	Grasslands, mountain forests with adjoining open grasslamds
Size	Up to 47 to 49 inches (120–125 cm), including a tail of up to 30 inches (75 cm) in the largest specimens
Weight	2 pounds, 8 ounces to 4 pounds, 4 ounces (1.1–2 kg)
Foods	Plants, seeds, grain, fruit, berries, and invertebrates

Flies can be made with every feather from a silver pheasant. From the crests for tails to the tail used in wings and all of the body and wing feathers in between, the silver in natural and dyed colors makes some striking flies. See an example in the Noir et Blanc (chapter 3, "The Flies").

Silver pheasant skin

Silver pheasant body
feather close-up

Straw-Necked Ibis

(*Threskiornis spinicollis*)

Natural ranges	Australia, New Guinea, southwest Tasmania, Indonesia
Habitat	Freshwater wetlands, pastures, edges of swamps and lagoons, and wet or dry grasslands
Size	24 to 30 inches (60–75 cm)
Weight	2 pounds, 6 ounces to 3 pounds, 4 ounces (1,100–1,500 g)
Foods	Aquatic insects, mollusks, frogs, grasshoppers, crickets, locusts, small lizards, skinks, and other small reptiles

The straw-necked ibis are very nomadic, constantly on the move in search of favored habitats and food. They are often seen standing on high branches of bare trees, silhouetted against the sky.

Straw-necked ibises feed on pests that would otherwise eat farm crops and, so, are often called the "farmer's friend."

The straw-necked ibis has an abundance of wing and body feathers with a glossy blue-black barring. Feathers have an ever-changing metallic purple, green, and bronze sheen. These are outstanding feathers to use for wings, shoulders, and sides in classic salmon flies. See the Swinhoe's Splendor for an example (chapter 3, "The Flies").

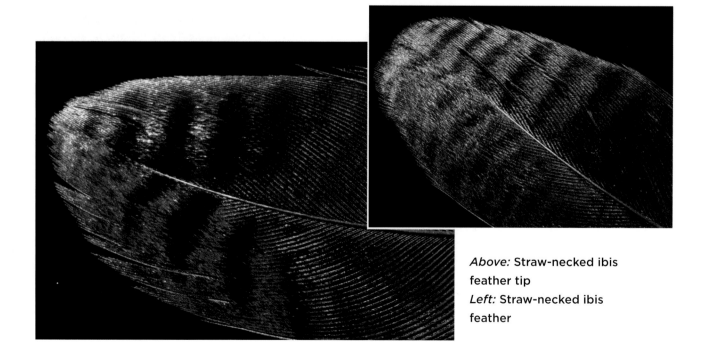

Above: Straw-necked ibis feather tip
Left: Straw-necked ibis feather

Swinhoe's Pheasant (*Lophura swinhoii*)

Natural ranges	Taiwan
Habitat	Mountain forests
Size	28 to 31 inches (70 to 79 cm)
Weight	2 pounds, 5 ounces (1,100 g)
Foods	Seeds, plant material, acorns, berries, flower buds, leaves, and insects, such as earthworms, millipedes, and termites

The Swinhoe's pheasant is limited in the wild to the mountains of central Taiwan, where it lives in forest habitat up to 7,550 feet (2,300 m) in elevation. The bird was named after the British naturalist Robert Swinhoe, who first described the species in 1862. Along with two other native birds of Taiwan, the mikado pheasant and Taiwan magpie, the Swinhoe's pheasant is sometimes considered an unofficial national symbol of Taiwan.

Swinhoe's pheasant males are large, brightly colored birds, with a glossy dark blue to black plumage with highlights of brilliant metallic blue, green, and maroon. Somewhat akin to the fireback's, they have a bold white patch on the upper back, crest, and long central tail feathers. The shoulders are a dark, shimmering maroon. The body, flank, and shoulder feathers are a rich addition to any classic salmon fly as an underwing, main wing, side, or shoulder. See my creation, the Swinhoe's Splendor, as an example (chapter 3, "The Flies").

Swinhoe's pheasant skin with clipped wings

Left: Swinhoe's pheasant
back patch
Below: Swinhoe's pheasant
single feather close-up

Temminck's Tragopan

(*Tragopan temminckii*)

Natural ranges	Northeast India, northwest Vietnam, Tibet, northern China
Habitat	Forests
Size	25.2 inches (64 cm)
Weight	2 pounds, 2 ounces to 3 pounds, 8 ounces (980–1,600 g)
Foods	Flowers, leaves, grass stalks, ferns, bamboo sprouts, mosses, berries, and seeds of a wide variety of plants

This colorful bird's common name and Latin binomial are in honor of the Dutch naturalist Coenraad Jacob Temminck. The Temminck's tragopan is a stocky medium-size bird that spends most of its time on the ground, foraging for food. The male's breast and abdomen feathers are deep orange with tear-shaped white centers tinted in pinkish gray. The back and rump feathers are dark reddish orange with tiny white centers edged in black similar to the satyr tragopan. His face is fluorescent light blue. When displaying, his neck is a bright light blue with a border of dark red markings. A colorful sight indeed!

The orange feathers on the body and flank are a great addition to any classic salmon pattern in the tail, throat, shoulder, or sides, and as wings and veilings. See the Spotted Tiger as an example (chapter 3, "The Flies").

Temminck's tragopan skin

Temminck's tragopan body
feather with dime

Toucan

Ariel Toucan (*Ramphastos ariel*)

Natural ranges	Southeast Amazon basin to coastal regions of Brazil
Habitat	Forest and woodlands in humid regions, especially along rivers
Size	Average 19 inches (48 cm) with a 3.5- to 5.5-inch (9–14 cm) bill
Weight	11 to 15 ounces (300–430 g)
Foods	Fruit, insects, small reptiles, eggs, and frogs

"Toucan" is the name for many similar species in South America. They are usually in the lowlands, but can be found up to an altitude of 5,600 feet (1,700 m). We will focus on the Ariel toucan as our example. It is a medium-size bird and a strong flyer, enabling it to reach a varied food supply and travel when needed to seek new territories. A distinctive feature is its large sickle-shaped bill. The bird is light and skilled at reaching any food item, whether living or waiting to be plucked and eaten. For fly tying, the soft, pale yellow breast feathers are used in several classic salmon flies in tails and as veilings and sides. See the Jock Scott and Black Argus for examples (chapter 3, "The Flies").

Above: Toucan breast feather pair with dime
Left: Toucan breast feather close-up

Twelve-Wired Bird of Paradise

(*Seleucidis melanoleucus*)

Natural ranges	New Guinea, Salawati Island, Indonesia
Habitat	Flat lowlands and swamp forests
Size	13 inches (33 cm)
Weight	6 to 7.7 ounces (170–217 g)
Foods	Fruits, arthropods, frogs, insects, and nectar

The twelve-wired bird of paradise is a velvet-black and yellow member of the Paradisaeidae family. It is a medium-size bird about the size of a small American crow. The male has a red iris, long black bill, and rich yellow feathers along his flanks. Twelve blackish, wirelike filaments emanate from within the tail, curving back near their bases to sweep forward over the bird's hindquarters. These are used in the males display "dance" to attract the female during courtship rituals. The black body feathers have an iridescent glistening surface when in sunlight with green on the tips. The outer breast feathers have a curved "sickle" shape and are used for tails, sides, cheeks, and throats on classic salmon flies. See the Glimpse of Paradise fly (chapter 3, "The Flies") for an example of how the outer curved breast feathers are used for the throat of the fly.

Above: Twelve-wired bird of paradise body feather pair
Left: Twelve-wired bird of paradise yellow tail feather with dime

Vulturine Guinea Fowl

(*Acryllium vulturinum*)

Natural ranges	Southern Ethiopia through Kenya and into northern Tanzania
Habitat	Forests and adjoining scrub and grasslands
Size	24 to 28 inches (61–71 cm)
Weight	2 pounds, 5 ounces to 3 pounds, 7 ounces (1,026–1,645 g)
Foods	Seeds and small invertebrates

The vulturine guinea fowl is the largest species of guinea fowl. This guinea fowl is a terrestrial ground dweller—it will run rather than fly when alarmed. It tends to keep to cover and roosts in trees.

The vulturine guinea fowl's vivid black-and-white-striped body feathers are used in many ways in classic salmon flies, from underwings to main wings, shoulders and sides, and also as hackles wrapped around the hook. See an example in the Noir et Blanc (chapter 3, "The Flies").

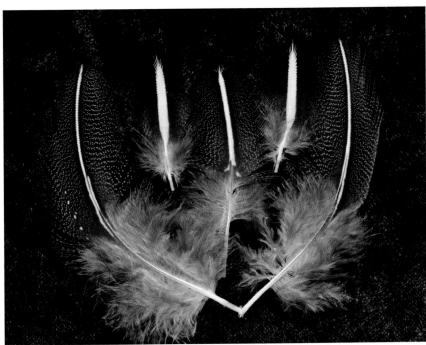

Vulturine guinea fowl body feathers

Vulturine guinea fowl skin

Vulturine guinea fowl
side with blue breast

Western Tragopan

(*Tragopan melanocephalus*)

Natural ranges	Himalayas from Hazara in northern Pakistan in the west to Uttarakhand in India to the east
Habitat	Upper-level dense coniferous and broad-leaved forests
Size	22 to 24 inches (55–60 cm)
Weight	4 pounds to 4 pounds, 10 ounces (1.8–2.2 kg)
Foods	Leaves, shoots, seeds, insects, and other invertebrates

The western tragopan, also known as the western horned tragopan, is found in a limited area in southeast Asia. Five populations are known from Kohistan, Kaghan Valley, Kishtwar, Chamba, Kullu, and an area east of the Satluj River. They are found at higher elevations, from 7,800 to 11,800 feet (2,400–3,600 m) in summer, and from 6,500 to 9,200 feet (2,000–2,800 m) in winter.

The western tragopan is a medium-size bird about the size of a North American Ringneck pheasant. They feed on the ground but roost in trees for safety. The females are well camouflaged during nesting; their natural-toned coloration blends in with ground-cover and vegetation. The male is dark colored with an overall gray and black appearance. Each body feather has a dark crimson base, a black tip half with a bright white spot in the center of each feather tip. It has deep crimson on the sides and back of the neck and a small black crest.

The unique body feathers are used for the Black Argus—a striking fly with three pairs of the white-spotted black-tipped feathers. I have come up with a simple, inexpensive substitute for these rare feathers (see chapter 4, "Substitute Feathers").

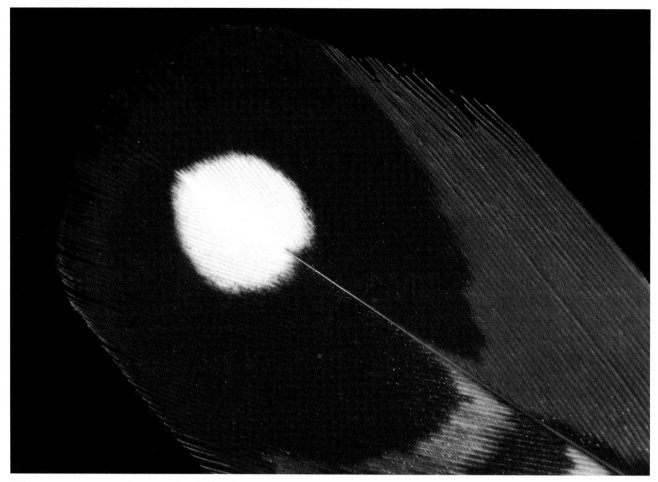

Western tragopan pheasant body feather tip close-up

Left: Western tragopan pheasant body feather group with dime
Below: Western tragopan pheasant body feather pairs with dime

Wood Duck (*Aix sponsa*)

Natural ranges	North America and western Mexico
Habitat	Wooded swamps, shallow lakes, marshes, ponds, and creeks
Size	19 to 21 inches (47–54 cm); wingspan from 26 to 29 inches (66–73 cm)
Weight	1 pound, 3 ounces to almost 2 pounds (544–862 g)
Foods	Berries, acorns, seeds, and insects

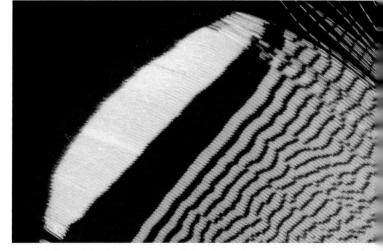

Wood duck black-barred flank feather close-up

The wood duck, or Carolina duck, is a species of water-loving perching duck. It is one of North America's most colorful waterfowl. It shares its genus with the equally beautiful Asian Mandarin duck (*Aix galericulata*). The wood duck is a medium-size perching duck. These birds feed by dabbling, which is feeding along the surface of the water or by tipping headfirst into the water to enjoy aquatic plants and vegetation. They also forage on land for seeds and insects. The prize feathers for fly tiers are the unique black-barred flank feathers, which are used in a wide variety of classic salmon patterns as shoulders and sides. See the Jock Scott and Black Argus (chapter 3, "The Flies").

Anatomy of a Feather and a Fly

Anatomy of a Feather

Feathers have been around much longer than the birds they now adorn. Since the 1990s several dinosaurs with simple feathers covering their bodies have been discovered in China and Canada. These early feathers may have been insulating or when colorful may have helped the dinosaurs show off or stay camouflaged. Some non-avian dinosaurs had feathers on their limbs that would not have functioned for flight, while other small dinosaur species grew longer feathers that were helpful in gliding, leading to the evolution of protobirds like the archaeopteryx and microraptor.

Feathers are epidermal growths that form the distinctive outer covering, or plumage, on birds. They are considered the most complex structures found in vertebrates and are an amazing example of a complex evolutionary structure. Although feathers cover most parts of a bird's body, they arise only from certain well-defined tracts on the skin. They aid in flight, thermal insulation, and waterproofing. In addition, coloration helps in communication, mating, and protection from predators. Plumology is the name for the science associated with the study of feathers for those interested in learning more. Next we'll look at the different types of feathers.

Feathers are classified into six distinct categories, although there is occasional overlap.

Flight feathers: Found on the wings and tail, flight feathers are the largest feathers on a bird. On the wings, one side of the vane is wider than the other. They also have stronger barbules, which give them more strength for flight.

Contour feathers: Also called "body" feathers, these give shape and color to the bird. A contour feather becomes downy at the base, which helps insulate the bird.

Down feathers: These have little or no shaft and are soft and fluffy to help insulate birds by trapping air. Next time you use your genuine down pillow or blanket, thank the birds for having those soft warming feathers.

Semiplume feathers: Feathers that are a cross between down and contour feathers. Unlike down, they do have a well-formed shaft. However, they do not have well-developed barbicels, which make them soft.

Bristle feathers: Feathers that are very stiff with only a few barbs found at the base.

Bristle feathers are found around the mouth of insect-eating birds, where they act as a funnel. They can also be found around the eyes, where they work like eyelashes.

Filoplume feathers: Feathers that are very small. They have a tuft of barbs at the end of the shaft. These feathers send messages to the brain that give information about the placement of feathers for flight, insulation, and preening.

Parts of a Feather

What makes up a feather? Let's look at the parts of a flight feather as an example.

Vane: The connected barbs forming a stiff, aerodynamic surface for flight.

Rachis: A typical feather features a main shaft, called the rachis, also commonly called the "stem" or "quill."

Barb: Fused to the rachis are a series of branches, or barbs.

Barbules: The barbs themselves are also branched and form the barbules.

Hooklets: These barbules have minute hooks called barbicels ("hooklets") for cross-attachment.

Afterfeather: The downy lower barbs not yet able to interconnect, as do the barbs above.

Calamus: The hollow shaft tip that connects to the bird's skin.

It is the ability of flight feathers to reconnect and join fibers back together and stay connected that the fly tier takes advantage of.

Feather Coloration—More than Meets the Eye

Color patterns serve as camouflage against predators for birds in their habitats and as camouflage for predators looking for a meal. As with fish, the top and bottom colors may be different, in order to provide camouflage during flight. Striking differences in feather patterns and colors are part of the sexual dimorphism (two sexes of the same species exhibiting different characteristics) of many bird species and are particularly important in mate selection. In some cases differences in the UV reflectivity of

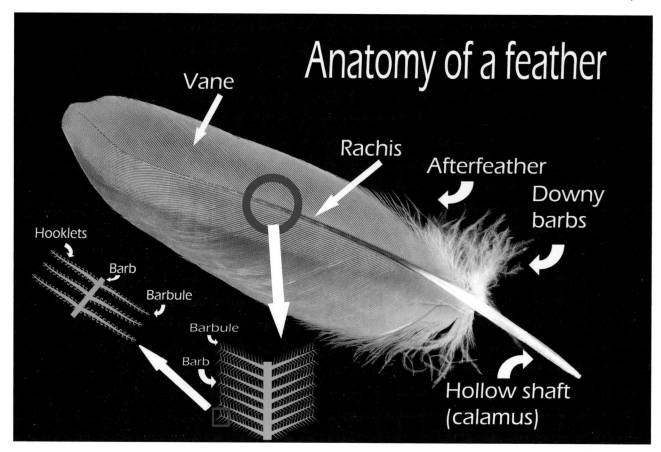

feathers occur across sexes, although no differences in color are noted in the visible range.

The colors of the feathers are produced in several ways: by pigments; by microscopic structures that can refract, reflect, or scatter selected wavelengths of light; or by a combination of both. White feathers lack pigment and scatter light diffusely.

Most colors are caused by a pigment. Yellows, oranges, and reds are pigment based. But what about blue or green? Structural coloration is involved in the production of blue colors through iridescence, reflectance, and enhancement of existing pigment colors. When light hits the blue feather, the feather is designed to reflect back only the blue light to our eyes. Cotinga feathers have this feature, as do all other naturally produced blue feathers. To get green, the yellow feather has reflectance to bounce back blue, and combined they create green. Turacos are the only birds that produce green pigments. All other green birds use a combination of pigments and reflecting blue wavelengths.

This can be shown in a simple experiment. If you take a blue feather and shine a flashlight on it from the top, you will see the bright blue. However,

if you shine the light from underneath the feather, the blue color disappears. If you repeat this experiment with a red feather, the feather will appear red no matter which direction the light passes through.

A bird's feathers undergo wear and tear and are replaced periodically during the bird's life through molting. New feathers, known when developing as blood or pin feathers, depending on the stage of growth, are formed through the same follicles from which the old ones were fledged.

How Feathers Are Used in Fly Tying

Fly tiers use all types of feathers in one manner or another. Whether wrapped around a hook or just tied to it, feathers are an essential part of the tradition and future of fly tying. Classic salmon flies take this pairing to the extreme. The properties of flight feathers from every bird—be it a swan, bustard, turkey, or pheasant—enable strands from the tail of one bird to be connected to the wing of another to literally build a wing feather strip to use in a classic salmon fly. It is truly amazing, like nature's own Velcro system.

Here is an example showing how the wing of the Jock Scott fly is created.

Collect the wing or tail feathers needed to "build" the wing: peacock secondary wing quill, yellow-dyed white goose shoulder, red-dyed white goose shoulder, blue-dyed white goose shoulder, kori bustard, florican bustard, and golden pheasant tail. All feathers for the near-side wing of the fly need to be from the left side of the bird. The near-side wing for right-handed tiers is the left-side wing of the fly when viewed from in front of the fly.

Once assembled, the left sides of the feathers are used to make the near-side wing. As listed in the pattern, the wing is assembled from the bottom up. The fly size will determine how many fibers per feather to use, but normally four to six fibers per material are used.

So to start, cut five fibers of peacock wing from the left side of the feather. Next, cut five fibers off of the yellow goose. Place the goose on edge above the peacock with the tips matching. Touch the tips together and then start stroking the strips back toward the base. Doing this once or twice will lift the barbules and hooklets. Now start stroking and weaving the strips toward the tips. This will get the strips to "marry" back together as if off of one bird. Repeat both

Golden Pheasant

Florican Bustard

Kori Bustard

Blue dyed Goose

Red dyed Goose

Yellow dyed Goose

Peacock wing

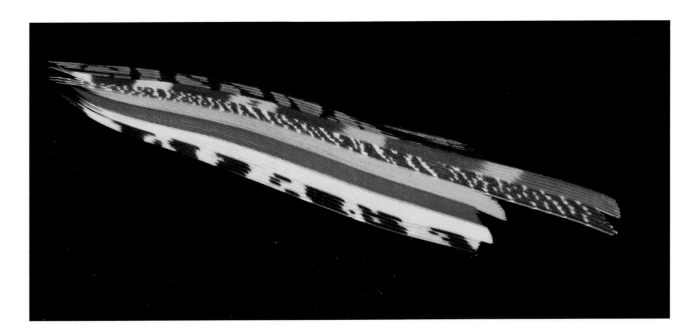

steps as needed to get to where the strips are fully joined. Now cut five strands of the red goose and lay it on top of the yellow. Repeat with all materials until the wing is fully assembled.

The photo above illustrates the finished near-side wing. Now repeat the entire process with feathers from the right side of the birds and assemble the far-side wing, and then you'll be ready to tie the fly. Most tiers actually build the wing as they make the fly, but it can be built up ahead of time—tier's preference.

Anatomy of a Classic Salmon Fly

This section is intended for those who may have never seen a fly made or are new to the process. For those who are experienced tiers, various proportions are discussed, so it may be worth a glance. Hopefully you find it helpful whatever your experience in fly tying. For this example, we'll look in depth at the Jock Scott, a famous classic salmon fly that is a favorite of many tiers.

Just as feathers have specific parts and makeup, so do the classic salmon flies made from them. Even the hook has parts to be aware of and use in the process of constructing any fly. Let's start there.

The Hook

Every hook has five parts: the eye, shank, bend, barb, and point. Following is a description of each part, what it is for, and where it is located.

Eye: The front of the hook the angler attaches the leader (fishing line) to the fly. The eye can be either rolled metal, as in modern hooks, or twisted silkworm gut material. The silkworm gut is drawn out thin and twisted together tightly. This twisted loop is then attached to a "blind-eye" hook, which was the only style available up until the early to mid-1900s. The twisted gut loop was traditionally tied onto the hook the full length of the shank, all the way from front to back, to ensure good strength when fighting and trying to land big Atlantic salmon of old. Modern hooks have a rolled looped eye for the leader to attach to. All flies in this book are tied on blind-eye hooks with silkworm-gut-looped eyes.

Shank: The level portion (or nearly so) of the hook from the eye back to the bend. The shank gives the fly a proportional length, so you can have a relatively larger fly without having to have a huge hook.

Bend: The curve of the hook from the shank down to the barb and point. Various shapes have different names, but all give the hook its unique appearance and style. The distance from the start to end of the bend is known as the gap, or gape, of the hook. This distance determines the hook size.

Barb: The thin, backward-pointing sliver on top of the point area intended to keep the hook locked in the fish's mouth after it has been hooked and the point has sunk in. Aesthetically part of a traditional fly hook, it is functionally detrimental. In reality a hook that is barbless—either manufactured without a barb or made barbless by crushing the barb down with pliers—allows the hook to penetrate and hold onto the fish much better and makes it easier and less harmful to remove from the fish's mouth. I always use barbless hooks for fishing. An added bonus is that it is also much easier to unhook yourself in the event of an accident.

Point: Whether rounded, drooping, shaped with cutting edges, or just plain sharp, the point is the business end of the hook.

The point is also an important reference position, like the barb, for where the body of the fly starts when the tying thread is hanging straight down from the shank.

Hooks can be a passionate subject of discussion all by themselves. Many styles are made, and there are a number of good hook makers. Some are long-standing names such as Partridge, while others are specialty makers of hand-produced hooks of the highest quality. One of the best is Ronn Lucas Sr. of Milwaukie, Oregon. You can see Ronn's offerings, along with a great essay on the history of hooks, at his website, www.ronnlucassr.com. In addition to hooks, he has many unique fly creations for sale as well.

The names most often associated with classic salmon fly hooks include Adlington; Allcock & Co.; Carlisle, Harrison & Co.; Hutchinson; O'Shaughnessy; Partridge; and Wm. Bartleet & Sons. These were the main players in the hooks of old and some are still around today with Partridge, as an example, continuing to produce good quality salmon fly hooks. As with most preferences, there are as many likes and dislikes as there are hooks to be used. Try a variety of styles

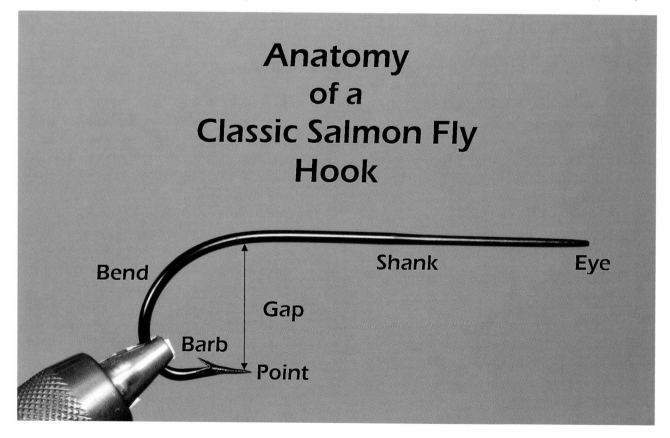

Anatomy of a Classic Salmon Fly Hook

Bend

Shank

Eye

Gap

Barb

Point

Anatomy of a Classic Salmon Fly

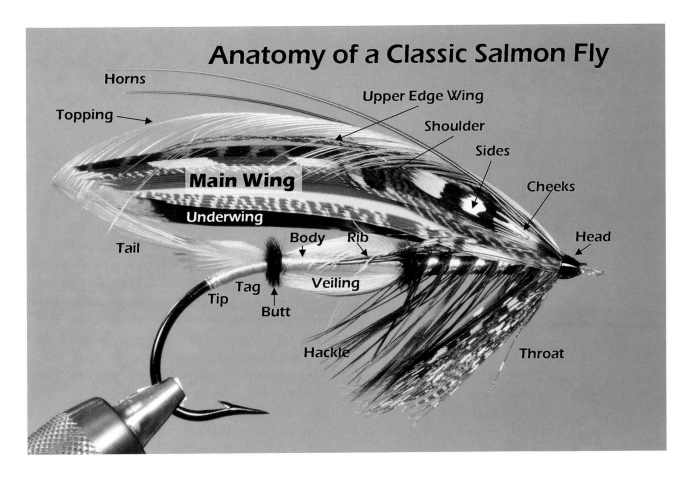

Horns
Topping
Upper Edge Wing
Shoulder
Sides
Cheeks
Main Wing
Underwing
Head
Tail
Body
Rib
Veiling
Tag
Tip
Butt
Hackle
Throat

Parts of the Fly

and find your favorite. And definitely get some of Dave McNeese's outstanding Blue Heron Spey Hooks at www.blueheronspey.com and/or ask for them at your local fly shop.

For additional resources on hooks, materials, and flies, be sure to search out and join a local fly club and frequent your local fly shop. Most if not all are a wealth of knowledge, experience, and help for any aspect of fly tying and fishing. Now on to an example fly and its makeup.

Parts of the Fly

Almost all flies are constructed from the inside out and from the back to the front. Fly-tying thread is wrapped around the hook either by hand or through a tool called a fly-tying bobbin. The bobbin hold the thread spool and the thread feeds out through a small-diameter tube, giving the tier great control over where the thread is placed. The exception to the back-to-front process is when you use a blind-eye hook. The first step is to fold the gut eye and tie it in at the front of the hook, and then move the thread back to

a position above the point or barb to begin constructing the fly.

The pattern listing, or recipe, for the Jock Scott is:

Tip: Fine oval silver tinsel

Tag: Yellow silk floss

Tail: Golden pheasant crest and Indian crow

Butt: Black ostrich herl

Body: Rear half: yellow silk floss veiled above and below with toucan and butted with black ostrich herl. Front half: black floss.

Rib: Fine oval silver tinsel over rear half of body; flat silver tinsel and medium oval silver tinsel over front half

Hackle: Black over front half of body

Underwing: White-tip turkey tail

Wing: Peacock; yellow, red, and blue swan or turkey; kori (speckled) bustard; florican bustard; golden pheasant tail. Over which is peacock sword and bronze mallard for upper edge wing.

Throat: Speckled gallina (guinea fowl)

Shoulders: Narrow married strips of teal and black-barred wood duck extending to butt

Sides: Jungle cock

Cheeks: Blue chatterer
Topping: Golden pheasant crest
Horns: Blue-and-gold macaw
Head: Black

We'll start at the back moving forward and list the parts as they would be created when tying the fly. The proportions listed are my preferences. Some will say this should be shorter or that should be longer. Again, try it and find what you like.

Tip: A fine metal tinsel, normally oval or round, wrapped three to six turns above the barb. Generally tied in and started above the barb.

Tag: Covering the remaining distance from the tip up the bend to a position above the point, the tag is typically a thin layer of fine-grade flat silk floss. The tag can also be just a tinsel alone, and in this case it is half the length of the combination of tip and tag.

Tail: Extends one and a half to two times the gap in length back from the tie-in position above the point. Can be a single material or often a combination. If more than one material, the second is typically half the length of the first material.

Butt: Covers the tie-in point of the tail and provides a visual starting point for the body of the fly.

Rib: If called for, it is tied in at the rear of the body section and is to be wrapped over prior to creating the body. Some patterns call for two ribs over one area, one flat and the other oval. The flat is wrapped first, then the oval follows the back edge of the flat. Tradition calls for five wraps, starting and ending on the bottom of the fly.

Body: The covering of the shank of the hook. Can be a single layer or multiple sections. Floss, tinsel, dubbing fur, chenille, and other materials can be called for. Thin and smooth is normally the preference, but styles and tastes vary greatly.

Veiling: If called for, feathers tied in flat at the top and bottom of the body section they cover.

Joint: Also called a butt, a divider between body sections.

Hackle: A feather, often chicken saddle or neck, wrapped tightly behind a rib. The fibers splay out and give the fly fullness and additional color.

Underwing: Can be made of strips from a larger feather—as in this case, turkey tail—or whole feathers placed back-to-back.

Main wing: Simple strips the same as the underwing, but more often "married" strips as shown in the finished fly pictured. Can also be whole feathers tied back-to-back. If an upper edge wing is called for, it is tied in over the main wing, lying over the top edge like a roof.

Throat: A longer-fibered feather complementing or contrasting the hackle (if used) tied in and pulled down around the sides and underside of the front of the fly. Always tied in with the fibers "swept back" and curving toward the back of the fly.

Shoulders: Strips of various types of feathers tied in on the sides of the main wing and extending back to about the rear butt if possible.

Sides: Additional feathers, often jungle cock neck "nails," tied in on the outside of the main wing and extending back to about the middle of the main wing.

Cheeks: Generally contrasting smaller feathers that are about half the length of the sides.

Topping: Generally a golden pheasant crest feather, but not always. Ideally it should reach back to meet the tip of the tail and form an enclosure for the tail and wing.

Horns: Often macaw center tail fibers, but not always. Tied in so they stand up and curve back lying over the top of the wings and are as long as possible to end at or just beyond the tip of the tail.

Whew! Enough parts for one fly? Some are simpler, others even more complex. Great tiers like Syd Glasso were known to take a full week or even more to tie one fly. Take your time, practice, and above all—have fun. You'll be amazed at what you can create, and practice makes perfect is never truer.

The Flies

For those unfamiliar with fly fishing, we will start at the beginning. Fly fishing is an angling method in which an artificial "fly" is created, often from fur and feather wrapped around a hook with thread, and used to catch fish. The fly is cast using a fly rod, reel, and specialized weighted line. Fly fishers use hand-tied flies that resemble natural insects, baitfish, other foods, or sometimes nothing found in nature to provoke the fish to bite at the fly.

Fly fishing can be done in fresh or salt water. North Americans usually distinguish freshwater fishing between coldwater species (trout, salmon, steelhead) and warmwater species, notably bass. In Britain, where natural water temperatures vary less, the distinction is between gamefishing for trout and salmon versus coarse fishing for other species. Techniques for fly fishing differ with habitat: lakes and ponds, small streams, large rivers, bays and estuaries, and deepwater or shallow flats ocean.

Many credit the first recorded use of an artificial fly to the Roman Claudius Aelianus near the end of the second century. The traditional Japanese method of fly fishing is known as *tenkara* (translated to English as "from heaven"). Tenkara originated in the mountains of Japan as a way for professional fishermen and innkeepers to harvest the local fish, ayu, along with trout and char, for selling and providing as a meal to their guests. It is primarily a small-stream fishing method that was preferred for being highly efficient, where the long rod allowed the fisherman to place the fly where the fish would be.

Izaak Walton's *The Compleat Angler*, published in 1653, helped popularize fly fishing as a sport. Prior to that, "A Treatyse of Fysshynge wyth an Angle," attributed to Dame Juliana Berners, was published in the 1496 edition of *The Boke of Saint Albans*. The essay contains instructions on rod, line, and hook making and dressings for different flies to use at different times of the year. By the 15th century, rods of approximately 14 feet length with a twisted line attached at the tip were probably used in England. As time progressed, so did the sophistication of the tackle, techniques, and flies used to try to fool the fish. Often the best waters in Europe belonged to the titled and wealthy landowners. As such, many had interests in foreign lands, and as their ships traveled farther around the globe, exotic cargo often returned, which included the many varied birds of the time.

The fly tiers of the 17th, 18th, and 19th centuries had more than they could deal with and started creating complex new patterns to be used to catch what was considered the fish of royalty, the Atlantic salmon. Atlantic salmon returned to the freshwater rivers after years of feasting in salt water to meet back where they hatched from eggs, to mate and expire to start the cycle of life again. They can be ready takers of a well-presented fly on their journey, and many involved patterns to do just that came into being.

Traditional versus Modern Classic Salmon Flies

Traditional flies, or "true" classics, are flies designed and created centuries ago, prior to or during the Victorian era. The Victorian era of British history was the period of Queen Victoria's reign from 1837 until her death in 1901. It was a long period of peace, prosperity, refined sensibilities, and national self-confidence for Britain. Modern flies are any patterns developed after the Victorian era.

Here is a breakdown of the flies in this book:

Traditional Classics

Black Argus
Bronze Pirate
Jock Scott
Lady Amherst
Nelly Bly
White Winged Akroyd

Modern Classics

Emerald Isle
Firebird
Glimpse of Paradise
Grand Argus
Jo's Jewel
Leopard
Noir et Blanc
Ocellation
Spotted Tiger
Swinhoe's Splendor

Other Flies Using Unusual Feathers

Classic salmon flies are not the only flies out there, of course. Many flies tied for other fish utilize the amazing feathers discussed herein. A good example are the wonderful streamer patterns developed in Maine and other areas for trout. Whether cast or trolled, these flies intended to suggest baitfish swimming through the water are indeed works of art in their own right. One of the masters was Carrie Stevens, who developed many patterns that are still considered masterpieces of functional and aesthetic design.

A newfound friend, Jon LeBretton, sent me a photo of one of his flies utilizing Crawford Kalij pheasant for the shoulder. An up-and-coming fly tier, Jon has deep family roots in the salmon and trout pools of the Penobscot River and central Maine. Carrying on the traditions of earlier generations, he specializes in tying the heritage wet fly and streamer patterns of Maine as well as full-dress Atlantic salmon flies.

Jon has fished the famed waters of New England most of his life and has learned, through trial and error, what works, and he strives to implement colors, materials, and patterns that have proven effective, regardless of convention. Now living in Boston, Massachusetts, and a registered nurse by profession, Jon focuses the same attention to detail he uses in his professional life into his tying. Whether he is trolling streamers, swinging wet flies, or casting dry flies to finicky fish, Jon's love of fly fishing is evident in every cast he makes and fly he ties.

Here is his description of the fly he tied for this book, the Austie's Special:

Hook: Partridge CS-15 "Carrie Stevens" 2/0
Tag: Wide silver tinsel
Body: Wide silver tinsel
Underbelly: Red bucktail
Throat: Red, then blue hackle fibers
Underwing: Peacock herl
Wing: 4 gray hackles
Shoulder: Crawford Kalij pheasant body feather
Cheek: Jungle cock
Head: Black with red stripe

Jon's pattern note: This pattern appears to be synonymous with the Austin's Special (Stevens). My research found both the shoulder feather and the names used interchangeably. Although I was not able to fully make a determination, even after consulting with authors of books on the subject, my assumption is that the Austie's Special is a less-popular pattern using a white-on-black lineated pheasant shoulder rather than the black-on-white silver pheasant shoulder of the Austin's Special. It is possible that the pattern evolved due to the relative difficulty in obtaining lineated pheasant feathers compared to silver pheasant.

A lot of flies used in all sorts of scenarios in fly angling utilize many of the feathers discussed herein. But it is the classics, as they are called, that call for many of the exotic feathers most often, are the most fascinating, and show the ultimate example of the art and science of fly tying.

Fly-Tying Tools

So what does it take to make a fly, be it for trout, salmon, tarpon, bluegill, or barracuda? Basically, a hook, thread, and the materials to attach to the hook. Tiers of old used to tie in hand, by hand, meaning they would hold the hook in their left hand (for right-handed tiers) and the thread, either a precut length or a small spool, in the other. Some great tiers of today still honor this tradition. The great Harry Lemire tied many a fly in this style, and his were some of the best. Whether his famous Greased Liner for steelhead, or a classic like the Gordon, he tied all in hand with no tools.

Luckily we have some great tools today to help those of us not quite as talented as Harry. I like to keep things fairly simple, though, using a limited number of tools. They include:

Vise: A clamp, either table edge or tabletop, that holds the hook. This gives us both hands free to work with, though at times I'd like to have another pair to hold, wrap, position, and get everything where I want it.

Bobbin: A small tube mounted to a pair of sprung legs to hold the thread spool. It gives great control of the placement of the thread wraps and provides weight to keep the wraps you've just made tight while you prepare the next materials.

Thread: Considered a material, to me it is literally the binding fiber that holds the fly together and is the tool of creating any fly. I use two threads: flat white monochord or flat waxed floss for the underbody, and UNI-Midge 8/0 for the wing and finishing of the fly. You want a flat thread to untwist and lie as thin as possible for the underbody. Then finishing with the 8/0 gives fine diameter and great strength for tying in and securing throats, wings, and all the fine finishing feathers from shoulders through sides and cheeks, toppings and horns, all the while maintaining a nice, small, packed head. Ideally the head is a small billet shape, smallest in front and tapering up to the materials it secures. All I can say is practice often and you'll get some nice, small heads with the techniques I'll show you and time spent behind the vise.

Scissors: Sharp with fine, small points are a must to trim materials and keep the fly's head as small as possible. Small heads keep the focus on the fly itself and not on a large, distracting ball of thread near the eye.

Hackle pliers: A small clamp to hold feathers as they are wrapped around the hook for hackle or as a throat. Can also hold smaller feathers to give you both hands free to position and tie down the material.

Bodkin: A needle set in a handle. Used to loosen or strip out fibers from a wing or tail quill for married wings. Also used to apply the finishing coating of head cement over the head after tying off the thread.

Body divider: Nearly essential to get evenly sectioned bodies on the many flies that call for multiple sections. This is used to mark off even body sections on the underbody thread wraps to determine where to start and stop each section.

You can download my body divider *free* at my website, www.modernclassicsflytying.com.

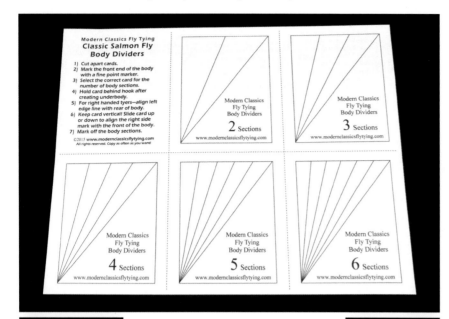

Download the MCFT (Modern Classics Fly Tying) Body Divider in PDF format and print it out.

Cut the six sections apart.

When you are tying a fly, complete the construction of the underbody. You can either use the sheet while the hook is in the vise or tie off the thread and take the hook out and mark it on a tabletop, as in the example shown here. I usually mark it up while still in the vise.

Select the sheet with the number of sections you need for your fly.

The sheets will tie the
smallest fly up to an
8/0 or even 10/0 if
you can find them.

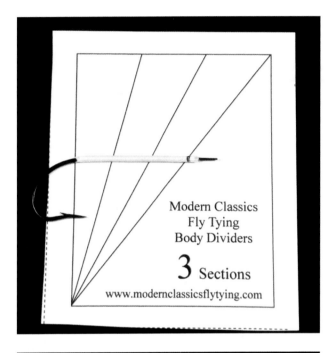

Mark the front end of the body with a fine-point
felt-tip marker. Make sure it is permanent so it
won't bleed later if you are going to fish the flies.
Now either hold the sheet behind the fly in the vise
or lay the hook down on the sheet. Either way, it
is **vital** that the line on the left side line up with
the back of the body (usually at an ostrich herl
butt) and that the sheet is kept **vertical** if holding
behind the hook in the vise. Slide the sheet up or
down until the line on the right side is even with
the mark at the front of the body. At this point the
rear of the body is over the left-side line and the
front of the body meets the right-side line.

Mark off the sections and that's it! You are
ready to continue tying with nice, even body
sections all laid out for your reference.

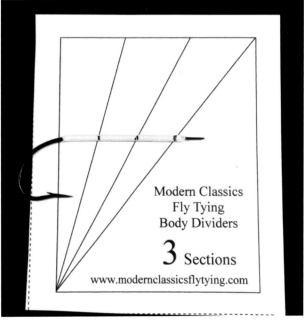

How Flies Are Made

All flies, from the smallest size 32 trout micromidge to the largest 10/0 tandem saltwater trolling fly, are made by hand-wrapping thread around the hook and binding the materials in place in the process. Right-handed tiers wrap from the front, over the top to the back, around underneath, and back up again. As long as you maintain this direction from start to finish, a well-constructed fly can be made.

Also important is walking the tightrope of using as tight of wraps as possible—but without breaking the thread. Tight wraps bind the materials securely to the hook so they won't come off or move around. It takes practice by trial and error to learn how much pressure you can put on the thread without breaking it. Again—practice, practice, practice.

Every part of each fly's construction is covered in the "How to Tie the Flies" instructions (page 111). If you go through every pattern, you will find some repetition in the descriptions. But that's how it is when tying the flies. You mount the hook in the vise the same way every time. You start out and attach a gut loop eye the same way every time. I could have

skipped the steps and said "refer to page . . .," but I know I hate to have to look up other pages and steps when I'm working on something. So I'm not going to make you do so either. Every fly has all steps start to finish. So forgive the repetition by understanding its intent. Whether you try one or all, each has everything you need. Good luck and have fun! I make no claim as to being an expert—I have much to learn and perfect, but that's part of the lifelong fun of fly tying. Every fly gets a bit better. You learn from mistakes and can add new techniques as you learn them. I just enjoy sharing what I've learned and hope others will enjoy what I am presenting here. Please keep in touch to let me know how your tying is going, if you have any trouble along the way, or need help sourcing materials, and send some photos of your flies to me at info@modernclassicsflytying.com. I'll be glad to help as I can and look forward to seeing your work!

Following are the step-by-step instructions and photos to tie all 16 flies in this book. Almost all of the 50 birds listed are utilized somewhere in these flies to showcase their unique properties and appearance.

How to Tie the Flies

BLACK ARGUS

The Black Argus is one of the many creative patterns designed by Major John Popkin Traherne in the mid-19th century. It is a whole-wing pattern, which was his mainstay pattern style. Major Traherne was born August 28, 1826, and caught his first salmon in 1850. From then on he fished most rivers in the United Kingdom until the time of his death in 1901.

The Black Argus has both high contrast of black and white in the wings and vivid color in the body of the fly. Bright orange with red-tip Indian crow breast feathers are displayed at the rear of the fly, adding a special hot spot of rich color. Below the body are two sets of blue chatterer, which are from the cotinga species. They have amazing "electric" blue body feathers, which add a striking burst of color to any fly.

The Black Argus wings feature body feathers from the western tragopan pheasant, which has unique reddish brown body feathers with black

ends highlighted with a bright round white spot. Matched pairs of feathers, tied in back-to-back, create a symmetrical appearance of simple beauty. In front of these, tips of wood duck black-barred flank feathers are tied in, providing a covering for the front of the pheasant feathers and a nice tapering transition to the eye of the fly. Add toucan for a bit of yellow and scarlet macaw for horns, and you have the materials to make the Black Argus.

Hook: Blind eye black salmon fly—style and size of your choice
Thread: Black
Tip: Fine oval silver tinsel
Tag: Claret silk floss
Tail: Golden pheasant crest
Butt: Black ostrich herl
Body: Three equal sections: First is flat gold tinsel veiled above and below with matched pairs of Indian crow back-to-back, set vertically and

butted with black ostrich herl. Middle and front sections are flat silver tinsel veiled below with matched pairs of blue chatterer back-to-back, set vertically and butted with black ostrich herl between the sections.

Wings: Three matched pairs of western tragopan pheasant spotted body feathers with progressively smaller spots. Each pair is outside the prior pair and shorter to show the full spot of the prior pair.

Sides: Black barred wood duck flank feather tip extending back to blend in with the taper of the tragopan feathers

Cheeks: Three golden toucan breast feathers, one over the other

Horns: Red macaw

Head: Black ostrich herl

Tying the Black Argus

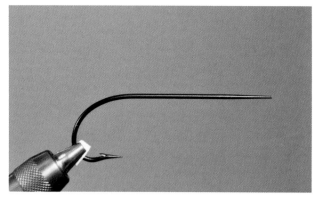

1 Create a liner to place between the hook wire and the vise jaws. I apply a single strip of Scotch tape to a 3-by-5-inch note card edge, then cut out a small rectangle about ½ by ¼ inch. Fold it over lengthwise with the tape on the inside. Taper the folded tip edges to match the jaw size and taper. Fold this piece around the hook bend where it will be placed in the vise jaws and move into place.

Secure the hook tightly in the vise with the hook shank level. Having the hook shank as level as possible is very important. The starting positions for material placement as well as overall proportions are based on where the tying thread hangs down from the hook. The positions of the thread as "even with the barb" or "even with the point" are starting positions for tags, tips, and the butt and/or body of the fly. If the hook shank is not level,

the position indicated will not be correct. If the hook shank is drooping excessively, the tag and body positions will be too far back. Same if the hook shank is tilted up too much—the tag and body will be too short. Likewise, be sure the hook is held securely so good, tight thread wraps and material positioning can be accomplished without the hook working loose.

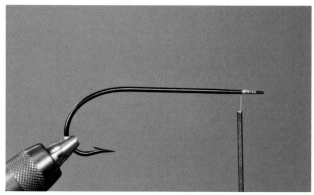

2 Attach the tying thread back from the end of the shank or eye. Be sure the wraps are tight and the thread end is secured well as a starting point for the entire fly. Create a single layer of wraps as a base for attaching the gut eye. Make sure to stay far enough back from the end of the shank tip. The tip of the shank on a blind-eye hook should be exposed ever so slightly and show over the gut loop eye.

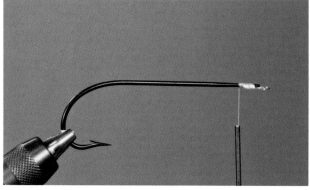

3 Secure the gut eye by folding it over and laying both "legs" under the shank and wrapping over them tightly. As genuine silkworm gut material is both hard to find and expensive, modern tiers use only a small length to form the eye. Traditional flies that were actually used for fishing had strands extending back for the full shank length, well secured to provide a strong and durable connection for hooking and landing the large Atlantic salmon of old.

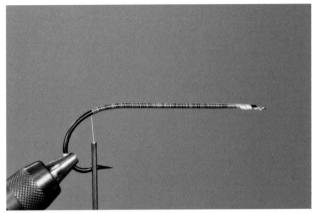

4 Create a smooth layer of thread all the way back on the shank to the starting point of the tag or tip. The underbody needs to be as smooth as possible; whatever the underbody shows as rough or inconsistent spots will often show through the body wrapped over it. I can always improve my underbody work and never seem to get it as consistent or smooth as I'd like it to be—stick with it and practice often.

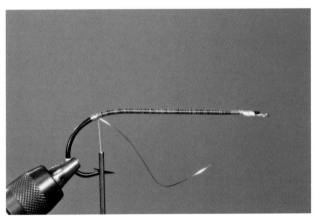

5 Attach the fine oval silver tinsel ("twist") for the tip immediately above the barb. Advance the thread five wide wraps forward to get it out of the way. Make five wraps of the tinsel spiraling forward with each wrap tightly touching the previous. Don't overlap—one single layer is all you want—and do not allow any gaps between wraps. Unwrap the five wide thread wraps until back at the end of the finished wraps of the tinsel. Tie off the tinsel securely with several tight wraps of thread spiraling forward. Trim off the excess.

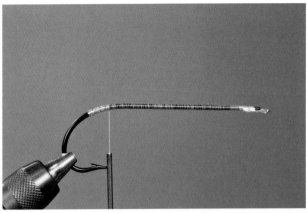

6 Advance the thread in a smooth layer to a position where the thread hangs down even with the hook point. Use a burnisher to smooth out and flatten the thread wraps if in doubt.

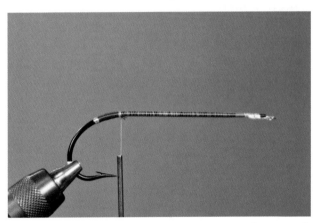

7 Unless your hands are very clean with smooth fingers to handle the silk floss, you may want to use silk gloves to provide a clean, smooth surface to handle the delicate floss.

Attach a single strand of claret silk floss with three tight wraps of thread. Make five open wraps of thread to the eye to move the thread and bobbin out of your way. Stroke the floss a few times to straighten and even the fibers. Wrap a single smooth layer of the floss back to the tinsel, then reverse direction, wrapping back up the bend to where the floss was tied in above the point. Once there, unwrap the five turns of thread over the shank and two more tie-down wraps, then tie off the end of the floss tightly and end up above the point again. Trim the excess floss, and you are now ready to tie in the tail.

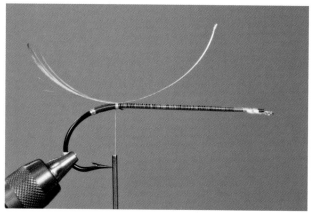

8 Select a single golden pheasant crest feather. Length and curvature depend on your fly style preference. A short, tightly curved tail will give a more traditional Old World look to the fly. It will require a high wing and tightly curved topping to match the tail's shape. A longer, less curved crest will result in a longer, shallower wing with a "sleeker," more streamlined appearance. Use a feather of size and quality as one that could be used as a topping. Smaller feathers just don't have the "body," curvature, or fiber length to match with a crest used for a topping. Strip fibers off the rachis to the tie-in point. Make a couple of tight wraps while holding the crest in position on top of the hook, then release to see how it sits. Untie and retie in as needed until properly set. Once set correctly, make a couple more tight wraps to lock it in place. Trim off the excess.

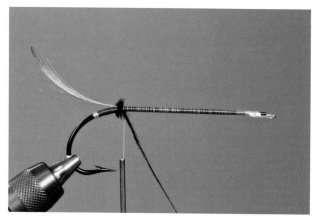

9 Attach a single strand of black ostrich herl. The herl has a slant to the fibers off of the core rachis. Ideally the herl is tied in so when wrapped, the fibers slant back toward the hook bend. Advance the tying thread slightly and make four to six wraps spiraling toward the hook eye.

Keep wraps close together with no gap between or overlap. Tie off and trim the excess herl.

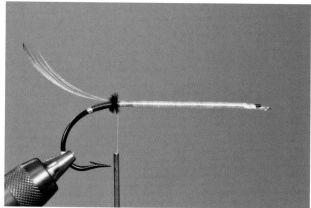

10 Construct the underbody. The purpose of the underbody is to provide a smooth tapering up to the ends of the gut loop which is attached underneath the hook shank. Attach a long single or paired strands of smooth, flat white floss at the front of the hook shank behind the gut loop ends on the underside of the hook. Make smooth, even wraps with the floss back to the rear of the body, then start wrapping back to the front. Stop at the ends of the gut loop and start wrapping toward the back again but this time stop about one-fifth of the body length away from the rear of the body. Repeat as needed, each time stopping farther away from the rear of the body. When built up sufficiently to match the diameter of the shank and gut eye ends, wrap forward to the end of the body. DO NOT GO TOO FAR FORWARD!!! Leave about one-fifth of the shank and eye uncovered to use for the winging and throat. Tie off the floss at the front of the body and add a couple of half-hitch knots to secure the thread temporarily. Cut the thread off. Use a burnisher to smooth out the underbody. Reattach the tying thread at the rear of the body. (For detailed steps, see Michael Radencich's excellent step-by-step instructional DVD *Tying the Classic Salmon Fly*. See "Recommended Reading and Viewing" for details.) Reattach the tying thread at the rear of the body.

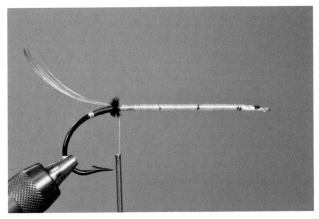

11 Use a body divider (get mine free at my website, www.modernclassicsflytying.com) and mark off the position of the end of the body near the eye; then divide the body into three equal sections, marking off the location of the two butts that will divide the body sections.

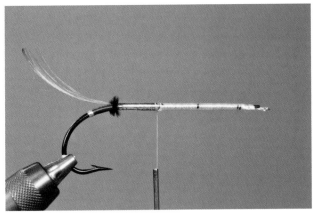

12 Advance the tying thread in a smooth single layer to the first mark. Attach the gold flat tinsel and wrap evenly back to the rear butt; then reverse direction, wrap back up to the thread position, and tie off. Keep tight, even wraps with no gaps or overlap.

13 Select two matched Indian crow feathers. Place back-to-back and position above the front of the body section just created. Tips should extend back to right above the ostrich herl butt. Where they will be tied in, strip the fibers off the rachis on both sides. This creates a flat area on both sides of the rachis that helps orient the feathers vertically, which is how you want to tie them in. Secure the feathers tightly on edge vertically above the end of the body section and extending back to the ostrich herl butt. Tie off tightly. Leave the excess extending forward while you complete the next step.

14 As in the last step, select two more matching Indian crow feathers. Place back-to-back and position below the front of the body section just created. Tips should extend back to right below the ostrich herl butt. As in the prior step, strip the fibers off the rachis on both sides. Secure the feathers tightly on edge vertically below the end of the body section and extending back to the ostrich herl butt. Tie off tightly.

15 Trim off the excess of the Indian crow feathers top and bottom. Select a black ostrich herl strand. Tie in and wrap four to six turns to form a "joint" between the body sections. Tie off and trim the excess closely.

16 Advance the tying thread in a single smooth layer to the next mark in the underbody. Tie in flat silver tinsel. Wrap the tinsel evenly to the ostrich herl joint just created and back up. Tie off tightly and trim the excess.

17 Select two matching medium-size blue chatterer (cotinga) feathers. Place back-to-back and measure for length. The tips should be even

with, or slightly longer than, the ostrich herl joint. Where they will be tied in, strip the fibers off both sides of the rachis to create a flat area on both sides to help orient the feathers vertically, which is how you want to tie them in. Secure the feathers tightly on edge vertically below the end of the body section and extending back to or just beyond the ostrich herl joint. Tie off tightly.

18 Trim off the excess of the blue chatterer feathers. Select a black ostrich herl strand. Tie in and wrap four to six turns to form a "joint" between the body sections. Tie off and trim the excess closely.

19 Advance the tying thread in a single smooth layer to the front mark at the end of the body. Tie in flat silver tinsel. Wrap the tinsel evenly to the ostrich herl joint just created and back up. Tie off tightly and trim the excess.

20 Select a matched pair of western tragopan pheasant body feathers with a vivid white spot and black tip. Place back-to-back and measure for length. The tips should extend back to the end of the tail and sit inside the tail's curve. Strip fibers off of both sides of the feather about halfway up. You need to strip this far up in order for the feather to lie flat and tuck into the curve of the tail. If fibers were left on the feather farther down, they would cause the feather to "stand up" and lift away from the tail. Additional feathers will cover the stripped sections as you proceed. Tie in carefully and check often to be sure the feathers stay aligned, fit in the tail correctly, sit on edge vertically, and are not crooked or lying off to one side or the other. They should be vertical and centered directly over the top of the hook shank.

21 Select another matched pair of western tragopan pheasant body feathers with a vivid white spot and black tip, but the spot should be slightly smaller than the first pair. Place this pair back-to-back outside of the first pair and measure for length. The tips should extend well back from the first pair, leaving the white spot and black tip of the first pair clearly visible underneath.

Strip fibers off of both sides of the feather about halfway up. Tie in securely and make sure the feathers are flat up against the first pair and are vertical. They should "tuck" in against the first pair and help press them together. If needed, untie and pinch the inside of the rachis to help curve the outer pair in against the first pair.

22 Repeat the last process with a third matched pair of the western tragopan pheasant body feathers. As before, the tips should extend well back from the last pair, leaving the white spot and black tip of all three pairs clearly visible. Strip fibers off of both sides of the feather about halfway up. Tie in securely and make sure the feathers are flat up against the last pair and are vertical. They should "tuck" in against the last pair and help press them together. If needed, untie and pinch the inside of the rachis to help curve the outer pair in against the last pair. Tie off securely and trim the rachis of all three pairs.

23 Select a matched pair of wood duck black barred flank feathers. Place back-to-back with the tips matched. Position so they will extend back to match the taper of the last pair of feathers and cover their base. Trim them slightly longer than needed. Trim off a few fibers on each side of the rachis to ensure they will lie flat when tied in on the side of the hook. Tie in tightly and trim the excess.

24 Select a long, full, well-colored golden pheasant crest feather for the topping. By tradition the tip of the feather should have a reddish cast. Lay it over the top of the wing and measure for length. The tip should meet the tip of the tail, and the curvature should match the curve of the wing. The center portion of the topping may need to be "straightened" a bit to match the shape of the wing. If needed, gently stroke the top edge of the topping with your fingernail. This will take out some of the curvature. Go slowly and little by little until it matches the upper edge curvature when you hold the crest over or beside the top edge of the wing. Strip off excess fibers beyond the tie-in point. Use a small pair of flat-nose smooth-jaw pliers to flatten the rachis at the tie-in point. Hold

the top of the wing tightly and make several wraps to tie in the topping. Lift it up a bit to be sure it is aligned with the top edge of the wing and doesn't twist or curve away. If it does, untie and retie until it sits correctly on its own. Trim off the excess.

25 Select two matching blue chatterer (cotinga) feathers larger than the prior pair. Place back-to-back and measure for length. The tips should be longer than the prior pair and extend well past the ostrich herl joint. Strip the fibers off both sides of the rachis where they will be tied in to create a flat area on both sides to help orient the feathers vertically, which is how you want to tie them in. Secure the feathers tightly on edge vertically below the end of the body. Tie off tightly.

26 Select three golden yellow toucan breast feathers per side. Lay one flat on top of another with the tip ends matching. Measure for length (typically halfway up the wood duck feathers underneath) and trim the fibers off the sides of the rachis to get the feathers to tie in flat. Tie in together, one on top of another, flat over the wood duck feathers for the cheeks. Repeat on the other side. Trim off the excess.

27 Select a matched pair of scarlet macaw tail fibers long enough to extend to the end of the wing or as close to it as possible. The fiber from the left side of the tail is tied in on the near side (for right-handed tiers), and the other fiber from the right side of the tail goes on the far side. The fibers should reach up just above the back of the wing and match in length and curvature to where they meet above the wing. Tie in tightly and trim the excess.

28 Tie in a single black ostrich herl fiber. Advance the thread toward the eye slightly, then wrap the ostrich herl six turns plus or minus. Tie off and trim the excess to create the head of the fly.

29 Tie the thread off by either using several half hitches or, my preferred method, whip finishing. Trim the thread, cement the head, and you are finished!

BRONZE PIRATE

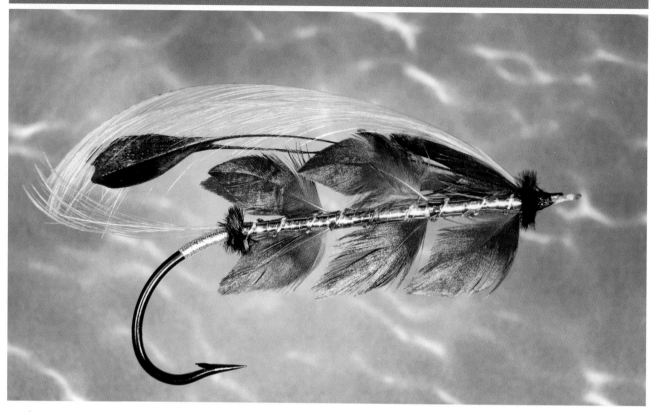

One of the many great flies Major John Traherne created in the mid-1800s, the Bronze Pirate features feathers from the Impeyan pheasant, also known as the Himalayan monal pheasant. Almost metallic in appearance, the crest feathers and bronze-colored neck feathers are both subtle and striking in appearance. Subdued until viewed at the correct angle with light, these feathers appear as if lit up from within. Vibrant greens and bronze colors shine through, and one can only imagine the fish's reaction as these colors flash on and off as the fly swims through the current.

While tradition states the fly should be tied on a size 7 hook, I took some creative liberty to tie it in a 7/0 to show the colors and character of the feathers and the beauty in the simplicity of the design.

Hook: Blind eye black salmon fly—style and size of your choice

Thread: BlackTag: Silver twist

Tail: Golden pheasant crest

Butt: Black ostrich herl

Body: Silver tinsel ribbed with silver twist, partially butted in three equal sections with Impeyan pheasant bronze neck feathers increasing in size

Wing: Two Impeyan pheasant crests back-to-back and two golden pheasant crest toppings

Head: Black herl

Tying the Bronze Pirate

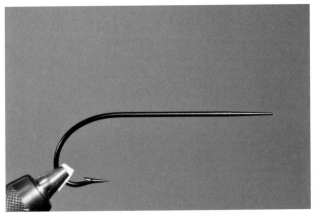

1 Create a liner to place between the hook wire and the vise jaws. I apply a single strip of Scotch tape to a 3-by-5-inch note card edge, then cut out a small rectangle about ½ by ¼ inch. Fold it over lengthwise with the tape on the inside. Taper the folded tip edges to match the jaw size and taper. Fold this piece around the hook bend where it will be placed in the vise jaws and move into place.

Secure the hook tightly in the vise with the hook shank level. Having the hook shank as level as possible is very important. The starting positions for material placement as well as overall proportions are based on where the tying thread hangs down from the hook. The positions of the thread as "even with the barb" or "even with the point" are starting positions for tags, tips, and the butt and/or body of the fly. If the hook shank is not level, the position indicated will not be correct. If the hook shank is drooping excessively, the tag and body positions will be too far back. Same if the hook shank is tilted up too much—the tag and body will be too short. Likewise, be sure the hook is held securely so good, tight thread wraps and material positioning can be accomplished without the hook working loose.

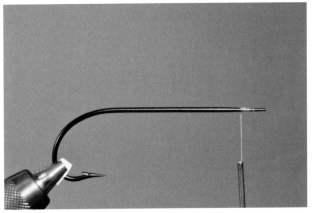

2 Attach the tying thread back from the end of the shank or eye. Be sure the wraps are tight and the thread end is secured well as a starting point for the entire fly. Create a single layer of wraps as a base for attaching the gut eye. Make sure to stay far enough back from the end of the shank tip. The tip of the shank on a blind-eye hook should be exposed ever so slightly and show over the gut loop eye.

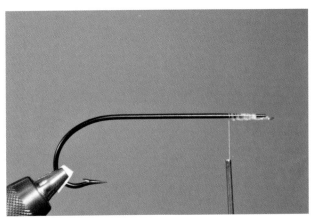

3 Secure the gut eye by folding it over and laying both "legs" under the shank and wrapping over them tightly. As genuine silkworm gut material is both hard to find and expensive, modern tiers use only a small length to form the eye. Traditional flies that were actually used for fishing had strands extending back for the full shank length, well secured to provide a strong and durable connection for hooking and landing the large Atlantic salmon of old.

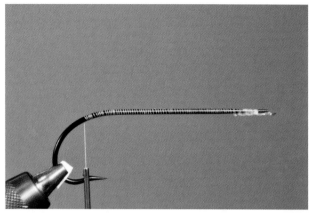

4 Create a smooth layer of thread all the way back on the shank to the starting point of the tag above the point. The underbody needs to be as smooth as possible; whatever the underbody shows as rough or inconsistent spots will often show through the body wrapped over it. I can always improve my underbody work and never seem to get it as consistent or smooth as I'd like it to be—stick with it and practice often.

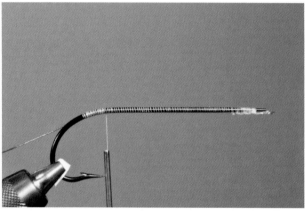

5 Attach the silver twist tinsel for the tag immediately above the point. Advance the thread five wide wraps forward to get it out of the way.

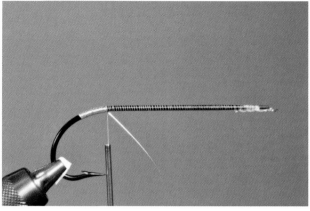

6 Wrap the tinsel spiraling forward with each wrap tightly touching the previous. Don't overlap—one single layer is all you want—and do not allow any gaps between wraps. Once above the point, unwrap the five wide thread wraps until back above the point at the end of the finished wraps of the tinsel. Tie off the tinsel securely with several tight wraps of thread spiraling forward. Trim off the excess.

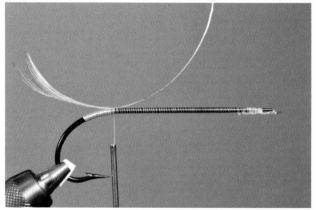

7 Select a single golden pheasant crest for the tail. Ideally it has a reddish cast to the tip. Length and curvature depend on your fly style preference. A short, tightly curved tail will give a more traditional Old World look to the fly. A longer, less curved crest will result in a longer, shallower wing with a "sleeker," more streamlined appearance. Use a feather of size and quality as one that could be used as a topping. Smaller feathers just don't have the "body," curvature, or fiber length to match with a crest used for a topping. Strip fibers off the rachis to the tie-in point. Make a couple of tight wraps while holding the crest in position on top of the hook, then release to see how it sits. Untie and retie in as needed until properly set. Once set correctly, make a couple more tight wraps to lock it in place.

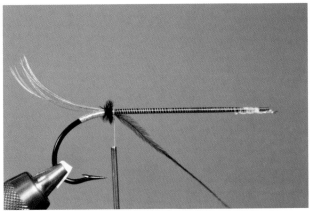

8 Tie in a single strand of black ostrich herl. The herl has a slant to the fibers off of the core rachis. Ideally the herl is tied in so when wrapped, the fibers slant back toward the hook bend. Advance the tying thread slightly and make four to six wraps spiraling toward the hook eye. Keep wraps close together with no gap between or overlap. Tie off and trim the excess herl.

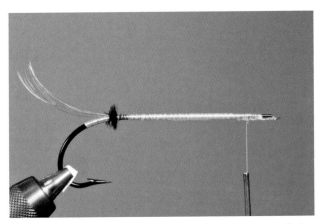

9 Construct the underbody. The purpose of the underbody is to provide a smooth tapering up to the ends of the gut loop which is attached underneath the hook shank. Attach a long single or paired strands of smooth, flat white floss at the front of the hook shank behind the gut loop ends on the underside of the hook. Make smooth, even wraps with the floss back to the rear of the body, then start wrapping back to the front. Stop at the ends of the gut loop and start wrapping toward the back again but this time stop about one-fifth of the body length away from the rear of the body. Repeat as needed, each time stopping farther away from the rear of the body. When built up sufficiently to match the diameter of the shank and gut eye ends, wrap forward to the end of the body. **DO NOT GO TOO FAR FORWARD!!!**

Leave about one-fifth of the shank and eye uncovered to use for the winging and throat. Tie off the floss at the front of the body and add a couple of half-hitch knots to secure the thread temporarily. Cut the thread off. Use a burnisher to smooth out the underbody. Reattach the tying thread at the rear of the body. See the aforementioned DVD for detailed steps for this process.

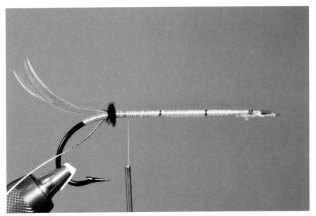

10 Use a body divider (get mine free at my website, www.modernclassicsflytying.com) and mark off the position of the end of the body near the eye; then divide the body into three equal sections. Attach the oval silver tinsel for the ribbing on the underside of the shank. Advance the thread in smooth, even wraps up to the first mark.

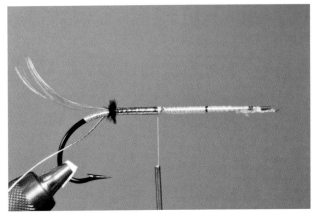

11 Attach the flat silver tinsel. Wrap back to the butt in smooth, even turns—not overlapping nor with any gaps. Once back to the butt, reverse direction and wrap back up to the thread. Tie off tightly and trim the excess.

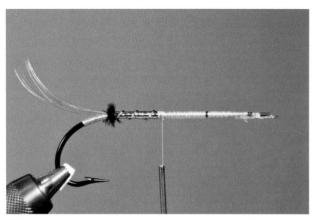

12 Wrap the rib three turns and tie off securely. Trim off the excess.

13 Select two matched pairs of the bronze-colored neck feathers from an Impeyan pheasant. Match the tips and measure for length. The tips when tied in should be even with or slightly past the ostrich herl butt. At the tie-in point, strip the fibers off of both sides of the rachis. This creates a flat area on both sides that helps orient the feathers vertically when tied in, which is how you want them to be. Tie in the first pair on top, with the tips curving inwards toward the hook.

14 Tie in the bottom pair to mirror the top pair in length and position.

15 Tie in the oval tinsel on the bottom of the shank. Advance the thread in a smooth, even layer to the next mark.

16 Tie in the flat silver tinsel. Wrap back to the front end of the first body section in smooth, even turns—not overlapping nor with any gaps. Once back to the butt, reverse direction and wrap back up to the thread. Tie off tightly and trim the excess. Wrap the rib in three turns and tie off underneath the shank.

17 Select two matched pairs of the bronze-colored neck feathers from an Impeyan pheasant. This second set should be slightly larger than the first set. Match the tips and measure for length. The feathers should extend past the end of the first body section—again, larger overall than the first pair. At the tie-in point, strip the fibers off of both sides of the rachis. This creates a flat area on both sides that helps orient the feathers vertically when tied in, which is how you want them to be. Tie in the first pair on top, with the tips curving inwards toward the hook.

18 Tie in the bottom pair to mirror the top pair in length and position.

19 Tie in the oval tinsel on the bottom of the shank. Advance the thread in a smooth, even layer to the next mark.

20 Tie in the flat silver tinsel. Wrap back to the front end of the second body section in smooth, even turns—not overlapping nor with any gaps. Once back to the butt, reverse direction and wrap back up to the thread. Tie off tightly and trim the excess. Wrap the rib in three turns and tie off underneath the shank.

21 Wrap the rib in three turns and tie off underneath the shank.

23 Tie in the bottom pair to mirror the top pair in length and position.

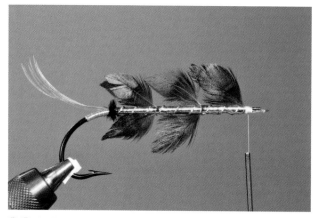

22 Select two matched pairs of the bronze-colored neck feathers from an Impeyan pheasant. This third set should be slightly larger than the second set. Match the tips and measure for length. The feathers should extend past the end of the second body section—about halfway back on the second body section and larger overall than the second pair. At the tie-in point, strip the fibers off of both sides of the rachis. This creates a flat area on both sides that helps orient the feathers vertically when tied in, which is how you want them to be. Tie in the first pair on top, with the tips curving inwards toward the hook.

24 Select a matched pair of Impeyan pheasant crest feathers. Place back-to-back and measure for length. The tips should extend back to just inside the tip of the tail. Tie in tightly, one on each side, and trim off the excess.

25 Select two golden pheasant crests for the remainder of the wing. By tradition the tips of the feathers should have a reddish cast. Lay them over the top of the Impeyan wing and measure for length. The tips should meet the tip of the tail, and the curvature should match the curve of the wing. The center portion of the toppings may need to be "straightened" a bit to match the shape of the wing. If needed, gently stroke the top edge of the toppings with your fingernail. This will take out some of the curvature. Go slowly and little by little until it matches the upper edge curvature when you hold the crest over or beside the top edge of the wing. Strip off excess fibers beyond the tie-in point. Use a small pair of flat-nose smooth-jaw pliers to flatten the rachis at the tie-in point. Tie in together or one at a time—your preference. Hold the top of the wing tightly and make several wraps to tie in the topping. Lift it up a bit to be sure it is aligned with the top edge of the wing and doesn't twist or curve away. If it does, untie and retie until it sits correctly on its own. Trim off the excess.

26 Tie in a single black ostrich herl fiber. Advance the thread toward the eye slightly, then wrap the ostrich herl six turns plus or minus. Tie off and trim the excess to create the head of the fly. Tie the thread off by either using several half hitches or, my preferred method, whip finishing. Trim the thread, cement the head, and you are finished!

EMERALD ISLE

I created this fly to display the beautiful, darker, and more richly colored Germain's peacock pheasant feathers. Add Nicobar pigeon, African emerald cuckoo, and resplendent quetzal, and you have a beautiful eyeful of green and feel like you've got the luck of the Irish in the palm of your hand.

Hook: Blind eye black salmon fly—style and size of your choice

Thread: Black

Tip: Fine oval gold tinsel

Tag: Golden yellow floss

Tail: Golden pheasant crest and resplendent quetzal

Butt: Black ostrich herl

Body: Rear half flat gold tinsel; front half peacock herl

Rib: Medium oval gold tinsel

Wing: Matched pair Germain's peacock pheasant eyed body feathers extending to just inside tail. Outside of which is a shorter matched pair of Nicobar pigeon feathers extending back to just short of the eye of the prior pair. Outside of which is another matched pair of Germain's peacock pheasant eyed body feathers extending to an equal distance back from the tip of the prior pair as that pair was back from the first pair. Outside of which is a matched pair of African emerald cuckoo extending back to just short of the eye of the prior pair. Outside of which is a final matched pair of Germain's peacock pheasant eyed body feathers extending to an equal distance back from the tip of the prior pair.

Shoulder: Nicobar pigeon feathers extending back to just short of the eye of the final pair

Throat: Java green peacock body feather

Sides: Resplendent quetzal

Cheeks: African emerald cuckoo

Topping: Golden pheasant crest

Horns: Blue-and-gold macaw tail fibers

Head: Black

Tying the Emerald Isle

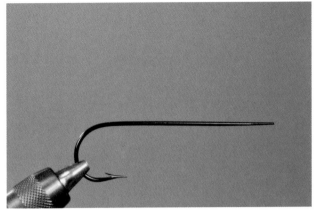

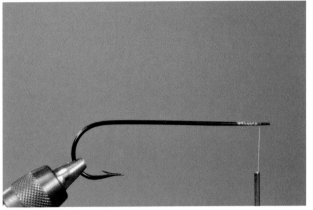

1 Create a liner to place between the hook wire and the vise jaws. I apply a single strip of Scotch tape to a 3-by-5-inch note card edge, then cut out a small rectangle about ½ by ¼ inch. Fold it over lengthwise with the tape on the inside. Taper the folded tip edges to match the jaw size and taper. Fold this piece around the hook bend where it will be placed in the vise jaws and move into place.

Secure the hook tightly in the vise with the hook shank level. Having the hook shank as level as possible is very important. The starting positions for material placement as well as overall proportions are based on where the tying thread hangs down from the hook. The positions of the thread as "even with the barb" or "even with the point" are starting positions for tags, tips, and the butt and/or body of the fly. If the hook shank is not level, the position indicated will not be correct. If the hook shank is drooping excessively, the tag and body positions will be too far back. Same if the hook shank is tilted up too much—the tag and body will be too short. Likewise, be sure the hook is held securely so good, tight thread wraps and material positioning can be accomplished without the hook working loose.

2 Attach the tying thread back from the end of the shank or eye. Be sure the wraps are tight and the thread end is secured well as a starting point for the entire fly. Create a single layer of wraps as a base for attaching the gut eye. Make sure to stay far enough back from the end of the shank tip. The tip of the shank on a blind-eye hook should be exposed ever so slightly and show over the gut loop eye.

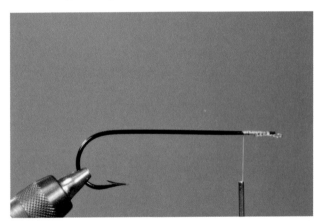

3 Secure the gut eye by folding it over and laying both "legs" under the shank and wrapping over them tightly. As genuine silkworm gut material is both hard to find and expensive, modern tiers use only a small length to form the eye. Traditional flies that were actually used for fishing had strands extending back for the full shank length, well secured to provide a strong and durable connection for hooking and landing the large Atlantic salmon of old.

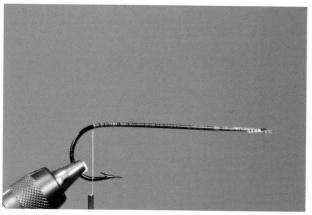

4 Create a smooth layer of thread all the way back on the shank to the starting point of the tag or tip. The underbody needs to be as smooth as possible; whatever the underbody shows as rough or inconsistent spots will often show through the body wrapped over it. I can always improve my underbody work and never seem to get it as consistent or smooth as I'd like it to be—stick with it and practice often.

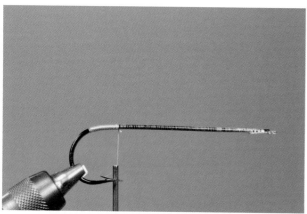

5 Attach the fine oval gold tinsel for the tip immediately above the barb. Advance the thread five wide wraps forward to get it out of the way. Make five wraps of the tinsel spiraling forward with each wrap tightly touching the previous. Don't overlap—one single layer is all you want—and do not allow any gaps between wraps. Unwrap the five wide thread wraps until back at the end of the finished wraps of the tinsel. Tie off the tinsel securely with several tight wraps of thread spiraling forward. Trim off the excess. Advance the thread in a smooth layer to a position where the thread hangs down even with the hook point. Use a burnisher to smooth out and flatten the thread wraps if in doubt.

Unless your hands are very clean with smooth fingers to handle the silk floss, you may want to use silk gloves to provide a clean, smooth surface to handle the delicate floss. Attach a single strand of yellow silk floss with three tight wraps of thread. Make five open wraps of thread to the eye to move the thread and bobbin out of your way. Stroke the floss a few times to straighten and even the fibers. Wrap a single smooth layer of the floss back to the tinsel, then reverse direction, wrapping back up the bend to where the floss was tied in above the point. Once there, unwrap the five turns of thread over the shank and two more tie-down wraps, then tie off the end of the floss tightly and end up above the point again. Trim the excess floss, and you are now ready to tie in the tail.

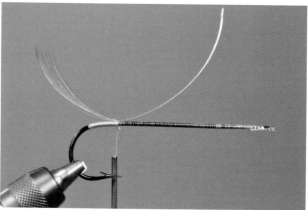

6 Select a single, full golden pheasant crest feather with good color. Length and curvature depend on your fly style preference. A short, tightly curved tail will give a more traditional Old World look to the fly. It will require a high wing and tightly curved topping to match the tail's shape. A longer, less curved crest will result in a longer, shallower wing with a "sleeker," more streamlined appearance. Use a feather of size and quality as one that could be used as a topping. Smaller feathers just don't have the "body," curvature, or fiber length to match with a crest used for a topping. Strip fibers off the rachis to the tie-in point. Make a couple of tight wraps while holding the crest in position on top of the hook, then release to see how it sits. Untie and retie in as needed until properly set.

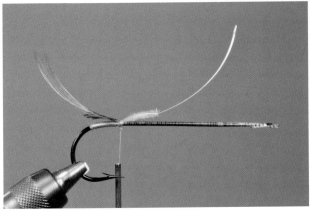

7 Select a single resplendent quetzal green body feather. Measure for length. The tips should extend back to about midpoint of the golden pheasant crest tail. At the tie-in point, trim several fibers off of both sides. This will orient the feather to lie flat. Position above the tail and tie in with the good, or shiny, side up. This sets the best color side of the feather on top and gets the curve of the fibers to go down and help press the golden pheasant tail underneath down for a sleeker fly.

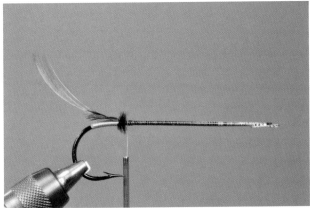

8 Tie in a single strand of black ostrich herl. The herl has a slant to the fibers off of the core rachis. Ideally the herl is tied in so when wrapped, the fibers slant back toward the hook bend. Advance the tying thread slightly and make four to six wraps spiraling toward the hook eye. Keep wraps close together with no gap between or overlap. Tie off and trim the excess herl.

9 Construct the underbody. For detailed steps, see Michael Radencich's excellent step-by-step instructional DVD in "Recommended Reading and Viewing." Reattach the tying thread at the rear of the body.

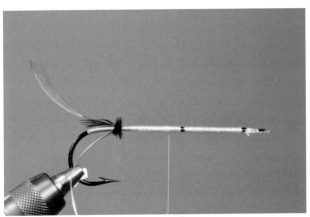

10 Use a body divider (get mine *free* at my website, www.modernclassicsflytying.com) and mark off the position of the end of the body near the eye, then divide the body into two equal sections, marking off the location of the butt that will divide the body sections. Attach the medium oval gold tinsel at the butt. Advance the tying thread in a smooth single layer to the first mark.

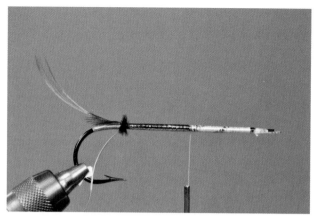

11 Attach the flat gold tinsel and wrap evenly back to the rear butt, then reverse direction, wrap back up to the thread position, and tie off. Keep tight, even wraps with no gaps or overlap.

12 At the midpoint of the body, attach several strands of peacock tail fibers (peacock herl), then advance the thread up to the mark at the front end of the body.

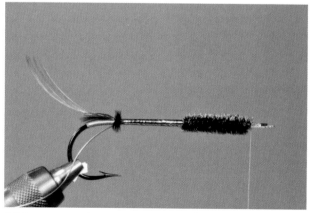

13 Twist and wrap the peacock herl forward in a smooth, even body and tie off at the mark for the end of the body. Secure tightly and trim off the excess.

14 Wrap the rib forward in five even turns and tie off on the bottom of the end of the entire body section.

15 Select two matched Germain's peacock pheasant eyed body feathers long enough to make the main wing with. Place back-to-back with the tips even and measure for length. The tips should extend back to the end of the tail and sit inside the tail's curve. Strip fibers off of both sides of the feather about halfway up. You need to strip this far up in order for the feather to lie flat and tuck into the curve of the tail. If fibers were left on the feather farther down, they would cause the feather to "stand up" and lift away from the tail. Additional feathers will cover the stripped sections as you proceed. Tie in carefully and check often to be sure the feathers stay aligned, fit in the tail correctly, sit on edge vertically, and are not crooked or lying off to one side or the other. They should be vertical and centered directly over the top of the hook shank.

THE FLIES ■ 133

16 Select a matched pair of Nicobar pigeon body or wing covert feathers. Place this pair back-to-back outside of the first pair and measure for length. The tips should be about one-fifth of the overall wing length back from the first pair, leaving the tip of the first pair with the eye clearly visible underneath. Strip fibers off of both sides of the feather about halfway up. Tie in securely and make sure the feathers are flat up against the first pair and are vertical. They should lie against the first pair and help press them together. If needed, untie and pinch the inside of the rachis to help curve the outer pair in against the first pair.

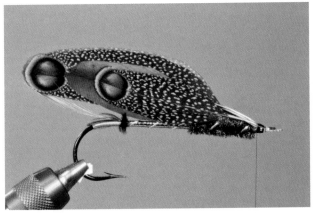

17 Select two matched Germain's peacock pheasant eyed body feathers long enough to make the main wing with. Place back-to-back with the tips even and measure for length. The tips should be about one-fifth of the overall wing length back from the second pair, leaving the tip of the second pair clearly visible underneath and the eyes separated by an equal distance. Strip fibers off of both sides of the feather about halfway up. Tie in securely and make sure the feathers are flat up against the first pair and are vertical. They should lie against the first pair and help press

them together. If needed, untie and pinch the inside of the rachis to help curve the outer pair in against the first pair.

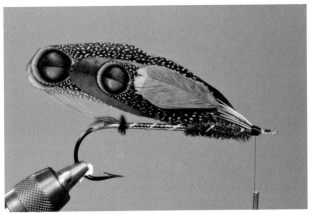

18 Select two matched African emerald cuckoo body feathers. Place back-to-back with the tips even and measure for length. The tips should be about one-fifth of the overall wing length back from the third pair, leaving the tip of the third pair clearly visible underneath and all tips separated by an equal distance. Strip fibers off of both sides of the feather about halfway up. Tie in securely and make sure the feathers are flat up against the first pair and are vertical. They should lie against the first pair and help press them together. If needed, untie and pinch the inside of the rachis to help curve the outer pair in against the first pair.

19 Select two matched Germain's peacock pheasant eyed body feathers for the final wing pair. Place back-to-back with the tips even and measure for length. The tips should be about one-fifth of the overall wing length back from the prior pair, leaving the tip of that pair clearly visible underneath and the eyes separated by an equal distance. Strip fibers off of both sides of the feather about halfway up. Tie in securely and make sure the feathers are flat up against the first pair and are vertical. They should lie against the first pair and help press them together. If needed, untie and pinch the inside of the rachis to help curve the outer pair in against the first pair.

20 Tie in and wrap about four or five turns of a Java green peacock body feather for the throat. Pull the fibers down underneath and even make a few wraps over them if needed to secure the fibers so they will lay properly.

21 Select a matched pair of Nicobar pigeon body or wing covert feathers. Place this pair back-to-back outside of the first pair and measure for length. The tips should be back about one-quarter of the overall wing length, leaving the tip of the prior pair's eyes clearly visible underneath. Trim the fibers off of both sides of the feather to create a flat profile to help the feather tie in flat against the wing. Tie in securely and make sure the feathers are flat up against the wing and are vertical. They should lie against the prior pair and help press them together. If needed, untie and pinch the inside of the rachis to help curve the outer pair in against the first pair.

22 Repeat the last process with a matched pair of resplendent quetzal body feathers for the sides. Place this pair back-to-back outside of the second pair and measure for length. The tips should extend back about halfway of the sides just tied in. Trim fibers off of both sides of the feather. Tie in securely and make sure the feathers are flat up against the first pair and are vertical. They should lie against the first pair and help press them together. If needed, untie and pinch the inside of the rachis to help curve the outer pair in against the first pair.

23 Select a matched pair of African emerald cuckoo body feathers for the cheeks. Place back-to-back with the tips matched. Position so they will extend back about halfway up the quetxal feathers. Trim off a few fibers on each side of the rachis to ensure they will lie flat when tied in on the side of the wing. Tie in tightly and trim the excess.

24 Select a long, full golden pheasant crest feather for the topping. Lay it over the top of the wing and measure for length. The tip should meet the tip of the tail, and the curvature should match the curve of the wing. The center portion of the topping may need to be "straightened" a bit to match the shape of the wing. If needed, *gently* stroke the top edge of the topping with your fingernail. This will take out some of the curvature. Go slowly and little by little until it matches the upper edge curvature when you hold the crest over or beside the top edge of the wing. Strip off excess fibers beyond the tie-in point. Use a small pair of flat-nose smooth-jaw pliers to flatten the rachis at the tie-in point. Hold the top of the wing tightly and make several wraps to tie in the topping. Lift it up a bit to be sure it is aligned

with the top edge of the wing and doesn't twist or curve away. If it does, untie and retie until it sits correctly on its own. Trim off the excess.

25 Select two long matching blue-and-gold macaw center tail fibers. Measure for length. The tips should extend to the end of the wing. Tie in angling up above the wing so the tips match well above the wing's upper edge. Secure the fibers tightly. Tie off and trim the excess.

26 Form the head of the fly and tie the thread off by either using several half hitches or, my preferred method, whip finishing. Trim the thread, cement the head, and you are finished!

FIREBIRD

For this fly, I combined Malayan crested fireback and Siamese fireback pheasant feathers for the wing. The gradual brightening of colors as you near the eye reminded me of getting closer to the flame, so the name was a natural. Andean cock of the rock and Indian crow light this one up.

Hook: Blind eye black salmon fly—style and size of your choice

Thread: Red

Tip: Fine oval silver twist

Tag: Yellow silk floss

Tail: Golden pheasant crest and yellow-over-blue golden-breasted starling feathers

Butt: Black ostrich herl

Body: Two equal sections of silk floss: first is orange veiled above and below with Andean cock of the rock and butted with black ostrich herl; second is red.

Rib: Fine oval gold over rear half; medium oval gold and flat gold over front half

Hackle: Orange-dyed Sebright rooster hackle over front half

Wing: Two matched pair jungle cock feathers to just inside the tip of the tail. Outside of which is a matched pair of Malayan crested fireback pheasant flank feathers with dark reddish purple tips shorter than the jungle cock by one-quarter. Outside of which is a matched pair of Malayan crested fireback back feathers with bright rust-colored tips tied shorter than the prior pair by one-quarter. Outside of which is a matched pair of Siamese fireback pheasant back feathers with orange tips one-quarter shorter than the prior pair. Outside of which is a matched pair of orange-colored hybrid macaw body feathers.

Throat: Purple-dyed guinea fowl

Sides: Jungle cock

Cheek: Indian crow

Topping: Golden pheasant crest

Horns: Siamese fireback pheasant crest feathers

Head: Red

Tying the Firebird

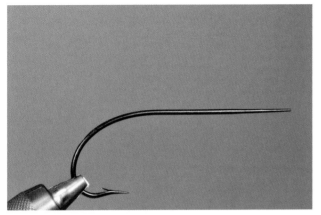

1 Create a liner to place between the hook wire and the vise jaws. I apply a single strip of Scotch tape to a 3-by-5-inch note card edge, then cut out a small rectangle about ½ by ¼ inch. Fold it over lengthwise with the tape on the inside. Taper the folded tip edges to match the jaw size and taper. Fold this piece around the hook bend where it will be placed in the vise jaws and move into place.

Secure the hook tightly in the vise with the hook shank level. Having the hook shank as level as possible is very important. The starting positions for material placement as well as overall proportions are based on where the tying thread hangs down from the hook. The positions of the thread as "even with the barb" or "even with the point" are starting positions for tags, tips, and the butt and/ or body of the fly. If the hook shank is not level, the position indicated will not be correct. If the hook shank is drooping excessively, the tag and body positions will be too far back. Same if the hook shank is tilted up too much—the tag and body will be too short. Likewise, be sure the hook is held securely so good, tight thread wraps and material positioning can be accomplished without the hook working loose.

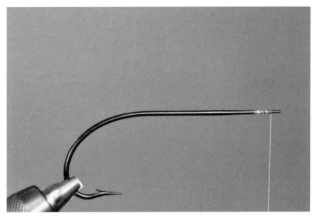

2 Attach the tying thread back from the end of the shank or eye. Be sure the wraps are tight and the thread end is secured well as a starting point for the entire fly. Create a single layer of wraps as a base for attaching the gut eye. Make sure to stay far enough back from the end of the shank tip. The tip of the shank on a blind-eye hook should be exposed ever so slightly and show over the gut loop eye.

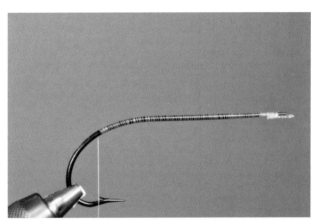

3 Secure the gut eye by folding it over and laying both "legs" under the shank and wrapping over them tightly. As genuine silkworm gut material is both hard to find and expensive, modern tiers use only a small length to form the eye. Traditional flies that were actually used for fishing had strands extending back for the full shank length, well secured to provide a strong and durable connection for hooking and landing the large Atlantic salmon of old.

Create a smooth layer of thread all the way back on the shank to the starting point of the tag or tip. The underbody needs to be as smooth as possible; whatever the underbody shows as rough or inconsistent spots will often show through the body wrapped over it. I can always improve my under-body work and never seem to get it as consistent or smooth as I'd like it to be—stick with it and practice often.

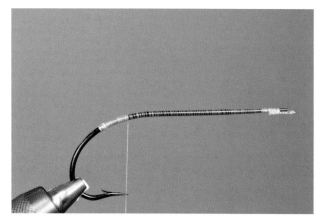

4 Attach the fine oval silver tinsel for the tip immediately above the barb. Advance the thread five wide wraps forward to get it out of the way. Make five wraps of the tinsel spiraling forward with each wrap tightly touching the previous. Don't overlap—one single layer is all you want—and do not allow any gaps between wraps. Unwrap the five wide thread wraps until back at the end of the finished wraps of the tinsel. Tie off the tinsel securely with several tight wraps of thread spiraling forward. Trim off the excess. Advance the thread in a smooth layer to a position where the thread hangs down even with the hook point. Use a burnisher to smooth out and flatten the thread wraps if in doubt.

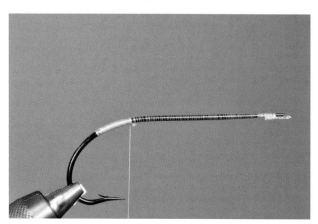

5 Unless your hands are very clean with smooth fingers to handle the silk floss, you may want to use silk gloves to provide a clean, smooth surface to handle the delicate floss. Attach a single

strand of yellow silk floss with three tight wraps of thread. Make five open wraps of thread to the eye to move the thread and bobbin out of your way. Stroke the floss a few times to straighten and even the fibers. Wrap a single smooth layer of the floss back to the tinsel, then reverse direction, wrapping back up the bend to where the floss was tied in above the point. Once there, unwrap the five turns of thread over the shank and two more tie-down wraps; then tie off the end of the floss tightly and end up above the point again. Trim the excess floss, and you are now ready to tie in the tail.

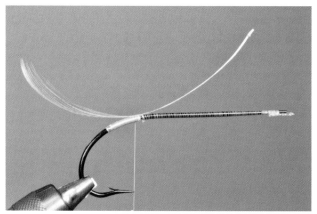

6 Select a single, full golden pheasant crest feather with good color. Length and curvature depend on your fly style preference. A short, tightly curved tail will give a more traditional Old World look to the fly. It will require a high wing and tightly curved topping to match the tail's shape. A longer, less curved crest will result in a longer, shallower wing with a "sleeker," more streamlined appearance. Use a feather of size and quality as one that could be used as a topping. Smaller feathers just don't have the "body," curvature, or fiber length to match with a crest used for a topping. Strip fibers off the rachis to the tie-in point. Make a couple of tight wraps while holding the crest in position on top of the hook, then release to see how it sits. Untie and retie in as needed until properly set.

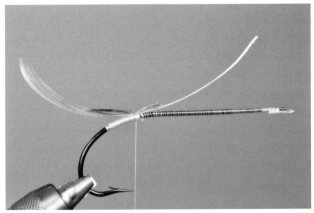

7 Select a single blue golden-breasted starling body feather. Measure for length. The tip should extend back to about midpoint of the golden pheasant crest tail. At the tie-in point, trim several fibers off of both sides. This will orient the feather to lie flat. Position it above the tail and tie in with the good, or shiny, side up. This sets the best color side of the feather on top and gets the curve of the fibers to go down and help press the golden pheasant tail underneath down for a sleeker fly.

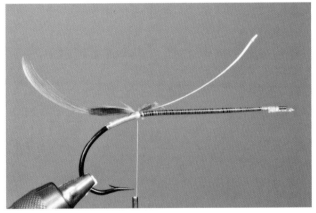

8 Repeat the last step with a single yellow golden-breasted starling feather tied in flat on top of the blue feather.

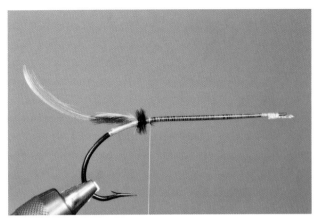

9 Tie in a single strand of black ostrich herl. The herl has a slant to the fibers off of the core rachis. Ideally the herl is tied in so when wrapped, the fibers slant back toward the hook bend. Advance the tying thread slightly and make four to six wraps spiraling toward the hook eye. Keep wraps close together with no gap between or overlap. Tie off and trim the excess herl.

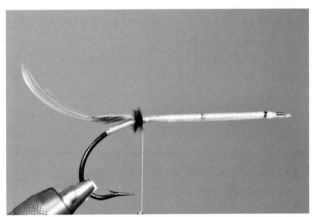

10 Construct the underbody. The purpose of the underbody is to provide a smooth tapering up to the ends of the gut loop which is attached underneath the hook shank. Attach a long single or paired strands of smooth, flat white floss at the front of the hook shank behind the gut loop ends on the underside of the hook. Make smooth, even wraps with the floss back to the rear of the body, then start wrapping back to the front. Stop at the ends of the gut loop and start wrapping toward the back again but this time stop about one-fifth of the body length away from the rear of the body. Repeat as needed, each time stopping farther away from the rear of the body. When built up sufficiently to match the diameter of the shank and gut eye ends, wrap forward to the end of the body. DO NOT GO

TOO FAR FORWARD!!! Leave about one-fifth of the shank and eye uncovered to use for the winging and throat. Tie off the floss at the front of the body and add a couple of half-hitch knots to secure the thread temporarily. Cut the thread off. Use a burnisher to smooth out the underbody. Reattach the tying thread at the rear of the body. See the aforementioned DVD for detailed steps for this process. Use a body divider (get mine *free* at my website, www.modernclassicsflytying.com) and mark off the position of the end of the body near the eye, then divide the body into two equal sections, marking off the location of the butt that will divide the body sections. Attach the medium oval gold tinsel.

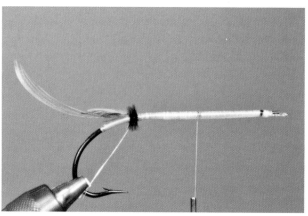

11 Attach the fine oval gold tinsel at the butt. Advance the tying thread in a smooth single layer to the first mark.

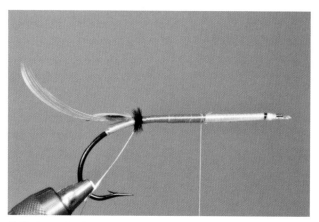

12 Attach the orange silk floss at the first mark. Wrap evenly back to the rear butt, then reverse direction, wrap back up to the thread position, and tie off. Keep tight, even wraps with no gaps or overlap. Use a burnisher if needed to smooth out the wraps.

13 Wrap the rib forward in five even turns and tie off on the bottom of the end of the body section.

14 Select two matching Andean cock of the rock feathers to be used for the veiling. Place back-to-back and position above the front of the body section just created. Tips should extend back to right above or slightly past the ostrich herl butt. Where they will be tied in, trim the fibers off the rachis on both sides. This creates a flat profile that helps orient the feathers horizontally, which is how you want to tie them in. Secure the feathers horizontally, one at a time, tightly above and below the end of the body section and extending back to the ostrich herl butt. Tie off tightly.

15 Tie in a single strand of black ostrich herl. The herl has a slant to the fibers off of the core rachis. Ideally the herl is tied in so when wrapped, the fibers slant back toward the hook bend. Advance the tying thread slightly and make four to six wraps spiraling toward the hook eye. Keep wraps close together with no gap between or overlap. Tie off and trim the excess herl.

16 Tie in the flat gold tinsel and medium oval gold tinsel underneath at the front side of the ostrich herl joint just created.

17 Attach the orange-dyed Sebright rooster neck hackle at the front end of the ostrich herl joint as well.

18 Advance the tying thread in a smooth single layer to the front end of the body to the first mark. Unless your hands are very clean with smooth fingers to handle the silk floss, you may want to use silk gloves to provide a clean, smooth surface to handle the delicate floss. Attach a single strand of red silk floss with three tight wraps of thread at the front mark at the end of the body. Stroke the floss a few times to straighten and even the fibers. Wrap a single smooth layer of the floss back to the ostrich joint, then reverse direction, wrapping back up to the thread. Tie off the end of the floss tightly and trim the excess.

19 Wrap the flat tinsel forward in five even turns and tie off. Repeat with the oval tinsel right behind the flat tinsel with no gaps. Finally, fold the feather and wrap tightly behind the oval tinsel. Tie off and trim the excess for all. Fold the fibers down and toward the back to provide an open base for the wing to be tied in next.

20 Select two matched jungle cock neck feathers long enough to reach the tip of the tail. Place back-to-back with the tips even and measure for length. The tips should extend back to the end of the tail and sit inside the tail's curve. Strip fibers off of both sides of the feather about halfway up. You need to strip this far up in order for the feather to lie flat and tuck into the curve of the tail. If fibers were left on the feather farther down, they would cause the feather to "stand up" and lift away from the tail. Additional feathers will cover the stripped sections as you proceed. Tie in carefully and check often to be sure the feathers stay aligned, fit in the tail correctly, sit on edge vertically, and are not crooked or lying off to one side or the other. They should be vertical and centered directly over the top of the hook shank.

21 Select two matched Malayan crested fireback pheasant flank feathers with a purple cast that are long enough to make the main wing with. Place back-to-back with the tips even and measure for length. The tips should be back to the front of the "eye" of the jungle cock feather. Strip fibers off of both sides of the feather about halfway up. Tie in securely and make sure the feathers are flat up against the first pair and are vertical. They should lie against the first pair and help press them together. If needed, untie and pinch the inside of the rachis to help curve the outer pair in against the first pair.

22 Select a matched pair of Malayan crested fireback "fire spot" back feathers. Place this pair back-to-back outside of the second pair and measure for length. The tips should be about one-quarter of the overall wing length back from the first pair, leaving the tip of the first pair clearly visible underneath. Strip fibers off of both sides of the feather about halfway up. Tie in securely and make sure the feathers are flat up against the first pair and are vertical. They should lie against the first pair and help press them together. If needed, untie and pinch the inside of the rachis to help curve the outer pair in against the first pair.

23 Select a matched pair of Siamese fireback pheasant "fireback" feathers. Place back-to-back with the tips matched. Position so they will extend back about one-third of the overall wing length. Trim off a few fibers on each side of the rachis to ensure they will lie flat when tied in on the side of the wing. Tie in tightly and trim the excess.

24 Select a matched pair of hybrid macaw orange body feathers. Place back-to-back with the tips matched. Position so they will extend back about one-quarter of the overall wing length and tie in tipped up to complete the taper of the wing top edge. Trim off a few fibers on each side of the rachis to ensure they will lie flat when tied in on the side of the wing. Tie in tightly and trim the excess.

25 Tie in the purple guinea fowl feather for the throat. Make four or five wraps and tie off. Fold down all fibers on the top and on the sides to collect the fibers under the hook shank. Make a few wraps of thread if needed to secure the fibers in place.

26 Select two matched jungle cock neck feathers for the sides. Place back-to-back and measure for length. The tips should go to the tips of the macaw feathers underneath. Trim off fibers on both sides of the rachis to create a flat profile to help the feather tie in flat against the wing. Tie in tightly and trim off the excess.

27 Select a matched pair of Indian crow breast feathers for the sides. Place this pair back-to-back outside of the second pair and measure for length. The tips should extend back about halfway of the sides just tied in. Trim fibers off of both sides of the feather. Tie in securely and make sure the feathers are flat up against the first pair and are vertical. They should lie against the first pair and help press them together. If needed, untie and pinch the inside of the rachis to help curve the outer pair in against the first pair.

28 Select a long, full golden pheasant crest feather for the topping. Lay it over the top of the wing and measure for length. The tip should meet the tip of the tail, and the curvature should match the curve of the wing. The center portion of the topping may need to be "straightened" a bit to match the shape of the wing. If needed, *gently* stroke the top edge of the topping with your fingernail. This will take out some of the curvature. Go slowly and little by little until it matches the upper edge curvature when you hold the crest over or beside the top edge of the wing. Strip off excess fibers beyond the tie-in point. Use a small pair of flat-nose smooth-jaw pliers to flatten

the rachis at the tie-in point. Hold the top of the wing tightly and make several wraps to tie in the topping. Lift it up a bit to be sure it is aligned with the top edge of the wing and doesn't twist or curve away. If it does, untie and retie until it sits correctly on its own. Trim off the excess.

29 Select two long matching Siamese fireback pheasant crest feathers for the horns. Measure for length. The tips should extend as far as possible, preferably to the end of the wing. Tie in angling up above the wing so the tips match well above the wing's upper edge. Secure the fibers tightly. Tie off and trim the excess.

30 Form the head of the fly and tie the thread off by either using several half hitches or, my preferred method, whip finishing. Trim the thread, cement the head, and you are finished!

GLIMPSE OF PARADISE

The beautiful, metallic colors of the magnificent riflebird and twelve-wired bird of paradise feathers were a natural together. Add the greater bird of paradise long display feathers and resplendent quetzal tail (substitute) for the wing, and you truly have a glimpse of paradise.

Hook: Blind eye black salmon fly—style and size of your choice

Thread: BlackTip: Fine oval gold tinsel

Tail: Golden pheasant crest and matched pair of magnificent riflebird set vertically

Butt: Black ostrich herl

Body: In equal thirds: Rear third is flat gold tinsel veiled above and below with a matched pair of magnificent riflebird set vertically. Middle third is dark green floss veiled above and below with a matched pair of twelve-wired bird of paradise black body feathers set vertically and butted with black ostrich herl. Final third is flat gold tinsel.

Rib: Gold twist over first and second body sections

Hackle: Resplendent quetxal tail (substitute green-dyed emu) wrapped closely and palmered over the front third of the body

Underwing: Matched pair of resplendent quetxal tail (substitute green-dyed emu) reaching to just past tip of the tail and placed between the twelve-wired bird of paradise feathers

Wing: Matched pair of greater bird of paradise yellow display feathers extending to just past the tip of the tail

Throat: Black schlappen with matched pair of twelve-wired bird of paradise feathers over the outside curving back toward hook bend

Shoulder: Palawan peacock pheasant teal-colored wing covert feathers with rounded tips

Sides: Jungle cock

Topping: Golden pheasant crest

Horns: Matched pair of male India peacock head crest (corona) feathers

Head: Black

Tying the Glimpse of Paradise

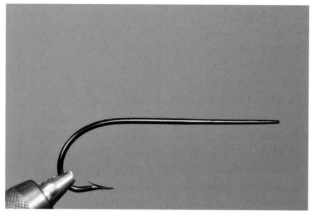

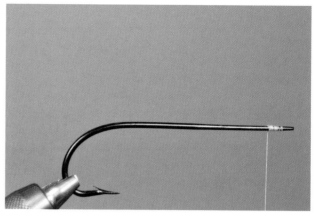

1 Create a liner to place between the hook wire and the vise jaws. I apply a single strip of Scotch tape to a 3-by-5-inch note card edge, then cut out a small rectangle about ½ by ¼ inch. Fold it over lengthwise with the tape on the inside. Taper the folded tip edges to match the jaw size and taper. Fold this piece around the hook bend where it will be placed in the vise jaws and move into place.

Secure the hook tightly in the vise with the hook shank level. Having the hook shank as level as possible is very important. The starting positions for material placement as well as overall proportions are based on where the tying thread hangs down from the hook. The positions of the thread as "even with the barb" or "even with the point" are starting positions for tags, tips, and the butt and/or body of the fly. If the hook shank is not level, the position indicated will not be correct. If the hook shank is drooping excessively, the tag and body positions will be too far back. Same if the hook shank is tilted up too much—the tag and body will be too short. Likewise, be sure the hook is held securely so good, tight thread wraps and material positioning can be accomplished without the hook working loose.

2 Attach the tying thread back from the end of the shank or eye. Be sure the wraps are tight and the thread end is secured well as a starting point for the entire fly. Create a single layer of wraps as a base for attaching the gut eye. Make sure to stay far enough back from the end of the shank tip. The tip of the shank on a blind-eye hook should be exposed ever so slightly and show over the gut loop eye.

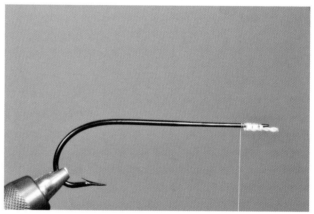

3 Secure the gut eye by folding it over and laying both "legs" under the shank and wrapping over them tightly. As genuine silkworm gut material is both hard to find and expensive, modern tiers use only a small length to form the eye. Traditional flies that were actually used for fishing had strands extending back for the full shank length, well secured to provide a strong and durable connection for hooking and landing the large Atlantic salmon of old.

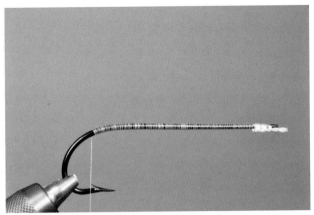

4 Create a smooth layer of thread all the way back on the shank to the starting point of the tag or tip. The underbody needs to be as smooth as possible; whatever the underbody shows as rough or inconsistent spots will often show through the body wrapped over it. I can always improve my underbody work and never seem to get it as consistent or smooth as I'd like it to be—stick with it and practice often.

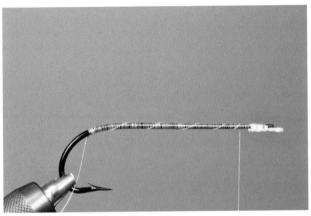

5 Attach the fine oval silver tinsel for the tip immediately above the barb. Advance the thread five wide wraps forward to get it out of the way. Make five wraps of the tinsel spiraling forward with each wrap tightly touching the previous. Don't overlap—one single layer is all you want—and do not allow any gaps between wraps.

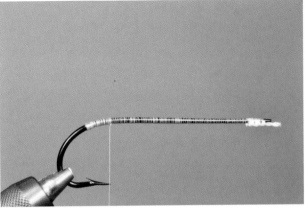

6 Unwrap the five wide thread wraps until back at the end of the finished wraps of the tinsel. Tie off the tinsel securely with several tight wraps of thread spiraling forward. Trim off the excess. Advance the thread in a smooth layer to a position where the thread hangs down even with the hook point. Use a burnisher to smooth out and flatten the thread wraps if in doubt.

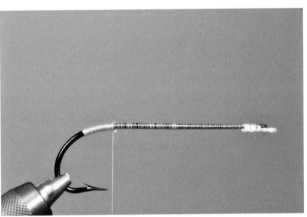

7 Unless your hands are very clean with smooth fingers to handle the silk floss, you may want to use silk gloves to provide a clean, smooth surface to handle the delicate floss. Attach a single strand of yellow silk floss with three tight wraps of thread. Make five open wraps of thread to the eye to move the thread and bobbin out of your way. Stroke the floss a few times to straighten and even the fibers. Wrap a single smooth layer of the floss back to the tinsel, then reverse direction, wrapping back up the bend to where the floss was tied in above the point. Once there, unwrap the five turns of thread over the shank and two more tie-down wraps, then tie off the end of the floss tightly and end up above the point again. Trim the excess floss, and you are now ready to tie in the tail.

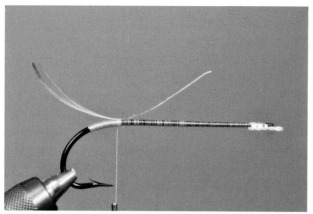

8 Select a single, full golden pheasant crest feather with good color. Length and curvature depend on your fly style preference. A short, tightly curved tail will give a more traditional Old World look to the fly. It will require a high wing and tightly curved topping to match the tail's shape. A longer, less curved crest will result in a longer, shallower wing with a "sleeker," more streamlined appearance. Use a feather of size and quality as one that could be used as a topping. Smaller feathers just don't have the "body," curvature, or fiber length to match with a crest used for a topping. Strip fibers off the rachis to the tie-in point. Make a couple of tight wraps while holding the crest in position on top of the hook, then release to see how it sits. Untie and retie in as needed until properly set.

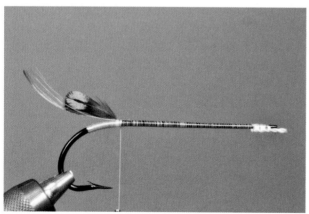

9 Select a matched pair of magnificent rifle-bird green breast feathers. Place back-to-back with the tips even and measure for length: The tip should extend back to about midpoint of the golden pheasant crest tail. At the tie-in point, strip several fibers off of both sides. This will orient the feather to tie in vertically as desired. Position above the golden pheasant crest tail and tie in vertically.

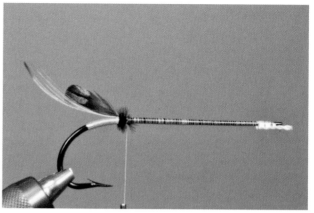

10 Trim off the excess of the tail materials. Tie in a single strand of black ostrich herl. The herl has a slant to the fibers off of the core rachis. Ideally the herl is tied in so when wrapped, the fibers slant back toward the hook bend. Advance the tying thread slightly and make four to six wraps spiraling toward the hook eye. Keep wraps close together with no gap between or overlap. Tie off and trim the excess herl.

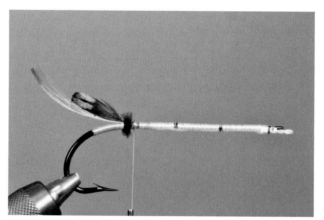

11 Construct the underbody. The purpose of the underbody is to provide a smooth tapering up to the ends of the gut loop which is attached underneath the hook shank. Attach a long single or paired strands of smooth, flat white floss at the front of the hook shank behind the gut loop ends on the underside of the hook. Make smooth, even wraps with the floss back to the rear of the body, then start wrapping back to the front. Stop at the ends of the gut loop and start wrapping toward the back again but this time stop about one-fifth of the body length away from the rear of the body. Repeat as needed, each time stopping farther away from the rear of the body. When built up sufficiently to match the diameter of the shank and gut eye ends, wrap forward to the end of the body. DO NOT GO TOO FAR FORWARD!!!

Leave about one-fifth of the shank and eye uncovered to use for the winging and throat. Tie off the floss at the front of the body and add a couple of half-hitch knots to secure the thread temporarily. Cut the thread off. Use a burnisher to smooth out the underbody. Reattach the tying thread at the rear of the body. See the aforementioned DVD for detailed steps for this process. Use a body divider (get mine *free* at my website, www.modernclassics flytying.com) and mark off the position of the end of the body near the eye; then divide the body into three equal sections, marking off the location of the butt that will divide the body sections.

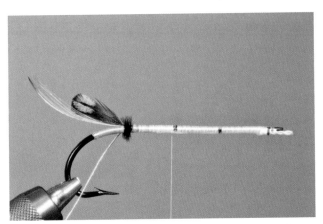

12 Attach the fine oval gold tinsel at the butt. Advance the tying thread in a smooth single layer to the first mark.

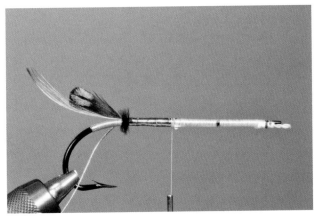

13 Attach the flat gold tinsel and make tight wraps back to the ostrich herl butt. Once there, reverse direction and make snug wraps back up to the mark, tie off, and trim the excess.

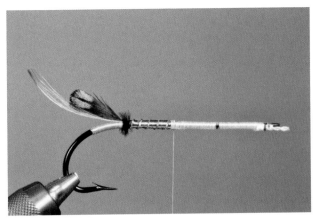

14 Wrap the rib forward in five even turns and tie off on the bottom of the end of the body section.

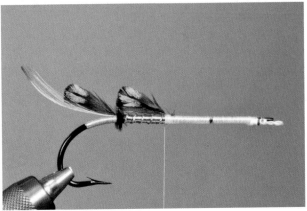

15 Select two matching pairs of magnificent riflebird feathers to be used for the veilings. Place back-to-back and measure for length. Tips should extend back to right above or slightly past the ostrich herl butt. Where they will be tied in, strip the fibers off the rachis on both sides. This creates a flat area that helps orient the feathers vertically, which is how you want to tie them in. Position above the front of the body section just created. Secure the top pair feathers vertically, one at a time, tightly above and below the end of the body section and extending back to the ostrich herl butt. Tie off tightly.

16 Repeat the process for the bottom pair of feathers and tie in the same as the last pair.

17 Tie in a single strand of black ostrich herl. The herl has a slant to the fibers off of the core rachis. Ideally the herl is tied in so when wrapped, the fibers slant back toward the hook bend. Advance the tying thread slightly and make four to six wraps spiraling toward the hook eye. Keep wraps close together with no gap between or overlap. Tie off and trim the excess herl.

18 Attach the oval gold tinsel for the ribbing on the underside of the hook shank. Advance the thread in smooth, even wraps back up to the next mark. Attach a single strand of green silk floss at the front mark for this body section. Wrap the floss back to the ostrich herl butt, reverse the wraps, and wrap smoothly and evenly back up to the last mark.

19 Wrap the rib in five even turns up to the thread. Tie off securely and trim the excess.

20 Select two matched pairs of twelve-wired bird of paradise black body feathers. Length is up to you, but I usually have the tips even with the midpoint of the magnificent riflebird feathers tied in above and below the first body section. At the tie-in point, strip fibers off both sides of both feathers. This creates a flat area on the rachis that helps orient the feathers to sit vertically when tied in, which is what you want. Tie in the first pair on top at the end of the body section you just created. They should stand vertically, with any curve to the feathers curving inwards toward the body.

21 Repeat with the other pair of magnificent riflebird feathers for the bottom pair. Place back-to-back with the tips even and measure for length. The tips should be back to the same point as the feathers above for a mirrorlike appearance. Tie in securely and make sure the feathers are centered over the hook from above and stand vertically above and below the hook shank.

22 Tie in a single strand of black ostrich herl. The herl has a slant to the fibers off of the core rachis. Ideally the herl is tied in so when wrapped, the fibers slant back toward the hook bend. Advance the tying thread slightly and make four to six wraps spiraling toward the hook eye. Keep wraps close together with no gap between or overlap. Tie off and trim the excess herl.

23 Select a single resplendent quetzal tail feather. As these are nearly impossible to get, use a great substitute in the form of a green-dyed emu feather. Tie in by the tip end near the ostrich herl butt.

24 Advance the thread smoothly to the mark at the front end of the body. Tie in a piece of flat gold tinsel and wrap evenly back to the butt and then back up again. Tie off and trim the excess.

25 Wrap the resplendent quetzal feather five to seven wraps and tie off at the front end of the body. Fold down all fibers on the top and on the sides to collect the fibers under the hook shank.

26 Select two matched resplendent quetzal tail feather tips (using the green-dyed emu substitute) for the underwing. Place back-to-back and measure for length. The tips should go just to or slightly beyond the tip of the tail. Strip fibers off both sides of the tie-in point to help prepare a flat side of the rachis to get the feathers to tie in vertically. Tie in securely and trim the excess. Place both feathers between the top pair of twelve-wired bird of paradise feathers.

27 Select another larger matched pair of twelve-wired bird of paradise feathers. Place this pair back-to-back outside of the resplendent quetzal feathers. Measure for length. The tips should extend to about halfway back on the mid-body pair of twelve-wired bird of paradise feathers. Trim fibers off of both sides of the feather at the tie-in point. Tie in securely and make sure the feathers are flat up against the resplendent quetzal feathers and are vertical. They should lay in and help press the underwing together. If needed, untie and pinch the inside of the rachis to help curve the outer pair in against the underwing.

28 Select a black schlappen hackle feather and tie in at the front of the wing. Make four to six wraps and tie off. Pull the fibers down below the hook and make a few wraps of thread over them if needed to secure in place.

29 Select a matched pair of greater bird of paradise display feathers and match the tips. As these are difficult to find, pale golden-yellow-dyed emu feathers can be substituted. Measure for length: They should extend just past the tip of the tail. Tie in tightly on top and make sure they curve into the center and lie flat against the underwing.

30 Select two matching Palawan peacock pheasant body feathers for the shoulders. Place back-to-back and with the tips even. Measure for length: The tips should extend to the middle of the hook shank. Trim fibers off both sides, tie in flat, and secure well with tight thread wraps. Trim off the excess.

31 Select a long, full golden pheasant crest feather for the topping. Lay it over the top of the wing and measure for length. The tip should meet the tip of the tail, and the curvature should match the curve of the wing. The center portion of the topping may need to be "straightened" a bit to match the shape of the wing. If needed, *gently* stroke the top edge of the topping with your fingernail. This will take out some of the curvature. Go slowly and little by little until it matches the upper edge curvature when you hold the crest over or beside the top edge of the wing. Strip off excess fibers beyond the tie-in point. Use a small pair of flat-nose smooth-jaw pliers to flatten the rachis at the tie-in point. Hold the top of the wing tightly and make several wraps to tie in the topping. Lift it up a bit to be sure it is aligned with the top edge of the wing and doesn't twist or curve away. If it does, untie and retie until it sits correctly on its own. Trim off the excess.

32 Select two matching jungle cock neck feathers for the sides. Measure for length: The tips should extend back near the end of the shoulder feathers underneath. Tie in angling up so the tips match the angle of the wing. Secure tightly. Tie off and trim the excess.

33 Select two long matching India blue peacock crest feathers for the horns. Measure for length. The tips should match and extend as far as possible, preferably to the end of the wing. Tie in angling up above the wing so the tips match well above the wing's upper edge. Secure the fibers tightly. Tie off and trim the excess.

34 Select a matched pair of twelve-wired bird of paradise sickle-shaped body feathers. Match tip-to-tip and place back-to-back. Tie in as a final throat over the black schlappen.

Form the head of the fly and tie the thread off by either using several half hitches or, my preferred method, whip finishing. Trim the thread, cement the head, and you are finished!

GRAND ARGUS

Created to highlight the amazing diversity of color and pattern in one bird, this fly uses almost everything, from body to wing and tail feathers. The Grand Argus is a relatively simple style, with a married wing; only two wide strips combined when tied in keep the center tail strip on the outside of the underwing in position by marrying it to the upper edge wing.

Hook: Blind eye black salmon fly—style and size of your choice

Thread: BlackTip: Fine oval silver tinsel

Tag: Yellow silk floss

Tail: Golden pheasant crest and argus center tail strips with red tips

Butt: Black ostrich herl

Body: Black silk floss

Rib: Two oval silver tinsels with a single strand of red floss between them

Hackle: Wine rooster saddle hackle wrapped snugly behind the rear oval silver tinsel rib

Underwing: Argus wing secondary strips to just inside the tip of tail

Wing: Argus center tail strips with red color extending back to be even with the tips of the argus tail used in the tail of the fly

Overwing: Argus wing secondary strips married to center tail and underwing tips extending to just inside the tip of the tail

Throat: Speckled guinea fowl

Sides: Argus body feather tip—dark with light spots

Cheek: Argus body feather tip—small golden tan with white spots

Topping: Golden pheasant crest

Horns: African crowned crane

Head: Black

Tying the Grand Argus

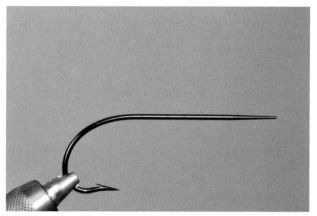

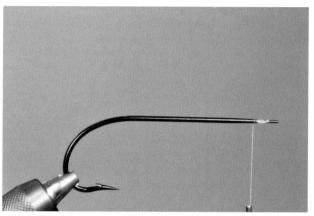

1 Create a liner to place between the hook wire and the vise jaws. I apply a single strip of Scotch tape to a 3-by-5-inch note card edge, then cut out a small rectangle about ½ by ¼ inch. Fold it over lengthwise with the tape on the inside. Taper the folded tip edges to match the jaw size and taper. Fold this piece around the hook bend where it will be placed in the vise jaws and move into place.

Secure the hook tightly in the vise with the hook shank level. Having the hook shank as level as possible is very important. The starting positions for material placement as well as overall proportions are based on where the tying thread hangs down from the hook. The positions of the thread as "even with the barb" or "even with the point" are starting positions for tags, tips, and the butt and/ or body of the fly. If the hook shank is not level, the position indicated will not be correct. If the hook shank is drooping excessively, the tag and body positions will be too far back. Same if the hook shank is tilted up too much—the tag and body will be too short. Likewise, be sure the hook is held securely so good, tight thread wraps and material positioning can be accomplished without the hook working loose.

2 Attach the tying thread back from the end of the shank or eye. Be sure the wraps are tight and the thread end is secured well as a starting point for the entire fly. Create a single layer of wraps as a base for attaching the gut eye. Make sure to stay far enough back from the end of the shank tip. The tip of the shank on a blind-eye hook should be exposed ever so slightly and show over the gut loop eye.

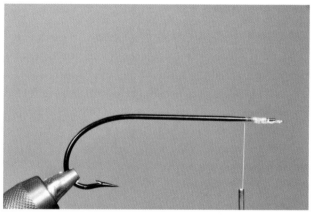

3 Secure the gut eye by folding it over and laying both "legs" under the shank and wrapping over them tightly. As genuine silkworm gut material is both hard to find and expensive, modern tiers use only a small length to form the eye. Traditional flies that were actually used for fishing had strands extending back for the full shank length, well secured to provide a strong and durable connection for hooking and landing the large Atlantic salmon of old.

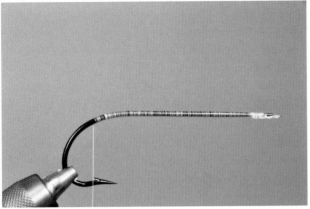

4 Create a smooth layer of thread all the way back on the shank to the starting point of the tip above the barb. The underbody needs to be as smooth as possible; whatever the underbody shows as rough or inconsistent spots will often show through the body wrapped over it. I can always improve my underbody work and never seem to get it as consistent or smooth as I'd like it to be—stick with it and practice often.

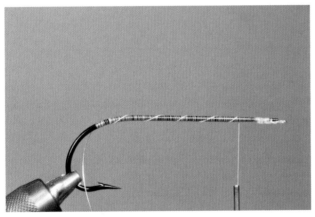

5 Attach the fine oval silver tinsel for the tip immediately above the barb. Advance the thread five wide wraps forward to get it out of the way. Make five wraps of the tinsel spiraling forward with each wrap tightly touching the previous. Don't overlap—one single layer is all you want—and do not allow any gaps between wraps.

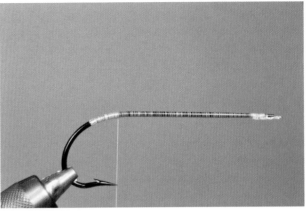

6 Unwrap the five wide thread wraps until back at the end of the finished wraps of the tinsel. Tie off the tinsel securely with several tight wraps of thread spiraling forward. Trim off the excess. Advance the thread in a smooth layer to a position where the thread hangs down even with the hook point. Use a burnisher to smooth out and flatten the thread wraps if in doubt.

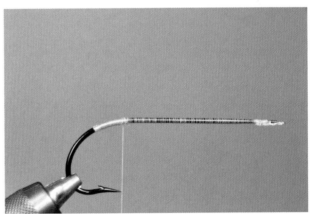

7 Unless your hands are very clean with smooth fingers to handle the silk floss, you may want to use silk gloves to provide a clean, smooth surface to handle the delicate floss. Attach a single strand of yellow silk floss with three tight wraps of thread. Make five open wraps of thread to the eye to move the thread and bobbin out of your way. Stroke the floss a few times to straighten and even the fibers. Wrap a single smooth layer of the floss back to the tinsel, then reverse direction, wrapping back up the bend to where the floss was tied in above the point. Once there, unwrap the five turns of thread over the shank and two more tie-down wraps, then tie off the end of the floss tightly and end up above the point again. Trim the excess floss, and you are now ready to tie in the tail.

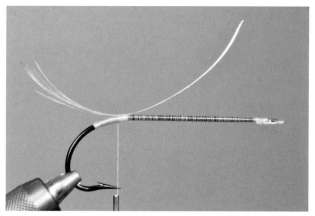

8 Select a single, full golden pheasant crest feather with good color. Length and curvature depend on your fly style preference. A short, tightly curved tail will give a more traditional Old World look to the fly. It will require a high wing and tightly curved topping to match the tail's shape. A longer, less curved crest will result in a longer, shallower wing with a "sleeker," more streamlined appearance. Use a feather of size and quality as one that could be used as a topping. Smaller feathers just don't have the "body," curvature, or fiber length to match with a crest used for a topping. Strip fibers off the rachis to the tie-in point. Make a couple of tight wraps while holding the crest in position on top of the hook, then release to see how it sits. Untie and retie in as needed until properly set.

9 Select a matched pair of narrow sections from a pair of argus center tails with red tips. Place back-to-back with the tips even. Measure for length: The tips should extend back to about midpoint of the golden pheasant crest tail. Hold together vertically with a tight grip above the tie-in point. When tied in, don't let the portion you are holding collapse or roll. The butt ends at and beyond the tie-in point are the only fibers that should compress vertically. Tie in tightly and inspect. The strips should lie together vertically above the golden pheasant crest and help press the golden pheasant tail underneath down for a sleeker fly.

10 Trim the excess from the tails and tie in a single strand of black ostrich herl. The herl has a slant to the fibers off of the core rachis. Ideally the herl is tied in so when wrapped, the fibers slant back toward the hook bend. Advance the tying thread slightly and make four to six wraps spiraling toward the hook eye. Keep wraps close together with no gap between or overlap. Tie off and trim the excess herl.

11 Construct the underbody. The purpose of the underbody is to provide a smooth tapering up to the ends of the gut loop which is attached underneath the hook shank. Attach a long single or paired strands of smooth, flat white floss at the front of the hook shank behind the gut loop ends on the underside of the hook. Make smooth, even wraps with the floss back to the rear of the body, then start wrapping back to the front. Stop at the ends of the gut loop and start wrapping toward the back again but this time stop about one-fifth of the body length away from the rear of the body. Repeat as needed, each time stopping farther away from the rear of the body. When built up sufficiently to match the diameter of the shank and gut eye ends, wrap forward to the end of the body. DO NOT GO TOO FAR FORWARD!!! Leave about one-fifth of the shank and eye uncovered to use for the winging and throat. Tie off the floss at the front of the body and add a couple of half-hitch knots to secure the thread temporarily. Cut the thread off. Use a burnisher to smooth out the underbody. Reattach the tying thread at the rear of the body. See the aforementioned DVD for detailed steps for this process.

12 Attach a single strand of red silk floss and the two pieces of fine oval silver tinsel at the butt. Use a body divider (get mine *free* at my website, www.modernclassicsflytying.com) and mark off the position of the end of the body near the eye, then divide the body into five equal sections to show the position of the rib as it is wrapped forward. Advance the thread in smooth, even wraps to the first mark, which is the start of the second wrap of ribbing.

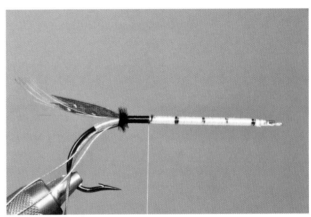

13 Tie in a single strand of black silk floss. Wrap smoothly and evenly back to the ostrich herl butt. Reverse direction and wrap back up to the thread. Tie off tightly and trim the excess.

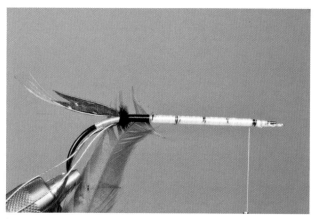

14 Tie in the hackle by the tip on the bottom of the shank. The good side should face down so when starting to wrap, it will face forward and give the classic "wet fly" style and back sweep of the fibers.

15 Advance the thread in smooth, even wraps up to the mark at the front end of the body. Attach a long single strand of black silk floss. Wrap in smooth, even turns back to the first mark where the hackle is tied in. Be sure not to leave a gap or overlap the first body section already created behind this point. Once there, reverse direction and wrap back up to the front end of the body. Tie off tightly and trim the excess.

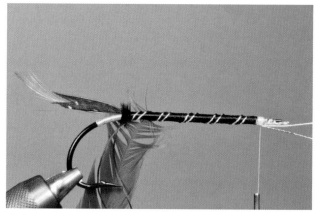

16 Wrap the ribs forward one at a time. Leave a gap between them for the red silk floss to follow. Tie down tightly and trim the excess.

17 Take the red floss and wrap in between the wraps of the oval silver tinsel. Make sure the floss is lying completely flat between the rib wraps and is not twisted—you want it to lie flat between the tinsel ribs. Tie off securely and trim the excess.

18 Double (fold all fibers from the good side toward the dull side so the fibers come off the rachis on the same side) and wrap the hackle behind the rear oval silver tinsel rib. Tie off securely in the front and trim the excess. Fold all fibers on top of the shank down to the sides and bottom to create a clear base to tie on the underwing.

19 Select a matched pair of argus secondary wing strips sized at about half the hook gap in width. Place the strips back-to-back and feel the fibers of both sides mesh into one another. Measure for length: The tips should extend back to just inside the tip of the tail. Hold tightly at the tie-in spot. Hold vertically, but slightly on your side of the hook. Allow the fibers to roll up into position when tied down rather than holding on top at first and trying to fight their tendency to roll. Make a full wrap around the strips and the hook so you are pulling up to tighten the thread. Most importantly, bring your middle finger around from behind and touch up against the butts in front of the tie-in point. Keep them from rolling as you tighten the thread. The quill strips should not be allowed to do anything except

compress vertically as tied in. Any twisting or rolling of the butts will affect the wings being tied in. After several tight wraps, release the strips and inspect. Adjust slightly if needed. If more than a slight adjustment is needed, untie and reposition; then tie back in correctly until the strips sit vertically on top of the hook.

20 Select two matched pairs of argus center tail strips with a red color. Match the tips and measure for length. The tips should extend back to be even with the tips of the argus center tail used in the tail of the fly. Tie in tightly and have the upper edges even with the upper edge of the underwing.

21 Select another matched pair of argus secondary wing strips about half the width of the underwing. Place above the edge of the underwing. The tips should extend back to be even with the tips of the underwing. Marry these strips to the red center tail strips just tied in and the tips of the underwing near the tail. Hold vertically and tie in tightly, making sure they stand vertically as the prior wing sections.

22 Trim off the excess of all wing sections and tie the butts down securely. Place a drop of head cement at the tie-in point and allow to dry.

23 Select a single speckled guinea fowl body feather with fibers about twice the hook gap in length. Trim the tip back slightly and tie in with the good side away from the hook.

24 Fold the fibers back to the dull side and make four or five wraps forward, one right next to the previous. Tie off tightly and trim the excess. Pull the fibers down under the hook and make a wrap or two over the base to secure them in place if needed.

25 Select a matched pair of small dark body feathers for the sides. Match tip to tip. Measure for length: The tips should extend back about one-quarter of the overall wing length. Trim the fibers off the rachis at the tie-in point to get them to lie flat when tied in. Tie one in on each side with the upper edge matching the curvature of the wing. Trim off the excess.

26 Select a matched pair of "leopard spot" argus body feathers. These are a golden tan color with white spots for the cheeks. Place back-to-back and measure for length: The tips should go back about halfway on the sides beneath them. Trim fibers off both sides of the tie-in point to help prepare a flat area to get the feathers to tie in flat against the sides beneath them. Tie in securely and trim the excess.

27 Select a long, full golden pheasant crest feather for the topping. Lay it over the top of the wing and measure for length. The tip should meet the tip of the tail, and the curvature should match the curve of the wing. The center portion of the topping may need to be "straightened" a bit to match the shape of the wing. If needed, *gently* stroke the top edge of the topping with your fingernail. This will take out some of the curvature. Go slowly and little by little until it matches the upper edge curvature when you hold the crest over or beside the top edge of the wing. Strip off excess fibers beyond the tie-in point. Use a small pair of flat-nose smooth-jaw pliers to flatten the rachis at the tie-in point. Hold the top of the wing tightly and make several wraps to tie in the topping. Lift it up a bit to be sure it is aligned with the top edge of the wing and doesn't twist or curve away. If it does, untie and retie until it sits correctly on its own. Trim off the excess.

28 Select a matched pair of African crowned crane crest feathers. Match the tips for length. The tips should extend as far as possible, preferably to the end of the wing. Tie in angling up above the wing so the tips match well above the wing's upper edge. Secure the fibers tightly. Tie off and trim the excess.

29 Form the head of the fly and tie the thread off by either using several half hitches or, my preferred method, whip finishing. Trim the thread, cement the head, and you are finished!

JO'S JEWEL

This fly is a more traditional style with a higher, more rounded wing used in flies such as those tied by Ron Alcott. It incorporates peacock shoulder and body feathers from the India blue and Java green for the underwing, a married strip wing of complementary colors, and sides of small peacock eyes and Palawan peacock pheasant. Named after my partner Betty Jo, it is an iridescent jewel indeed.

Hook: Blind eye black salmon fly—style and size of your choice

Thread: BlackTip: Silver twist

Tag: Yellow silk floss

Tail: Golden pheasant crest and peacock sword fibers

Butt: Black ostrich herl

Body: Two equal sections: First is dark green floss veiled above and below with resplendent quetzal and butted with black ostrich herl. Front half is peacock herl.

Rib: Oval gold tinsel over rear half. Flat gold tinsel and oval gold tinsel over front half.

Hackle: Resplendent quetzal tail (substitute green-dyed emu)

Underwing: Matched pair of India blue peacock shoulder feather extending to just inside the tip of the tail. Outside of which is a matched pair of Java green peacock shoulder feather one-quarter shorter than the prior pair. Outside of which is another matched pair of Java green peacock shoulder feather one-quarter shorter than the prior pair. Outside of which is a final matched pair of Java green peacock shoulder feather one-quarter shorter than the prior pair.

Wing: Married strips of kori (speckled) bustard, green-dyed white turkey tail, argus pheasant secondary wing, blue-dyed white turkey tail, and kori (speckled) bustard

Throat: Java green peacock body feather

Sides: Small matched pair of immature eyed peacock tail feathers

Cheeks: Palawan peacock pheasant feather

Topping: Golden pheasant crest

Horns: Male Java green peacock head crests

Head: Black

Tying the Jo's Jewel

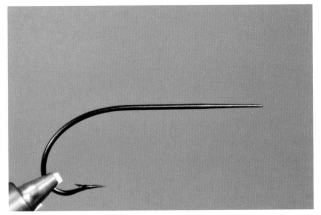

1 Create a liner to place between the hook wire and the vise jaws. I apply a single strip of Scotch tape to a 3-by-5-inch note card edge, then cut out a small rectangle about ½ by ¼ inch. Fold it over lengthwise with the tape on the inside. Taper the folded tip edges to match the jaw size and taper. Fold this piece around the hook bend where it will be placed in the vise jaws and move into place.

Secure the hook tightly in the vise with the hook shank level. Having the hook shank as level as possible is very important. The starting positions for material placement as well as overall proportions are based on where the tying thread hangs down from the hook. The positions of the thread as "even with the barb" or "even with the point" are starting positions for tags, tips, and the butt and/or body of the fly. If the hook shank is not level, the position indicated will not be correct. If the hook shank is drooping excessively, the tag and body positions will be too far back. Same if the hook shank is tilted up too much—the tag and body will be too short. Likewise, be sure the hook is held securely so good, tight thread wraps and material positioning can be accomplished without the hook working loose.

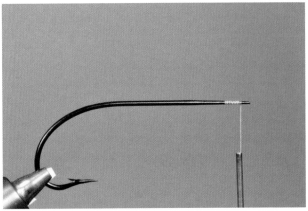

2 Attach the tying thread back from the end of the shank or eye. Be sure the wraps are tight and the thread end is secured well as a starting point for the entire fly. Create a single layer of wraps as a base for attaching the gut eye. Make sure to stay far enough back from the end of the shank tip. The tip of the shank on a blind-eye hook should be exposed ever so slightly and show over the gut loop eye.

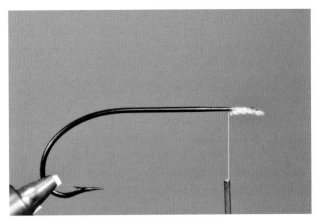

3 Secure the gut eye by folding it over and laying both "legs" under the shank and wrapping over them tightly. As genuine silkworm gut material is both hard to find and expensive, modern tiers use only a small length to form the eye. Traditional flies that were actually used for fishing had strands extending back for the full shank length, well secured to provide a strong and durable connection for hooking and landing the large Atlantic salmon of old.

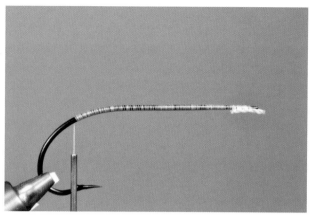

4 Create a smooth layer of thread all the way back on the shank to the starting point of the tag or tip. The underbody needs to be as smooth as possible; whatever the underbody shows as rough or inconsistent spots will often show through the body wrapped over it. I can always improve my underbody work and never seem to get it as consistent or smooth as I'd like it to be—stick with it and practice often.

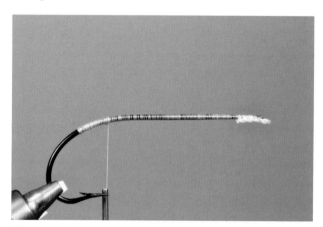

5 Attach the silver twist tinsel for the tip immediately above the barb. Advance the thread five wide wraps forward to get it out of the way. Make five wraps of the tinsel spiraling forward with each wrap tightly touching the previous. Don't overlap—one single layer is all you want—and do not allow any gaps between wraps. Unwrap the five wide thread wraps until back at the end of the finished wraps of the tinsel. Tie off the tinsel securely with several tight wraps of thread spiraling forward. Trim off the excess. Advance the thread in a smooth layer to a position where the thread hangs down even with the hook point. Use a burnisher to smooth out and flatten the thread wraps if in doubt.

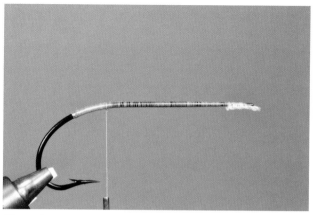

6 Unless your hands are very clean with smooth fingers to handle the silk floss, you may want to use silk gloves to provide a clean, smooth surface to handle the delicate floss. Attach a single strand of yellow silk floss with three tight wraps of thread. Make five open wraps of thread to the eye to move the thread and bobbin out of your way. Stroke the floss a few times to straighten and even the fibers. Wrap a single smooth layer of the floss back to the tinsel, then reverse direction, wrapping back up the bend to where the floss was tied in above the point. Once there, unwrap the five turns of thread over the shank and two more tie-down wraps, then tie off the end of the floss tightly and end up above the point again. Trim the excess floss, and you are now ready to tie in the tail.

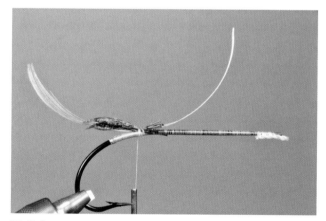

7 Select a single, full golden pheasant crest feather with good color. Length and curvature depend on your fly style preference. A short, tightly curved tail will give a more traditional Old World look to the fly. It will require a high wing and tightly curved topping to match the tail's shape. A longer, less curved crest will result in a longer, shallower wing with a "sleeker," more streamlined appearance. Use a feather of size and quality as one that could be used as a topping. Smaller feathers just don't have the "body," curvature, or fiber length to match with a crest used for a topping. Strip fibers off the rachis to the tie-in point. Make a couple of tight wraps while holding the crest in position on top of the hook, then release to see how it sits. Untie and retie in as needed until properly set. Select a few peacock sword fibers. The sword is a side tail with short, richly colored fibers. Tie these in with the tips extending halfway up the golden pheasant crest tail and curving down to help lower the tail profile.

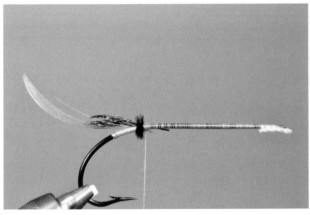

8 Tie in a single strand of black ostrich herl. The herl has a slant to the fibers off of the core rachis. Ideally the herl is tied in so when wrapped, the fibers slant back toward the hook bend. Advance the tying thread slightly and make four to six wraps spiraling toward the hook eye. Keep wraps close together with no gap between or overlap. Tie off and trim the excess herl.

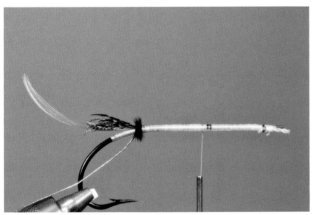

9 Construct the underbody. The purpose of the underbody is to provide a smooth tapering up to the ends of the gut loop which is attached underneath the hook shank. Attach a long single

or paired strands of smooth, flat white floss at the front of the hook shank behind the gut loop ends on the underside of the hook. Make smooth, even wraps with the floss back to the rear of the body, then start wrapping back to the front. Stop at the ends of the gut loop and start wrapping toward the back again but this time stop about one-fifth of the body length away from the rear of the body. Repeat as needed, each time stopping farther away from the rear of the body. When built up sufficiently to match the diameter of the shank and gut eye ends, wrap forward to the end of the body. DO NOT GO TOO FAR FORWARD!!! Leave about one-fifth of the shank and eye uncovered to use for the winging and throat. Tie off the floss at the front of the body and add a couple of half-hitch knots to secure the thread temporarily. Cut the thread off. Use a burnisher to smooth out the underbody. Reattach the tying thread at the rear of the body. See the aforementioned DVD for detailed steps for this process.

Use a body divider (get mine *free* at my website, www.modernclassicsflytying.com) and mark off the position of the end of the body near the eye; then divide the body into two equal sections, marking off the location of the butt that will divide the body sections.

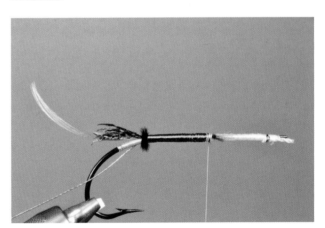

10 Attach the fine oval gold tinsel at the butt. Advance the tying thread in a smooth single layer to the first mark. Attach a single strand of green silk floss at the first mark. Wrap evenly back to the rear butt, then reverse direction, wrap back up to the thread position, and tie off. Keep tight even wraps with no gaps or overlap. Use a burnisher if needed to smooth out the wraps.

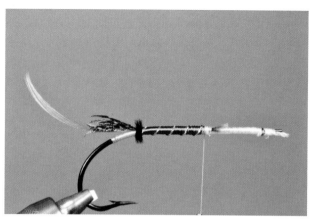

11 Wrap the rib in five even turns and tie it off securely on the underside of the hook. Trim off the excess.

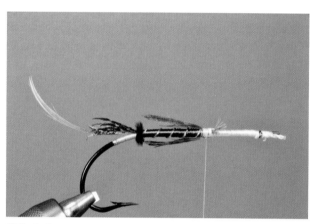

12 Select two matching resplendent quetzal green body feathers for the veilings. Match the tips and measure for length. The tips should extend back to the butt. At the tie-in point, trim fibers off of both sides of the rachis. This will orient the feathers to lie flat when tied in top and bottom. Tie in the top feather first, ensuring it lays flat and is in line with the hook. Repeat for the bottom feather. Trim off the excess and add a few wraps to secure the feathers in place.

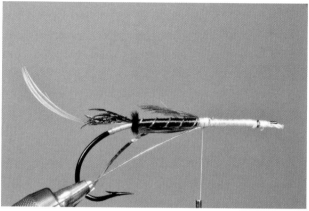

13 Attach the flat gold tinsel and oval gold tinsel at the midpoint of the body.

14 Select a single resplendent quetzal tail feather (substitute green-dyed emu) for the hackle. Trim back the tip and tie in tip-first at the midpoint of the body.

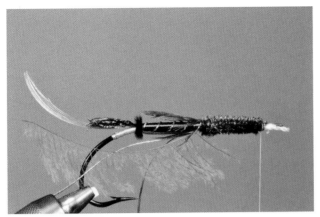

15 Tie in several thick, long peacock herl strands at the midpoint of the body. Advance the thread to the mark at the end of the body. Take the peacock herl strands and start wrapping forward. You may need to roll the strands together a bit to keep them somewhat even as you wrap. Once up to the front end of the body, tie down tightly with several good wraps of thread, then trim off the excess.

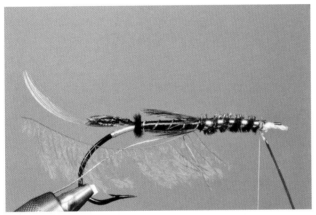

16 Wrap five turns of the flat gold tinsel to the front of the body. Tie off securely and trim the excess.

17 Wrap the oval gold tinsel along the back edge of the flat tinsel. Tie off and trim the excess.

18 Wrap the hackle snugly behind the oval gold tinsel rib. Tie off securely and trim the excess. Fold all fibers down to the sides and bottom of the hook to prepare a clear base for the wings.

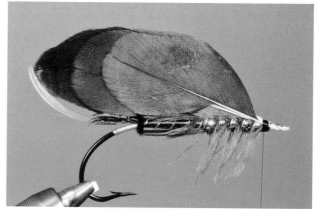

19 Select a matched pair of India blue peacock shoulder feathers for the start of the underwing. Place back-to-back with the tips even and measure for length. The tips should extend back to fit just inside the tip of the tail. Strip off fibers on both sides of the feathers and flatten the rachis even further with pliers at the tie-in point. You need to strip this far up in order for the feather to lie low and tuck into the curve of the tail. If fibers were left on the feather farther down, they would cause the feather to "stand up" and lift away from the tail. Additional feathers will cover the stripped sections as you proceed. Tie in securely. Repeat with the next matched pair of Java green peacock shoulder feathers. Tie in shorter than the prior pair with the tips even with the middle of the tail to show the tips of the India blue feathers underneath.

20 Select two more matching Java green peacock shoulder feathers. Place back-to-back with the tips even and measure for length. The tips should extend back to the end of the tag and tip. Strip fibers off of both sides of the feather about halfway up. Tie in carefully and check often to be sure the feathers stay aligned, sit on edge vertically, and are not crooked or lying off to one side or the other. They should press in against the other feathers to help flatten the wing profile. If not, untie them and crimp the inside of the rachis lightly with your fingernail to force an inward curvature. Retie and again check for position and alignment.

21 Select two smaller Java green peacock shoulder feathers. Place back-to-back with the tips even and measure for length. The tips should extend back to the ostrich herl butt. Strip fibers off of both sides of the feather about halfway up. Tie in securely and make sure the feathers are flat up against the first pair and are vertical. They should lie tight against the prior pair and help press them together. If needed, untie and pinch the inside of the rachis to help curve the outer pair in against the first pair.

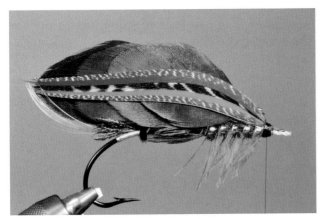 

22 Create the married main wing consisting of kori (speckled) bustard, green-dyed white turkey tail, argus pheasant secondary wing, blue-dyed white turkey tail, and kori (speckled) bustard. Place the strips back-to-back over the outside of the underwing. Measure for length: The tips should extend back to just inside the tip of the tail. Hold tightly at the tie-in spot. Hold vertically but slightly on your side of the hook. Allow the fibers to roll up into position when tied down rather than holding on top at first and trying to fight their wanting to roll. Make a full wrap around the strips and the hook so you are pulling up to tighten the thread. Most importantly, bring your middle finger around from behind and touch up against the butts in front of the tie-in point. Keep them from rolling as you tighten the thread. The quill strips should not be allowed to do anything except compress vertically as tied in. Any twisting or rolling of the butts will affect the wings being tied in. After several tight wraps, release the strips and inspect. Adjust slightly if needed. If more than a slight adjustment is needed, untie and reposition, then tie back in correctly until the strips sit vertically on top of the hook. They should lie against the underwing and help press everything together.

23 Select a Java green peacock body feather to be used for the throat. Fold the fibers back toward the dull side to ensure all fibers lie swept back toward the rear of the fly after being wrapped. Tie it in at the front end of the body, then make four to six wraps and tie off. Fold down all fibers on the top and the sides to collect the fibers under the hook shank. Make a few wraps of thread if needed to secure the fibers in place.

24 Select a matched pair of small immature eyed peacock tail feathers for the sides. Place back-to-back with the tips matched. Position so they will extend back to the midpoint of the body. Trim off fibers at the tie-in point to help orient the feathers to lie flat against the wing underneath. Tie in tipped up to complete the taper of the wing top edge. Tie in tightly on both sides and trim the excess.

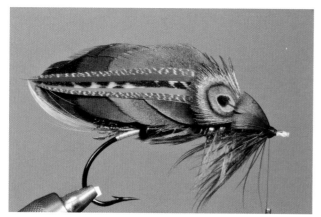

25 Select two matched Palawan peacock pheasant body feathers for the cheeks. Place back-to-back and measure for length. The tips should go just to the edge of the ring of the eyed feathers underneath. Trim off fibers on both sides of the rachis to create a flat profile to help the feather tie in flat against the wing. Tie in tightly and trim off the excess.

26 Select a long, full golden pheasant crest feather for the topping. Lay it over the top of the wing and measure for length. The tip should meet the tip of the tail, and the curvature should match the curve of the wing. The center portion of the topping may need to be "straightened" a bit to match the shape of the wing. If needed, *gently* stroke the top edge of the topping with your fingernail. This will take out some of the curvature. Go slowly and little by little until it matches the upper edge curvature when you hold the crest over or beside the top edge of the wing. Strip off excess fibers beyond the tie-in point. Use a small pair of flat-nose smooth-jaw pliers to flatten the rachis at the tie-in point. Hold the top of the wing tightly and make several wraps to tie in the topping. Lift it up a bit to be sure it is aligned

with the top edge of the wing and doesn't twist or curve away. If it does, untie and retie until it sits correctly on its own. Trim off the excess.

27 Select a matched pair of male Java green peacock crest feathers. Measure for length: The tips should extend as far as possible, preferably to the end of the wing. Tie in angling up above the wing so the tips match well above the wing's upper edge. Secure the fibers tightly. Tie off and trim the excess.

28 Form the head of the fly and tie the thread off by either using several half hitches or, my preferred method, whip finishing. Trim the thread, cement the head, and you are finished!

JOCK SCOTT

A true traditional classic, the Jock Scott was designed by John Scott around 1850. Without a doubt, the Jock Scott is one of the most popular classic salmon flies today. It is probably tied more often by tiers of traditional classic salmon flies than any other flies of old.

The first part is the body of the fly. A golden pheasant crest feather is used for the main portion of the tail. Added to that, shorter and laid flat on top, is a single Indian crow breast feather with its rich orange color and red tip. Then single ostrich feather strands called herl are wrapped around the hook to form the butt. This part provides a break between body sections and covers work completed on the feathers and materials tied in before it. The rear part of the body has several toucan breast feathers, both top and bottom, tied flat and curving inward, called "veilings." These add some color and subtle movement in the water as the fly swims in the current. Another ostrich herl butt is at the midpoint of the hook. The front half of the fly has a hackle—a single ordinary chicken neck or saddle feather dyed black and wrapped tightly behind the rib. In the front of the fly is a throat.

This feather (of speckled guinea fowl on the Jock Scott) adds a complementary or contrasting color, depending on what the pattern, or recipe, calls for. In addition, it provides fullness at the front of the fly and additional movement when the fly is fished.

The Jock Scott is a great example of a built, or married, wing style. An underwing of white-tipped turkey tail is a base for the married wing. The married wing consists of the same number of fibers from wings or tails of various birds that are then joined, or "married," as if all the joined fibers together had been taken from the same bird. To make the wing for the Jock Scott, you take strands from the same side of a peacock secondary wing; dyed swan, goose, or turkey in each of yellow, red, and blue wing or tail; kori bustard wing or tail; florican bustard wing or tail; and golden pheasant tail—all of which are joined together to form the single wing slip. This process is repeated for the other matching wing side. The two constructed wings are then laid together and tied in for the main wing. The strands will remain together and provide the appearance of a single strip of one feather with multiple colors and textures. Over the main wing are two strands of peacock sword fibers and what is termed a "roof," or upper edge wing, of two long strips of bronze mallard flank.

The Jock Scott is finished with "shoulders" of married strands of teal and black-barred wood duck flank. Over these go "sides" of jungle cock neck feathers called "nails"; next are the "cheeks" of blue chatterer (cotinga) body feathers; then a "topping" of golden pheasant crest feather; and finally "horns" of blue-and-gold macaw center tail fibers. All together a lot of feathers combined to create a true classic favorite of both fish and angler.

I highly recommend Michael Radencich's excellent DVD *Tying the Classic Salmon Fly* (see "Recommended Reading and Viewing") as this is the fly he shows how to tie—and he does it very well indeed!

Hook: Blind eye black salmon fly—style and size of your choice

Thread: Black

Tip: Fine oval silver tinsel

Tag: Yellow silk floss

Tail: Golden pheasant crest and Indian crow

Butt: Black ostrich herl

Body: Rear half: yellow silk floss veiled above and below with toucan and butted with black ostrich herl. Front half: black floss.

Rib: Fine oval silver tinsel over rear half of body. Flat silver tinsel and medium oval silver tinsel over front half.

Hackle: Black over front half of body

Underwing: White-tip turkey tail

Wing: Peacock; yellow, red, and blue swan or turkey; kori (speckled) bustard; florican bustard; and golden pheasant tail. Over which is peacock sword and bronze mallard for upper edge wing.

Throat: Speckled gallina (guinea fowl)

Shoulders: Narrow married strips of teal and black-barred wood duck extending to butt

Sides: Jungle cock

Cheeks: Blue chatterer

Topping: Golden pheasant crest

Horns: Blue-and-gold macaw

Head: Black

Tying the Jock Scott

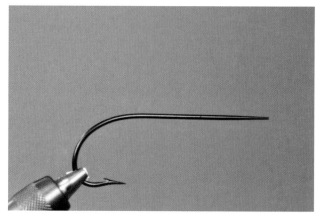

1 Create a liner to place between the hook wire and the vise jaws. I apply a single strip of Scotch tape to a 3-by-5-inch note card edge, then cut out a small rectangle about ½ by ¼ inch. Fold it over lengthwise with the tape on the inside. Taper the folded tip edges to match the jaw size and taper. Fold this piece around the hook bend where it will be placed in the vise jaws and move into place.

Secure the hook tightly in the vise with the hook shank level. Having the hook shank as level as possible is very important. The starting positions for material placement as well as overall proportions are based on where the tying thread hangs down from the hook. The positions of the thread as "even with the barb" or "even with the point" are starting positions for tags, tips, and the butt and/ or body of the fly. If the hook shank is not level, the position indicated will not be correct. If the hook shank is drooping excessively, the tag and body positions will be too far back. Same if the hook shank is tilted up too much—the tag and body will be too short. Likewise, be sure the hook is held securely so good, tight thread wraps and material positioning can be accomplished without the hook working loose.

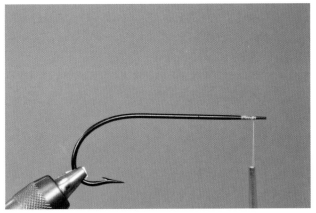

2 Attach the tying thread back from the end of the shank or eye. Be sure the wraps are tight and the thread end is secured well as a starting point for the entire fly. Create a single layer of wraps as a base for attaching the gut eye. Make sure to stay far enough back from the end of the shank tip. The tip of the shank on a blind-eye hook should be exposed ever so slightly and show over the gut loop eye.

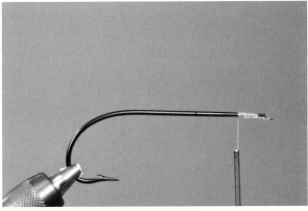

3 Secure the gut eye by folding it over and laying both "legs" under the shank and wrapping over them tightly. As genuine silkwo rm gut material is both hard to find and expensive, modern tiers use only a small length to form the eye. Traditional flies that were actually used for fishing had strands extending back for the full shank length, well secured to provide a strong and durable connection for hooking and landing the large Atlantic salmon of old.

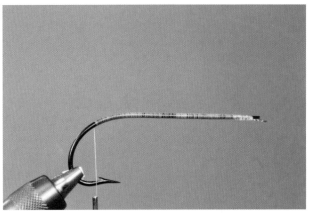

4 Create a smooth layer of thread all the way back on the shank to the starting point of the tag or tip. The underbody needs to be as smooth as possible; whatever the underbody shows as rough or inconsistent spots will often show through the body wrapped over it. I can always improve my underbody work and never seem to get it as consistent or smooth as I'd like it to be—stick with it and practice often.

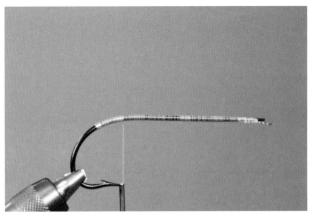

5 Attach the fine oval silver tinsel for the tip immediately above the barb. Advance the thread five wide wraps forward to get it out of the way. Make five wraps of the tinsel spiraling forward with each wrap tightly touching the previous. Don't overlap—one single layer is all you want—and do not allow any gaps between wraps. Unwrap the five wide thread wraps until back at the end of the finished wraps of the tinsel. Tie off the tinsel securely with several tight wraps of thread spiraling forward. Trim off the excess. Advance the thread in a smooth layer to a position where the thread hangs down even with the hook point. Use a burnisher to smooth out and flatten the thread wraps if in doubt.

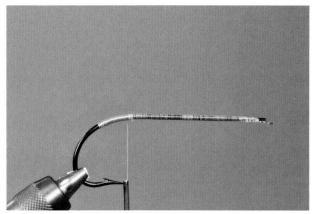

6 Unless your hands are very clean with smooth fingers to handle the silk floss, you may want to use silk gloves to provide a clean, smooth surface to handle the delicate floss. Attach a single strand of yellow silk floss with three tight wraps of thread. Make five open wraps of thread to the eye to move the thread and bobbin out of your way. Stroke the floss a few times to straighten and even the fibers. Wrap a single smooth layer of the floss back to the tinsel, then reverse direction, wrapping back up the bend to where the floss was tied in above the point. Once there, unwrap the five turns of thread over the shank and two more tie-down wraps, then tie off the end of the floss tightly and end up above the point again. Trim the excess floss, and you are now ready to tie in the tail.

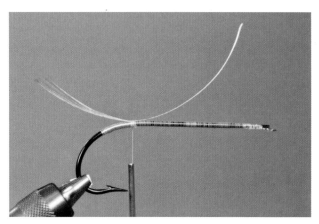

7 Select a single, full golden pheasant crest feather with good color. Length and curvature depend on your fly style preference. A short, tightly curved tail will give a more traditional Old World look to the fly. It will require a high wing and tightly curved topping to match the tail's shape. A longer, less curved crest will result in a longer, shallower wing with a "sleeker," more

streamlined appearance. Use a feather of size and quality as one that could be used as a topping. Smaller feathers just don't have the "body," curvature, or fiber length to match with a crest used for a topping. Strip fibers off the rachis to the tie-in point. Make a couple of tight wraps while holding the crest in position on top of the hook, then release to see how it sits. Untie and retie in as needed until properly set.

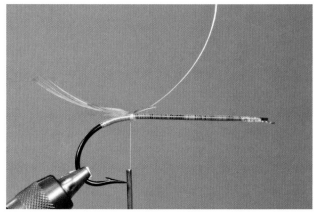

8 Select a single Indian crow breast feather and measure for length. The tip should extend back to the midpoint of the golden pheasant crest feather underneath. At the tie-in point, trim off fibers from both sides of the feather. Position on top of the golden pheasant tail with the good side up and tie in flat on top. Be sure it lies centered on the golden pheasant tail and doesn't twist or roll. Once secured, trim off the excess of both feathers.

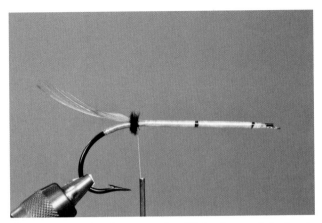

9 Tie in a single strand of black ostrich herl. The herl has a slant to the fibers off of the core rachis. Ideally the herl is tied in so when wrapped, the fibers slant back toward the hook bend. Advance the tying thread slightly and make four to six wraps spiraling toward the hook eye. Keep wraps close together with no gap between or overlap. Tie off and trim the excess herl.

Construct the underbody. The purpose of the underbody is to provide a smooth tapering up to the ends of the gut loop which is attached underneath the hook shank. Attach a long single or paired strands of smooth, flat white floss at the front of the hook shank behind the gut loop ends on the underside of the hook. Make smooth, even wraps with the floss back to the rear of the body, then start wrapping back to the front. Stop at the ends of the gut loop and start wrapping toward the back again but this time stop about one-fifth of the body length away from the rear of the body. Repeat as needed, each time stopping farther away from the rear of the body. When built up sufficiently to match the diameter of the shank and gut eye ends, wrap forward to the end of the body. DO NOT GO TOO FAR FORWARD!!! Leave about one-fifth of the shank and eye uncovered to use for the winging and throat. Tie off the floss at the front of the body and add a couple of half-hitch knots to secure the thread temporarily. Cut the thread off. Use a burnisher to smooth out the underbody. Reattach the tying thread at the rear of the body. See the aforementioned DVD for detailed steps for this process.

Use a body divider (get mine *free* at my website, www.modernclassicsflytying.com) and mark off the position of the end of the body near the eye; then divide the body into two equal sections, marking off the location of the butt that will divide the body sections.

10 Attach the fine oval silver tinsel. Advance the thread in smooth, even wraps to the first mark. Attach a single strand of yellow floss and wrap it back in a smooth, even layer to the ostrich herl butt. Once there, reverse the direction and wrap back up to the first mark. Tie off securely and trim the excess.

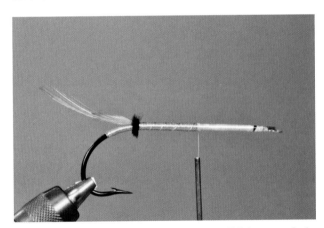

11 Make five even wraps of the ribbing and tie off securely.

12 Select four to six matching toucan breast feathers. Place half together one on top of the other, "stacking" them if you will. Measure for length: The tips should line up even with the ostrich herl butt. Trim off fibers from both sides at the tie-in point. Tie in half the feathers on top, lying flat when viewed from the side. Follow the same process for the feathers tied in on the bottom. Be sure both sets lie flat above and below the shank.

13 Tie in a single strand of black ostrich herl. The herl has a slant to the fibers off of the core rachis. Ideally the herl is tied in so when wrapped, the fibers slant back toward the hook bend. Advance the tying thread slightly and make four to six wraps spiraling toward the hook eye. Keep wraps close together with no gap between or overlap. Tie off and trim the excess herl. Attach the flat silver tinsel, oval silver tinsel, and black hackle by the tip end.

14 Advance the thread in a smooth, even layer up to the mark at the front end of the body. Attach a single strand of black silk floss and wrap back to the ostrich herl butt. Reverse the direction and wrap back up to the thread. Tie off securely and trim the excess.

15 Wrap the flat silver tinsel rib forward in five even turns and tie off on the bottom of the end of the body section.

16 Wrap the oval silver tinsel rib forward right up against the flat tinsel and tie off on the bottom of the end of the body section.

17 Fold the fibers back to the dull side so all fibers come off of one side of the rachis. Wrap the hackle snugly up against the oval tinsel rib and tie off tightly at the end of the body section.

18 Select two matching strips of white-tipped turkey tail with the white tips showing. Place the strips back-to-back and feel the fibers of both sides mesh into one another. Measure for length: The tips should extend back to just inside the tip of the tail. Hold tightly at the tie-in spot. Hold vertically but slightly on your side of the hook. Allow the fibers to roll up into position when tied down rather than holding on top at first and trying to fight their wanting to roll. Make a full wrap around the strips and the hook so you are pulling up to tighten the thread. Most importantly, bring your middle finger around from behind and touch up against the butts in front of the tie-in point. Keep them from rolling as you tighten the thread. The quill strips should not be allowed to do anything except compress vertically as tied in. Any twisting or rolling of the butts will affect the wings being tied in. After several tight wraps, release the strips and inspect. Adjust slightly if needed. If more than a slight adjustment is needed, untie

and reposition, then tie back in correctly until the strips sit vertically on top of the hook.

19 Build up both sides of the married wings. They consist of peacock secondary wing, yellow swan, red swan, blue swan, kori (speckled) bustard, florican bustard, and golden pheasant tail. For this fly, due to its size, I substituted Arabian bustard for the peacock wing, white-dyed turkey tail for the swan, and argus secondary wing dyed reddish brown for the golden pheasant tail: another example where the substitutes work better than the originals. The wings are tied in over and above the underwing so the underwing still shows beneath. Tie in with the same process detailed for the underwing. Trim off all of the excess and add a drop or two of head cement to secure the wing.

20 Select a single speckled guinea fowl feather for the throat. Trim back the tip and tie in by the tip. Make four or five wraps next to each other, advancing toward the eye. Tie off securely and trim the excess. Pull down the fibers and make a few thread wraps over them if needed to secure them in place. Also tie in two peacock sword fibers over the top edge of the wing.

21 Marry together strips from a teal flank feather and a wood duck black-barred flank feather for the shoulders. Fibers from the left side of the feathers join to form the near wing side, and fibers from the right side form the far wing side. Tips extend back to the butt. Tie in both sides, normally one at a time, tightly and to lie flat against the wing and be centered within the height of the wing. Also tie in the bronze mallard flank strips to form a flat upper edge wing that envelops the top of the front half of the wing. This provides a cover over the front edge of the main wing and a nice taper to the eventual head of the fly.

22 Select two matching jungle cock neck feathers to make the sides with. Match the tips and measure for length. The tips should extend back to the middle of the body above the ostrich herl joint. Trim fibers off of both sides at the tie-in point to help orient the feathers to lie flat against the wing. Tie in tightly and inspect. If they don't press in against the wing, untie them and crimp slightly on the inside with your fingernail to "bend" the rachis in toward the wing. Retie in and when satisfied, trim off the excess.

23 Select a single resplendent quetzal tail feather. As these are nearly impossible to get, use a great substitute in the form of a green-dyed emu feather. Tie in by the tip end near the ostrich herl butt.

24 Select two matching blue chatterer (cotinga) feathers for the cheeks. Measure for length: The tips should extend back halfway on the sides. Trim off fibers on both sides of the rachis to help orient them to lie flat. Tie in tightly and trim off the excess.

25 Select a long, full golden pheasant crest feather for the topping. Lay it over the top of the wing and measure for length. The tip should meet the tip of the tail, and the curvature should match the curve of the wing. The center portion of the topping may need to be "straightened" a bit to match the shape of the wing. If needed, gently stroke the top edge of the topping with your fingernail. This will take out some of the curvature. Go slowly and little by little until it matches the upper edge curvature when you hold the crest over or beside the top edge of the wing. Strip off excess fibers beyond the tie-in point. Use a small pair of flat-nose smooth-jaw pliers to flatten the rachis at the tie-in point. Hold the top of the wing tightly and make several wraps to tie in the topping. Lift it up a bit to be sure it is aligned with the top edge of the wing and doesn't twist or

curve away. If it does, untie and retie until it sits correctly on its own. Trim off the excess.

26 Select two matching fibers from a blue-and-gold macaw center tail. Measure for length: The tips should match and extend as far as possible, preferably to the end of the wing. Tie in angling up above the wing so the tips match well above the wing's upper edge. Secure the fibers tightly. Tie off and trim the excess.

27 Form the head of the fly and tie the thread off by either using several half hitches or, my preferred method, whip finishing. Trim the thread, cement the head, and you are finished!

LADY AMHERST

Created in post-Victorian Canada (ca. 1925) and attributed to George B. Bonbright, the Lady Amherst is most closely associated with the large salmon of Québec's Grand Cascapedia. The Lady Amherst is an early-season fly, most commonly tied on large hooks for deep, cold, heavy-flowing, spring rivers. While not a true Victorian-era pattern, it is nonetheless in every way a traditional classic design. Based perhaps on the Ranger series of classic patterns, it has simple, sleek lines and a high-contrast appearance well suited for many conditions. My version is a bit different from the true original. I have added Sebright feathers as underwings for the jungle cock and again for the hackle. The true original does not have the underwings and uses "badger" hackle—a white chicken feather with a black center stripe. I leave the version you tie up to you.

Hook: Blind eye black salmon fly—style and size of your choice

Thread: Black

Tip: Fine oval silver tinsel

Tag: Golden yellow floss

Tail: Golden pheasant crest and blue chatterer (cotinga)

Butt: Black ostrich herl

Body: Flat silver tinsel

Rib: Oval silver tinsel

Hackle: Natural black Sebright rooster hackle

Throat: Teal flank

Wing: Matched pair of natural Sebright rooster hackles tied back-to-back reaching to just inside the tip of the tail. Over which is a matched pair of jungle cock feathers set back-to-back. Over which are two sets of Amherst pheasant tippets, the longer pair with squared ends and the shorter pair with rounded ends.

Sides: Natural Sebright rooster feathers over which are jungle cock feathers

Cheeks: Blue chatterer (cotinga)

Topping: Golden pheasant crest

Horns: Blue-and-gold macaw

Head: Black

Tying the Lady Amherst

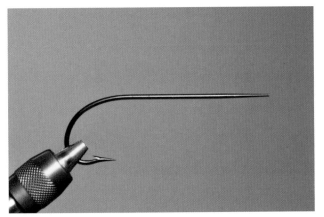

1 Create a liner to place between the hook wire and the vise jaws. I apply a single strip of Scotch tape to a 3-by-5-inch note card edge, then cut out a small rectangle about ½ by ¼ inch. Fold it over lengthwise with the tape on the inside. Taper the folded tip edges to match the jaw size and taper. Fold this piece around the hook bend where it will be placed in the vise jaws and move into place.

Secure the hook tightly in the vise with the hook shank level. Having the hook shank as level as possible is very important. The starting positions for material placement as well as overall proportions are based on where the tying thread hangs down from the hook. The positions of the thread as "even with the barb" or "even with the point" are starting positions for tags, tips, and the butt and/or body of the fly. If the hook shank is not level, the position indicated will not be correct. If the hook shank is drooping excessively, the tag and body positions will be too far back. Same if the hook shank is tilted up too much—the tag and body will be too short. Likewise, be sure the hook is held securely so good, tight thread wraps and material positioning can be accomplished without the hook working loose.

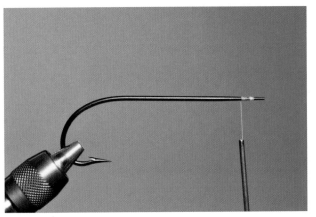

2 Attach the tying thread back from the end of the shank or eye. Be sure the wraps are tight and the thread end is secured well as a starting point for the entire fly. Create a single layer of wraps as a base for attaching the gut eye. Make sure to stay far enough back from the end of the shank tip. The tip of the shank on a blind-eye hook should be exposed ever so slightly and show over the gut loop eye.

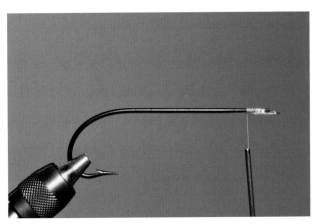

3 Secure the gut eye by folding it over and laying both "legs" under the shank and wrapping over them tightly. As genuine silkworm gut material is both hard to find and expensive, modern tiers use only a small length to form the eye. Traditional flies that were actually used for fishing had strands extending back for the full shank length, well secured to provide a strong and durable connection for hooking and landing the large Atlantic salmon of old.

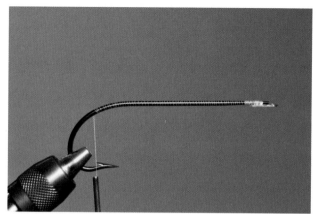

4 Create a smooth layer of thread all the way back on the shank to the starting point of the tag or tip. The underbody needs to be as smooth as possible; whatever the underbody shows as rough or inconsistent spots will often show through the body wrapped over it. I can always improve my underbody work and never seem to get it as consistent or smooth as I'd like it to be—stick with it and practice often.

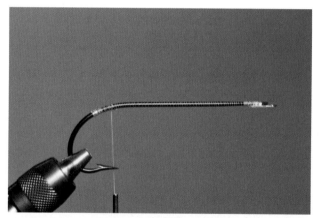

5 Attach the fine oval silver tinsel for the tip immediately above the barb. Advance the thread five wide wraps forward to get it out of the way. Make five wraps of the tinsel spiraling forward with each wrap tightly touching the previous. Don't overlap—one single layer is all you want—and do not allow any gaps between wraps. Unwrap the five wide thread wraps until back at the end of the finished wraps of the tinsel. Tie off the tinsel securely with several tight wraps of thread spiraling forward. Trim off the excess. Advance the thread in a smooth layer to a position where the thread hangs down even with the hook point. Use a burnisher to smooth out and flatten the thread wraps if in doubt.

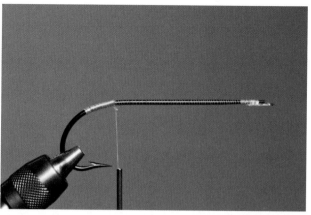

6 Unless your hands are very clean with smooth fingers to handle the silk floss, you may want to use silk gloves to provide a clean, smooth surface to handle the delicate floss. Attach a single strand of yellow silk floss with three tight wraps of thread. Make five open wraps of thread to the eye to move the thread and bobbin out of your way. Stroke the floss a few times to straighten and even the fibers. Wrap a single smooth layer of the floss back to the tinsel, then reverse direction, wrapping back up the bend to where the floss was tied in above the point. Once there, unwrap the five turns of thread over the shank and two more tie-down wraps, then tie off the end of the floss tightly and end up above the point again. Trim the excess floss, and you are now ready to tie in the tail.

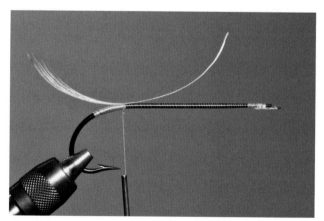

7 Select a single, full golden pheasant crest feather with good color. Length and curvature depend on your fly style preference. A short, tightly curved tail will give a more traditional Old World look to the fly. It will require a high wing and tightly curved topping to match the tail's shape. A longer, less curved crest will result in a longer, shallower wing with a "sleeker," more streamlined appearance. Use a feather of size and quality as one that could be used as a topping. Smaller feathers just don't have the "body," curvature, or fiber length to match with a crest used for a topping. Strip fibers off the rachis to the tie-in point. Make a couple of tight wraps while holding the crest in position on top of the hook, then release to see how it sits. Untie and retie in as needed until properly set.

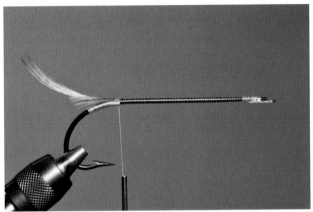

8 Select a single blue chatterer (cotinga) feather. Measure for length: The tip should extend back to the midpoint of the golden pheasant crest feather. Trim off fibers on both sides of the rachis to get the feather to lie flat when tied in. Tie in with the good side up (curving down) and lying flat to help lower the tail profile. Trim off the excess.

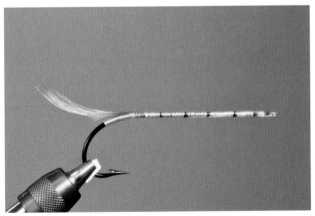

9 Construct the underbody. The purpose of the underbody is to provide a smooth tapering up to the ends of the gut loop which is attached underneath the hook shank. Attach a long single or paired strands of smooth, flat white floss at the front of the hook shank behind the gut loop ends on the underside of the hook. Make smooth, even wraps with the floss back to the rear of the body,

then start wrapping back to the front. Stop at the ends of the gut loop and start wrapping toward the back again but this time stop about one-fifth of the body length away from the rear of the body. Repeat as needed, each time stopping farther away from the rear of the body. When built up sufficiently to match the diameter of the shank and gut eye ends, wrap forward to the end of the body. DO NOT GO TOO FAR FORWARD!!! Leave about one-fifth of the shank and eye uncovered to use for the winging and throat. Tie off the floss at the front of the body and add a couple of half-hitch knots to secure the thread temporarily. Cut the thread off. Use a burnisher to smooth out the underbody. Reattach the tying thread at the rear of the body. See the aforementioned DVD for detailed steps for this process.

Use a body divider (get mine *free* at my website, www.modernclassicsflytying.com) and mark off the position of the end of the body near the eye; then divide the body into five equal sections representing the points at which the rib will be wrapped over the body.

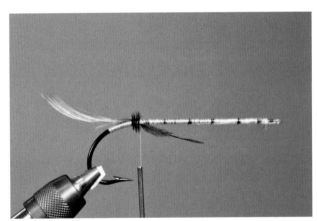

10 Tie in a single strand of black ostrich herl. The herl has a slant to the fibers off of the core rachis. Ideally the herl is tied in so when wrapped, the fibers slant back toward the hook bend. Advance the tying thread slightly and make four to six wraps spiraling toward the hook eye. Keep wraps close together with no gap between or overlap. Tie off and trim the excess herl.

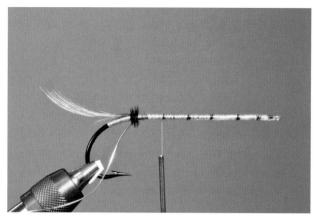

11 Attach the oval silver tinsel at the butt. Advance the tying thread in a smooth single layer to the first mark.

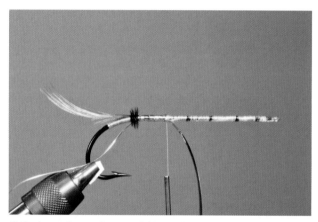

12 Attach a piece of flat silver tinsel at the first mark. Wrap evenly back to the rear butt, then reverse direction, wrap back up to the thread position, and tie off. Keep tight even wraps with no gaps or overlap.

13 Select a natural Sebright rooster hackle and trim off the tip fibers on both sides of the rachis. Attach it to the bottom of the shank at the first mark.

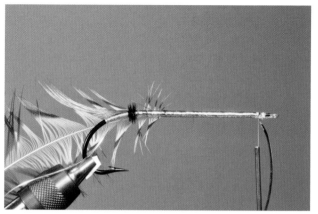

14 Advance the thread in smooth, even wraps up to the front of the body. Attach a length of fat silver tinsel. Wrap in smooth, even turns back to the first mark and up against the first small section of flat tinsel. Reverse the wraps and work back up to the thread. Tie off tightly and inspect. The body should look as if it were made in one complete section with no breaks, gaps, or overlaps.

15 Wrap five turns of the oval silver tinsel to the front of the body. The second wrap should go right in front of the feather tip so when the feather is wrapped, it will be tucked in behind the ribbing. Tie off securely and trim the excess.

16 Carefully double (fold over to one side the fibers) the hackle and wrap it behind and touching the rib to the front of the body. Tie off securely and trim the excess.

17 Reach up and pull and fold all of the fibers of the hackle down the sides so most, if not all, lie underneath the hook. This creates a clear space for the wing to be tied in and allows it to lie low against the body for a more streamlined appearance.

18 Select a matched pair of Sebright rooster hackles. Match up back-to-back with the tips even and measure for length. The tips should

extend back to sit just inside the tip of the tail. Strip off fibers on both sides of the rachis at the tie-in point. Flatten the rachis further with smooth flat-nose pliers if needed. Tie in tightly on top, ensuring the feathers stand up vertically when viewed from the side and are in line with the hook when viewed from above. Trim off the excess and make an extra wrap or two of thread.

19 Select a matched pair of jungle cock neck feathers. Place back-to-back with the tips even and measure for length. The tips should extend back to fit just inside the tip of the tail. Strip off fibers on both sides of the feathers up to the mid-way point and flatten the rachis even further with pliers at the tie-in point. You need to strip this far up in order for the feather to lie low and tuck into the curve of the tail. If fibers were left on the feather farther down, they would cause the feather to "stand up" and lift away from the tail. Additional feathers will cover the stripped sections as you proceed. Tie in securely and trim the excess.

20 Select a matching pair of Lady Amherst pheasant tippet feathers with squared tips rather than rounded. Place back-to-back with the tips even and measure for length. The tips should extend back to the middle spot on the jungle cock feathers just tied in. Strip fibers off of both sides of the feathers about one-third of the way up. Tie in carefully and check often to be sure the feathers stay aligned, sit on edge vertically, and are not crooked or lying off to one side or the other. They should press in against the other feathers to help flatten the wing profile. If not, untie them and crimp the inside of the rachis lightly with your fingernail to force an inward curvature. Retie and again check for position and alignment.

21 Select a smaller pair of Lady Amherst pheasant tippet feathers with rounded tips. Place back-to-back with the tips even and measure for length. The tips should extend back to the first bar of the pair of tippets underneath. Strip fibers off of both sides of the feather a short way up. Tie in securely and make sure the feathers are flat up against the first pair and are vertical. They should lie tight against the prior pair and help press them together. If needed, untie and pinch the inside of the rachis to help curve the outer pair in against the first pair. Tie back in securely and trim off the excess.

22 Select a teal flank feather and tie in by the tip for the throat. Fold the fibers back (double) and wrap a few turns for the throat. Tie off securely and trim the excess. Pull all fibers down and to the back. Select a matched pair of Sebright rooster hackles for the base for the sides. Place back-to-back with the tips even and measure for length: The tips should extend back to the first bar of the pair of tippets underneath. Trim a few fibers off the sides of the rachis and tie in tightly. They should lie against the underwing and help press everything together. Trim off the excess.

matches the upper edge curvature when you hold the crest over or beside the top edge of the wing. Strip off excess fibers beyond the tie-in point. Use a small pair of flat-nose smooth-jaw pliers to flatten the rachis at the tie-in point. Hold the top of the wing tightly and make several wraps to tie in the topping. Lift it up a bit to be sure it is aligned with the top edge of the wing and doesn't twist or curve away. If it does, untie and retie until it sits correctly on its own. Trim off the excess.

23 Select a matched pair of jungle cock neck feathers for the sides. Place back-to-back with the tips matched. Position so they will extend back to the first bar of the tippets and cover the Sebright hackles beneath. Trim off fibers at the tie-in point to help orient the feathers to lie flat against the wing underneath. Tie in tipped up to align with the center of the wing. Tie both sides in tightly and trim the excess. Select two blue chatterer (cotinga) body feathers for the cheeks. Place back-to-back and measure for length. The tips should extend to the midpoint of the jungle cock sides beneath. Trim off fibers on both sides of the tie-in point. Tie one in on each side tightly and trim off the excess.

25 Select a matched pair of blue-and-gold macaw center tail fibers. Measure for length: The tips should extend as far as possible, preferably to the end of the wing. Tie in angling up above the wing so the tips match well above the wing's upper edge. Secure the fibers tightly. Tie off and trim the excess.

Form the head of the fly and tie the thread off by either using several half hitches or, my preferred method, whip finishing. Trim the thread, cement the head, and you are finished!

24 Select a long, full golden pheasant crest feather for the topping. Lay it over the top of the wing and measure for length. The tip should meet the tip of the tail, and the curvature should match the curve of the wing. The center portion of the topping may need to be "straightened" a bit to match the shape of the wing. If needed, *gently* stroke the top edge of the topping with your fingernail. This will take out some of the curvature. Go slowly and little by little until it

LEOPARD

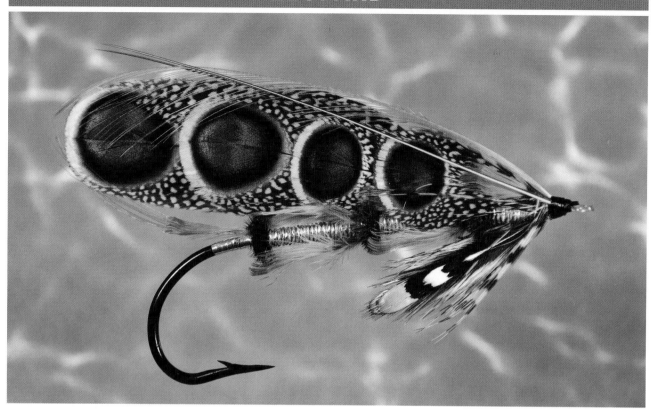

The Leopard is a modern classic created by Paul Schmookler, coauthor of *Rare and Unusual Fly Tying Materials: A Natural History*. Paul's original designs are a combination of the natural beauty found in the materials he selects and an aesthetically pleasing form for the fly tier, angler, and any fish lucky enough to get to see one in the water.

The Leopard features golden pheasant crest and Indian crow breast feathers in the tail. Additional Indian crow pairs are utilized as veilings at the top and bottom of the fly's body. For the wing, one of my favorite feathers, the gray peacock pheasant, is the showpiece. Four pairs in progressively smaller sizes are carefully layered over one another to create the impression of a single four-eyed feather tied in to make the wing. Add more Indian crow, some jungle cock, and guinea fowl for a throat, and you have a striking pattern showcasing the natural and man-made beauty of classic salmon flies.

Hook: Blind eye black salmon fly—style and size of your choice

Thread: Black

Tag: Flat silver tinsel

Tail: Golden pheasant crest and Indian crow

Butt: Black ostrich

Body: Three sections of 40/40/20 percent from back to front of silver lace butted with black ostrich herl. First and second sections veiled above and below with Indian crow reaching fully back to the prior butt. Third section veiled below with back-to-back jungle cock extending just past the second butt.

Wing: Four pairs of gray peacock pheasant eyed feathers, each shorter and smaller than the previous pair so all eyes show fully back to front

Throat: Guinea fowl (substitute for banded gymnogene)

Cheeks: Indian crow

Topping: Golden pheasant crest

Horns: Blue-and-gold macaw

Head: Black

Tying the Leopard

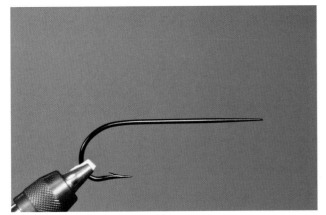

1 Create a liner to place between the hook wire and the vise jaws. I apply a single strip of Scotch tape to a 3-by-5-inch note card edge, then cut out a small rectangle about ½ by ¼ inch. Fold it over lengthwise with the tape on the inside. Taper the folded tip edges to match the jaw size and taper. Fold this piece around the hook bend where it will be placed in the vise jaws and move into place.

Secure the hook tightly in the vise with the hook shank level. Having the hook shank as level as possible is very important. The starting positions for material placement as well as overall proportions are based on where the tying thread hangs down from the hook. The positions of the thread as "even with the barb" or "even with the point" are starting positions for tags, tips, and the butt and/ or body of the fly. If the hook shank is not level, the position indicated will not be correct. If the hook shank is drooping excessively, the tag and body positions will be too far back. Same if the hook shank is tilted up too much—the tag and body will be too short. Likewise, be sure the hook is held securely so good, tight thread wraps and material positioning can be accomplished without the hook working loose.

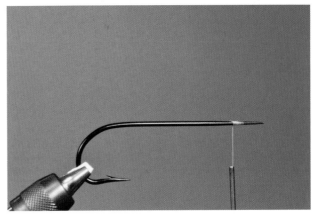

2 Attach the tying thread back from the end of the shank or eye. Be sure the wraps are tight and the thread end is secured well as a starting point for the entire fly. Create a single layer of wraps as a base for attaching the gut eye. Make sure to stay far enough back from the end of the shank tip. The tip of the shank on a blind-eye hook should be exposed ever so slightly and show over the gut loop eye.

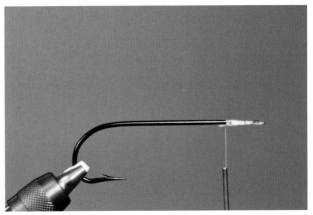

3 Secure the gut eye by folding it over and laying both "legs" under the shank and wrapping over them tightly. As genuine silkworm-gut material is both hard to find and expensive, modern tiers use only a small length to form the eye. Traditional flies that were actually used for fishing had strands extending back for the full shank length, well secured to provide a strong and durable connection for hooking and landing the large Atlantic salmon of old.

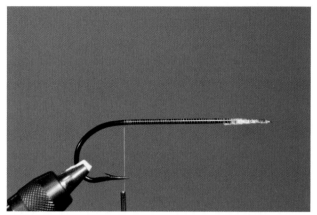

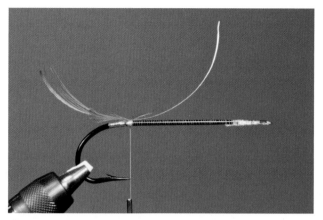

4 Create a smooth layer of thread all the way back on the shank to the starting point of the tag or tip. The underbody needs to be as smooth as possible; whatever the underbody shows as rough or inconsistent spots will often show through the body wrapped over it. I can always improve my underbody work and never seem to get it as consistent or smooth as I'd like it to be—stick with it and practice often. For the Leopard, stop the tying thread to where it is even with the point when hanging freely under the shank.

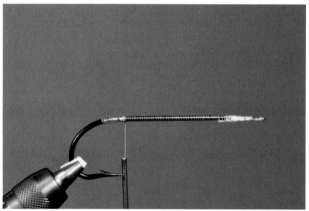

5 Attach the flat silver tinsel for the tag above the point. Advance the thread five wide wraps forward to get it out of the way. Wrap the tinsel spiraling back over the bend of the hook with each wrap tightly touching the previous. Don't overlap—one single layer is all you want—and do not allow any gaps between wraps. Once above the barb, reverse direction and wrap tightly over the top of the first layer with another even, smooth layer back up to the point. Unwrap the five wide thread wraps until back at the end of the finished wraps of the tinsel. Tie off the tinsel securely with several tight wraps of thread spiraling forward. Trim off the excess.

6 Select a single golden pheasant crest feather. Length and curvature depend on your fly style preference. A short, tightly curved tail will give a more traditional Old World look to the fly. It will require a high wing and tightly curved topping to match the tail's shape. A longer, less curved crest will result in a longer, shallower wing with a "sleeker," more streamlined appearance. Use a feather of size and quality as one that could be used as a topping. Smaller feathers just don't have the "body," curvature, or fiber length to match with a crest used for a topping. Strip fibers off the rachis to the tie-in point. Make a couple of tight wraps while holding the crest in position on top of the hook, then release to see how it sits. Untie and retie in as needed until properly set.

Once set correctly, make another couple of tight wraps to lock it in place. *Do not yet* trim off the excess. Select a single Indian crow breast feather and measure for use in the tail. The tips should go halfway up the golden pheasant crest or as close to this as possible. At the tie-in point, trim fibers off the sides close to the rachis. Hold the feather flat on top of the hook with the shiny, or "good," side up. This is the part with the best color and appearance, and with the good side up, the fibers curve down. This helps keep the golden pheasant crest tail from standing up too much and helps achieve a sleeker, more streamlined finished fly.

7 Here is a top view of the tail. The golden pheasant crest is standing up vertically and the Indian crow is lying flat. Both should be symmetrical and in line with the hook shank.

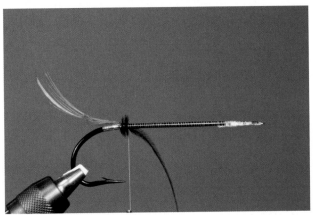

8 Attach a single strand of black ostrich herl. The herl has a slant to the fibers off of the core rachis. Ideally the herl is tied in so when wrapped, the fibers slant back toward the hook bend. Advance the tying thread slightly and make four to six wraps spiraling toward the hook eye. Keep the wraps close together with no gap between or overlap. Tie off and trim the excess herl.

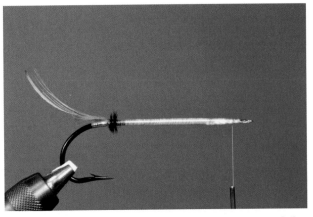

9 Construct the underbody. The purpose of the underbody is to provide a smooth tapering up to the ends of the gut loop which is attached underneath the hook shank. Attach a long single or paired strands of smooth, flat white floss at the front of the hook shank behind the gut loop ends on the underside of the hook. Make smooth, even wraps with the floss back to the rear of the body, then start wrapping back to the front. Stop at the ends of the gut loop and start wrapping toward the back again but this time stop about one-fifth of the body length away from the rear of the body. Repeat as needed, each time stopping farther away from the rear of the body. When built up sufficiently to match the diameter of the shank and gut eye ends, wrap forward to the end of the body. DO NOT GO TOO FAR FORWARD!!! Leave about one-fifth of the shank and eye uncovered to use for the winging and throat. Tie off the floss at the front of the body and add a couple of half-hitch knots to secure the thread temporarily. Cut the thread off. Use a burnisher to smooth out the underbody. Reattach the tying thread at the rear of the body. See the aforementioned DVD for detailed steps for this process.

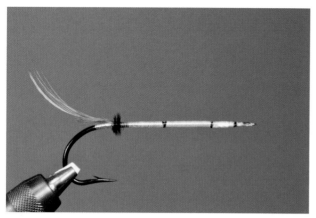

10 Use a body divider (get mine *free* at my website, www.modernclassicsflytying.com) and mark off the position of the end of the body near the eye, then divide the body into three sections. The first two, from the hook bend moving forward, make up 40 percent each of the body length, and the last makes up the final 20 percent. Mark off the location of the two butts that will divide the body sections.

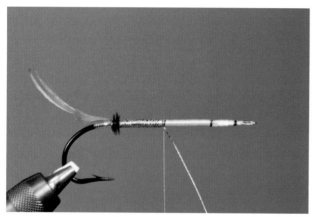

11 Attach the silver lace tinsel at the butt. Advance the tying thread in a smooth single layer to the first mark. Wrap the lace evenly and keep tight wraps with no gaps or overlap all the way up to the first mark. Tie it off at the thread position and trim off the excess after several tight wraps.

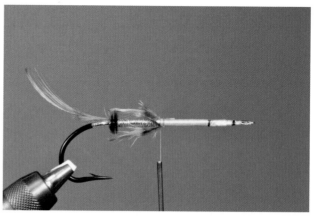

12 Select two matching Indian crow breast feathers to be used for the veilings. Place back-to-back and position above the front of the body section just created. Tips should extend back to right above or slightly past the ostrich herl butt. Where they will be tied in, trim the fibers off the rachis on both sides. This creates a flat profile that helps orient the feathers horizontally, which is how you want to tie them in. Secure the feathers horizontally, one at a time, tightly above and below the end of the body section and extending back to the ostrich herl butt. Tie off tightly.

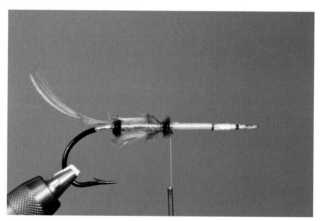

13 Trim off the excess of the Indian crow feathers top and bottom. Select a black ostrich herl strand. Tie in and wrap four to six turns to form a "joint" between the body sections. Tie off and trim the excess closely.

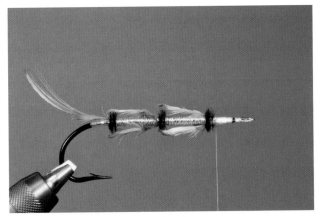

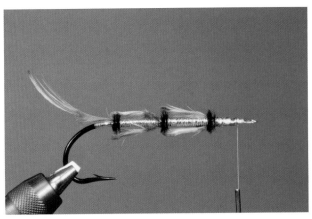

14 As in the previous steps, attach silver lace tinsel at the butt. Advance the tying thread in a smooth single layer to the first mark. Wrap the lace evenly and keep tight wraps with no gaps or overlap. Tie it off at the thread position. Select two more matching Indian crow breast feathers for the front veilings. Place back-to-back and position above the front of the body section just created. Tips should extend back to right above the ostrich herl butt. Where they will be tied in, trim the fibers off the rachis on both sides. This creates a flat profile that helps orient the feathers horizontally, which is how you want to tie them in. Secure the feathers horizontally, one at a time, tightly above and below the end of the body section and extending back to the ostrich herl butt. Tie off tightly and trim the excess of the Indian crow feathers top and bottom. Select a black ostrich herl strand. Tie in and wrap four to six turns to form a "joint" between the body sections. Tie off and trim the excess closely.

15 Advance the tying thread in a single smooth layer to the next mark in the underbody. Tie in silver lace tinsel. Wrap the tinsel evenly to the mark at the front of the body. Tie off tightly and trim the excess.

16 Select two matching gray peacock pheasant eyed body feathers. Place back-to-back and measure for length. The tips should extend to the end of the tail and fit just inside the curve of the golden pheasant crest feather. Where they will be tied in, strip the fibers off both sides of the rachis about halfway up to create a flat area on both sides to help orient the feathers vertically, which is how you want to tie them in. You need to strip fibers off this far up to allow the feathers to lie relatively flat on top of the hook. If this were not done, the fibers near the tie-in point would tend to lift the feathers up rather than lying low against the body of the fly. Secure the feathers tightly on edge vertically at the end of the body section. Be sure they sit in line with the hook shank and do not twist or curve in any direction. Tie off tightly.

the outside of the prior pair and tie off tightly. Be sure the feathers press in snugly against the prior pair, creating a flat wing profile from above.

17 Select two more gray peacock pheasant eyed body feathers slightly shorter and with a smaller "eye" than the prior pair. Place back-to-back and measure for length. The tips should extend to the edge of the eye on the prior pair. Fit to ensure there is not any overlap or large gap. Where they will be tied in, strip the fibers off both sides of the rachis about halfway up to create a flat area on both sides to help orient the feathers vertically, which is how you want to tie them in. Place on the outside of the first pair and tie off tightly. Be sure the feathers press in snugly against the first pair, creating a flat wing profile from above.

19 Repeat one last time. Select two more gray peacock pheasant eyed body feathers slightly shorter and with a smaller "eye" than the prior pair. Place back-to-back and measure for length. The tips should extend to the edge of the "eye" on the prior pair. Fit to ensure there is not any overlap or large gap. Where they will be tied in, strip the fibers off both sides of the rachis about halfway up to create a flat area on both sides to help orient the feathers vertically, which is how you want to tie them in. Place on the outside of the prior pair and tie off tightly. Be sure the feathers press in snugly against the prior pair, creating a flat wing profile from above. Tie in carefully and check often to be sure the feathers stay aligned, fit in line correctly, sit on edge vertically, and are not crooked or lying off to one side or the other. They should be vertical and centered directly over the top of the hook shank. Make a few extra wraps over all rachises and trim off the excess.

18 Repeat the previous step again. Select two more gray peacock pheasant eyed body feathers slightly shorter and with a smaller "eye" than the prior pair. Place back-to-back and measure for length. The tips should extend to the edge of the "eye" on the prior pair. Fit to ensure there is not any overlap or large gap. Where they will be tied in, strip the fibers off both sides of the rachis about halfway up to create a flat area on both sides to help orient the feathers vertically, which is how you want to tie them in. Place on

will take out some of the curvature. Go slowly and little by little until it matches the upper edge curvature when you hold the crest over or beside the top edge of the wing. Strip off excess fibers beyond the tie-in point. Use a small pair of flat-nose smooth-jaw pliers to flatten the rachis at the tie-in point. Hold the top of the wing tightly and make several wraps to tie in the topping. Lift it up a bit to be sure it is aligned with the top edge of the wing and doesn't twist or curve away. If it does, untie and retie until it sits correctly on its own. Trim off the excess.

Select two matching Indian crow breast feathers for the cheeks. Trim the fibers off both sides of the rachis where they will be tied in to create a flat area to help orient the feathers flat against the wing. Secure the feathers tightly.

Select a matched pair of blue-and-gold macaw tail fibers long enough to extend to the end of the wing or as close to it as possible. The fiber from the left side of the tail is tied in on the near side (for right-handed tiers), and the other fiber from the right side of the tail goes on the far side. The fibers should reach up just above the back of the wing and match in length and curvature to where they meet above the wing. Tie in tightly and trim the excess.

20 Select two matched jungle cock eyed feathers from the neck. Place back-to-back with tips even and measure for length. They should be long enough to extend even with or slightly beyond the mid-body joint of black ostrich herl. At the tie-in point on the feather, strip the fibers off of both sides. This creates a flat area that will help orient the feathers vertically, which is how you want them tied in. Tie in under the body, slanting back toward the hook point, and wrap tightly. Trim off the excess. Wrap a spotted guinea fowl hackle (a good substitute for the banded gymnogene hackle called for in the original pattern) as a throat and secure the fibers on the underside of the hook.

21 Select a long, full, well-colored golden pheasant crest feather for the topping. By tradition the tip of the feather should have a reddish cast. Lay it over the top of the wing and measure for length. The tip should meet the tip of the tail, and the curvature should match the curve of the wing. The center portion of the topping may need to be "straightened" a bit to match the shape of the wing. If needed, *gently* stroke the top edge of the topping with your fingernail. This

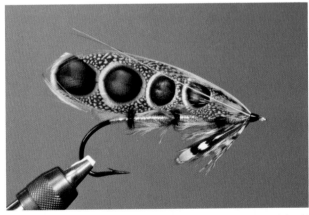

22 Tie the thread off by either using several half hitches or, my preferred method, whip finishing. Trim the thread, cement the head, and you are finished!

NELLY BLY

Another wonderful, colorful creation from Major John Traherne. As in the Black Argus, paired feathers make the main wing, but this time it is a pair of scarlet macaw shoulder feathers with an orange cast. These are surrounded by bright complementary colors of blue, white, and black barred Eurasian jay and orange-tipped jungle cock. A feast for the eyes of the tier, angler, and hopefully the salmon as well.

Hook: Blind eye black salmon fly—style and size of your choice

Thread: Black

Tip: Fine oval silver tinsel

Tag: Green silk floss

Tail: Golden pheasant crest

Butt: Black ostrich herl

Body: Four equal sections of silk floss: First is an orange-red, as in the Indian crow color, veiled top and bottom with Indian crow and butted with black ostrich herl. Second is blue veiled top and bottom with Eurasian jay reaching back to first butt. Third is green veiled top and bottom with jungle cock reaching back to the second butt. Fourth is magenta.

Rib: Flat silver tinsel over every section

Wing: Two red/orange macaw feathers

Throat: Jungle cock reaching back to third butt

Sides: Eurasian jay reaching back to second butt

Cheeks: Jungle cock reaching back to third butt

Topping: Two golden pheasant crests

Horns: Blue-and-gold macaw

Head: Black ostrich herl

THE FLIES • 199

Tying the Nelly Bly

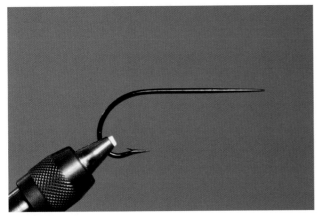

1 Create a liner to place between the hook wire and the vise jaws. I apply a single strip of Scotch tape to a 3-by-5-inch note card edge, then cut out a small rectangle about ½ by ¼ inch. Fold it over lengthwise with the tape on the inside. Taper the folded tip edges to match the jaw size and taper. Fold this piece around the hook bend where it will be placed in the vise jaws and move into place.

Secure the hook tightly in the vise with the hook shank level. Having the hook shank as level as possible is very important. The starting positions for material placement as well as overall proportions are based on where the tying thread hangs down from the hook. The positions of the thread as "even with the barb" or "even with the point" are starting positions for tags, tips, and the butt and/or body of the fly. If the hook shank is not level, the position indicated will not be correct. If the hook shank is drooping excessively, the tag and body positions will be too far back. Same if the hook shank is tilted up too much—the tag and body will be too short. Likewise, be sure the hook is held securely so good, tight thread wraps and material positioning can be accomplished without the hook working loose.

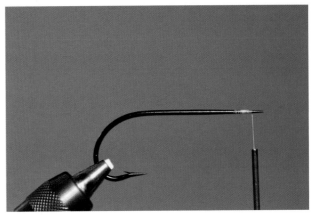

2 Attach the tying thread back from the end of the shank or eye. Be sure the wraps are tight and the thread end is secured well as a starting point for the entire fly. Create a single layer of wraps as a base for attaching the gut eye. Make sure to stay far enough back from the end of the shank tip. The tip of the shank on a blind-eye hook should be exposed ever so slightly and show over the gut loop eye.

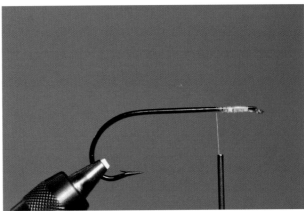

3 Secure the gut eye by folding it over and laying both "legs" under the shank and wrapping over them tightly. As genuine silkworm gut material is both hard to find and expensive, modern tiers use only a small length to form the eye. Traditional flies that were actually used for fishing had strands extending back for the full shank length, well secured to provide a strong and durable connection for hooking and landing the large Atlantic salmon of old.

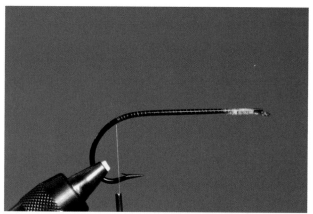

4 Create a smooth layer of thread all the way back on the shank to the starting point of the tag or tip. The underbody needs to be as smooth as possible; whatever the underbody shows as rough or inconsistent spots will often show through the body wrapped over it. I can always improve my underbody work and never seem to get it as consistent or smooth as I'd like it to be—stick with it and practice often.

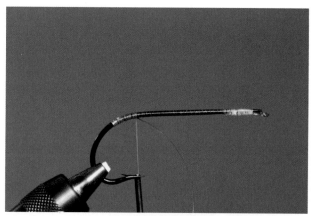

5 Attach the fine oval silver tinsel for the tip immediately above the barb. Advance the thread five wide wraps forward to get it out of the way. Make five wraps of the tinsel spiraling forward with each wrap tightly touching the previous. Don't overlap—one single layer is all you want—and do not allow any gaps between wraps. Unwrap the five wide thread wraps until back at the end of the finished wraps of the tinsel. Tie off the tinsel securely with several tight wraps of thread spiraling forward. Trim off the excess.

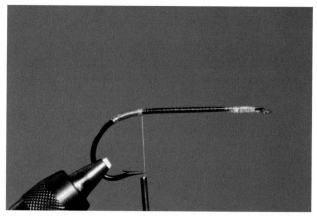

6 Advance the thread in a smooth layer to a position where the thread hangs down even with the hook point. Use a burnisher to smooth out and flatten the thread wraps if in doubt. Unless your hands are very clean with smooth fingers to handle the silk floss, you may want to use silk gloves to provide a clean, smooth surface to handle the delicate floss. Attach a single strand of light green silk floss with three tight wraps of thread. Make five open wraps of thread to the eye to move the thread and bobbin out of your way. Stroke the floss a few times to straighten and even the fibers. Wrap a single smooth layer of the floss back to the tinsel, then reverse direction, wrapping back up the bend to where the floss was tied in above the point. Once there, unwrap the five turns of thread over the shank and two more tie-down wraps, then tie off the end of the floss tightly and end up above the point again. Trim the excess floss, and you are now ready to tie in the tail.

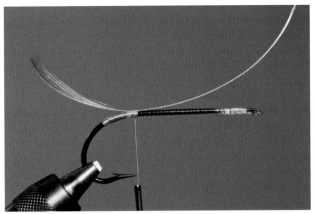

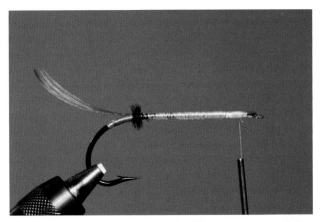

7 Select a single golden pheasant crest feather. Length and curvature depend on your fly style preference. A short, tightly curved tail will give a more traditional Old World look to the fly. It will require a high wing and tightly curved topping to match the tail's shape. A longer, less curved crest will result in a longer, shallower wing with a "sleeker," more streamlined appearance. Use a feather of size and quality as one that could be used as a topping. Smaller feathers just don't have the "body," curvature, or fiber length to match with a crest used for a topping. Strip fibers off the rachis to the tie-in point. Make a couple of tight wraps while holding the crest in position on top of the hook, then release to see how it sits. Untie and retie in as needed until properly set. Once set correctly, make a couple more tight wraps to lock it in place. Trim off the excess.

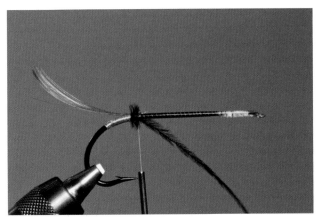

8 Attach a single strand of black ostrich herl. The herl has a slant to the fibers off of the core rachis. Ideally the herl is tied in so when wrapped, the fibers slant back toward the hook bend. Advance the tying thread slightly and make four to six wraps spiraling toward the hook eye. Keep wraps close together with no gap between or overlap. Tie off and trim the excess herl.

9 Construct the underbody. The purpose of the underbody is to provide a smooth tapering up to the ends of the gut loop which is attached underneath the hook shank. Attach a long single or paired strands of smooth, flat white floss at the front of the hook shank behind the gut loop ends on the underside of the hook. Make smooth, even wraps with the floss back to the rear of the body, then start wrapping back to the front. Stop at the ends of the gut loop and start wrapping toward the back again but this time stop about one-fifth of the body length away from the rear of the body. Repeat as needed, each time stopping farther away from the rear of the body. When built up sufficiently to match the diameter of the shank and gut eye ends, wrap forward to the end of the body. **DO NOT GO TOO FAR FORWARD!!!** Leave about one-fifth of the shank and eye uncovered to use for the winging and throat. Tie off the floss at the front of the body and add a couple of half-hitch knots to secure the thread temporarily. Cut the thread off. Use a burnisher to smooth out the underbody. Reattach the tying thread at the rear of the body. See the aforementioned DVD for detailed steps for this process.

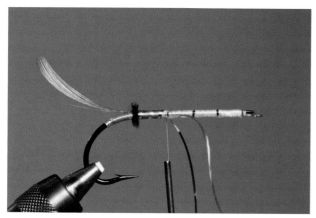

10 Use a body divider (get mine *free* at my website, www.modernclassicsflytying.com) and mark off the position of the end of the body near the eye; then divide the body into four equal sections, marking off the location of the three butts that will divide the body sections. Tie in the flat silver tinsel rib at the rear of the body against the butt.

Advance the tying thread in a smooth single layer to the first mark. Attach a single strand of reddish orange silk floss. Wrap evenly back to the second butt, then reverse direction, wrap back up to the thread position, and tie off.

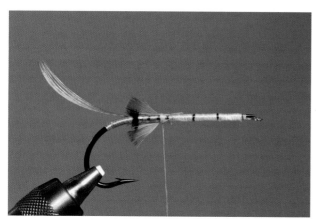

11 Select two matched pairs of Indian crow breast feathers and place back-to-back. Take the first pair and position above the front of the body section just created. Tips should extend back to right above the ostrich herl butt. Where they will be tied in, strip the fibers off the rachis on both sides. This creates a flat area on both sides of the rachis that helps orient the feathers vertically, which is how you want to tie them in. Secure the feathers tightly on edge vertically above the end of the body section and extending back to the ostrich herl butt. Tie off tightly. Leave the excess extending forward while you complete the next

step. Repeat the process with the remaining pair and tie in below the hook to mirror the top pair.

12 Trim off the excess of the Indian crow feathers top and bottom. Select a black ostrich herl strand. Tie in and wrap four to six turns to form a "joint" between the body sections. Tie off and trim the excess closely. Tie in the flat silver tinsel rib. Advance the tying thread in a smooth single layer to the first mark. Attach a single strand of the blue silk floss. Wrap evenly back to the rear butt, then reverse direction, wrap back up to the thread position, and tie off. Wrap the rib forward, tie off tightly, and trim the excess.

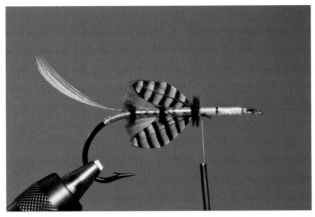

13 Select two matching medium-size pairs of Eurasian jay wing covert feathers. Both sides of the rachis should have equivalent markings and be evenly barred on both sides. Place back-to-back with the tip ends even. Measure for length: The tips should be even with, or slightly longer than, the rearmost ostrich herl butt at the tail. Where they will be tied in, strip the fibers off both sides of the rachis to create a flat area on both sides to help orient the feathers vertically, which is how you want to tie them in. Secure the feathers tightly on edge vertically, one pair above and the other below the end of the body section and extending back to or just at or beyond the first ostrich herl butt at the tail. Tie off tightly and trim the excess of the Eurasian jay feathers. Select a black ostrich herl strand. Tie in and wrap four to six turns to form a "joint" between the body sections. Tie off and trim the excess closely.

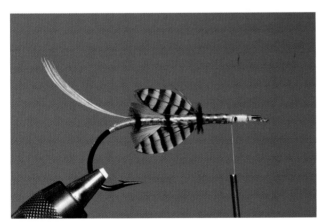

14 Tie in the flat silver tinsel rib. Advance the tying thread in a smooth single layer to the first mark. Attach a single strand of the green silk floss. Wrap evenly back to the rear butt, then reverse direction, wrap back up to the thread position, and tie off. Wrap the rib forward, tie off tightly, and trim the excess.

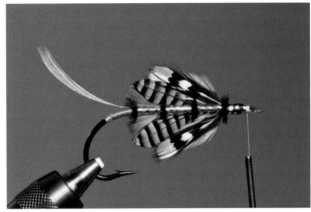

15 Select two matching medium-size pairs of jungle cock neck feathers. Place back-to-back with the tip ends even. Measure for length: The tips should be even with, or slightly longer than, the second ostrich herl butt—actually the first "joint" in the body between the orange and blue floss sections. Where they will be tied in, strip the fibers off both sides of the rachis to create a flat area on both sides to help orient the feathers vertically, which is how you want to tie them in. Secure the feathers tightly on edge vertically, one pair above and the other below the end of the body section and extending back to or just at or beyond the ostrich herl joint between the first and second body sections. Tie off tightly and trim the excess. Select a black ostrich herl strand. Tie in and wrap four to six turns to form a "joint" between the body sections. Tie off and trim the excess closely. Tie in the flat silver tinsel rib. Advance the tying thread in a smooth single layer to the mark at the front end of the body. Attach a single strand of the magenta silk floss. Wrap evenly back to the rear butt, then reverse direction, wrap back up to the thread position, and tie off. Wrap the rib forward, tie off tightly, and trim the excess.

16 Select a matched pair of scarlet macaw reddish-orange-toned wing covert feathers, often with a green tip. Place together back-to-back and measure for length. The tips should extend back to fit just inside the tip of the tail. Where the feathers will be tied in, strip the fibers off both side of the rachis. This creates a flat area on each side that helps orient the feathers to stand up vertically when tied in. Tie in tightly and secure with several thread wraps. Trim off the excess closely. They should be vertical and centered directly over the top of the hook shank.

Select a matching pair of jungle cock neck feathers larger than the previous pairs. Place back-to-back with the tip ends even. Measure for length: The tips should be even with, or slightly longer than, the previous pair of jungle cock feathers. Ideally if a straight line were made from the Eurasian jay tips through the tips of the prior pair of jungle cock, this new pair's tips would be where the line ended. Where they will be tied in, strip the fibers off both sides of the rachis to create a flat area on both sides to help orient the feathers vertically, which is how you want to tie them in. Secure the feathers tightly on edge vertically below the end of the body section and extending back to the position just described. Tie off tightly and trim the excess.

17 Select a matched pair of larger Eurasian jay feathers for the sides. They should be similar in appearance to the prior pairs. Both sides of the rachis should have equivalent markings and be evenly barred on both sides. Tips should extend back to the first joint of black ostrich herl between the reddish orange and blue floss. Tie one in on each side of the wing, standing up at an angle matching the prior jay and jungle cock positions.

18 Select a two long, full, well-colored golden pheasant crest feathers for the topping. By tradition the tip of the feather should have a reddish cast. Lay both over the top of the wing and measure for length. The tips should meet the tip of the tail, and the curvature should match the curve of the wing. The center portion of the topping may need to be "straightened" a bit to match the shape of the wing. If needed, *gently* stroke the top edge of the topping with your fingernail. This will take out some of the curvature. Go slowly and little by little until it matches the upper edge curvature when you hold the crest over or beside the top edge of the wing. Strip off excess fibers beyond the tie-in point. Use a small pair of flat-nose smooth-jaw pliers to flatten the rachis at the tie-in point. Hold both toppings on top of the wing tightly and make several wraps to tie in the topping. Lift up a bit to be sure they are aligned with the top edge of the wing and do not twist or curve away. If either does, untie and retie until they sit correctly on their own. Trim off the excess.

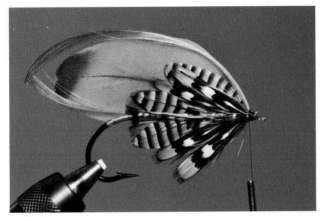

19 Select two matching jungle cock neck feathers equal in size and length to the pair used for the throat. Place back-to-back with the tip ends even. Measure for length: The tips should be the same length as the throat. Where they will be tied in, trim the fibers off both sides of the rachis to create a flat across the rachis to help orient the feathers flat. Secure the feathers, one on each side of the wing, tightly against the wing, extending back the same distance as the tip of the throat. Tie off tightly and trim the excess.

20 Select a matched pair of blue-and-gold macaw tail fibers long enough to extend to the end of the wing or as close to it as possible. The fiber from the left side of the tail is tied in on the near side (for right-handed tiers), and the other fiber from the right side of the tail goes on the far side. The fibers should reach up just above

the back of the wing and match in length and curvature to where they meet above the wing. Tie in tightly and trim the excess.

21 Tie in a single black ostrich herl fiber. Advance the thread toward the eye slightly, wrap the ostrich six turns plus or minus, then tie off and trim the excess to create the head of the fly.

22 Tie the thread off by either using several half hitches or, my preferred method, whip finishing. Trim the thread, cement the head, and you are finished!

NOIR ET BLANC

While so many classic salmon flies utilize the most colorful feathers and materials possible, I thought it would be a fun challenge to try to come up with a totally monochrome, purely black and white fly. The result is the Noir et Blanc (French for "black and white"). The main wing consists of varied-length feather pairs from the silver pheasant family. Longest are the white-with-thin-black-stripes silver pheasant body feathers. Next are the Crawford Kalij pheasant body feather pair—almost half-and-half black and white stripes. Finally a pair of Lewis's silver pheasant, which are like negatives of the silver with thin white stripes on a black feather. Vulturine guinea for sides and Mearn's quail for cheeks, and voila—a fly for all light conditions.

Hook: Blind eye black salmon fly—style and size of your choice

Thread: Black

Tip: Fine oval silver tinsel

Tag: White floss

Tail: Black-dyed golden pheasant crest and black-barred wood duck flank fibers

Butt: Black ostrich herl

Body: Rear half is flat embossed silver tinsel veiled above and below with black francolin black-barred flank feathers and butted with black ostrich herl. Front half is black silk floss.

Rib: Medium oval silver tinsel over rear half. Flat silver followed by medium oval silver tinsel.

Hackle: Black rooster saddle

Wing: Matched pair of silver pheasant body feathers extending to just inside tail. Outside of which is a matched pair of Crawford pheasant feathers about one-third shorter than the prior pair. Outside of which is a matched pair of Lewis's Silver pheasant feathers about one-third shorter than the prior pair.

Throat: Lewis's pheasant

Side: Vulturine guinea fowl with a vivid white center stripe extending to tip of Crawford pheasant feathers

Cheeks: Mearn's quail

Topping: Black-dyed golden pheasant crest

Horns: Lady Amherst's pheasant tail fibers

Head: Black

THE FLIES ■ 207

Tying the Noir et Blanc

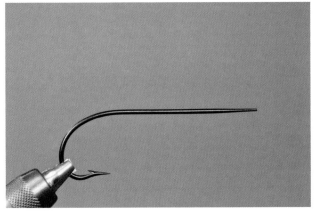

1 Create a liner to place between the hook wire and the vise jaws. I apply a single strip of Scotch tape to a 3-by-5-inch note card edge, then cut out a small rectangle about ½ by ¼ inch. Fold it over lengthwise with the tape on the inside. Taper the folded tip edges to match the jaw size and taper. Fold this piece around the hook bend where it will be placed in the vise jaws and move into place.

Secure the hook tightly in the vise with the hook shank level. Having the hook shank as level as possible is very important. The starting positions for material placement as well as overall proportions are based on where the tying thread hangs down from the hook. The positions of the thread as "even with the barb" or "even with the point" are starting positions for tags, tips, and the butt and/or body of the fly. If the hook shank is not level, the position indicated will not be correct. If the hook shank is drooping excessively, the tag and body positions will be too far back. Same if the hook shank is tilted up too much—the tag and body will be too short. Likewise, be sure the hook is held securely so good, tight thread wraps and material positioning can be accomplished without the hook working loose.

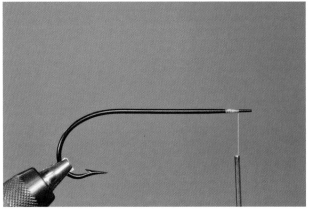

2 Attach the tying thread back from the end of the shank or eye. Be sure the wraps are tight and the thread end is secured well as a starting point for the entire fly. Create a single layer of wraps as a base for attaching the gut eye. Make sure to stay far enough back from the end of the shank tip. The tip of the shank on a blind-eye hook should be exposed ever so slightly and show over the gut loop eye.

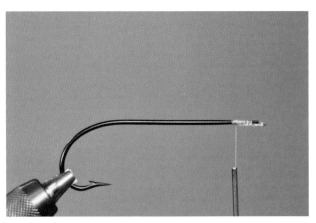

3 Secure the gut eye by folding it over and laying both "legs" under the shank and wrapping over them tightly. As genuine silkworm gut material is both hard to find and expensive, modern tiers use only a small length to form the eye. Traditional flies that were actually used for fishing had strands extending back for the full shank length, well secured to provide a strong and durable connection for hooking and landing the large Atlantic salmon of old.

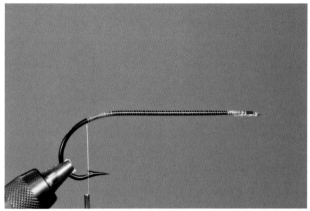

4 Create a smooth layer of thread all the way back on the shank to the starting point of the tag or tip. The underbody needs to be as smooth as possible; whatever the underbody shows as rough or inconsistent spots will often show through the body wrapped over it. I can always improve my underbody work and never seem to get it as consistent or smooth as I'd like it to be—stick with it and practice often.

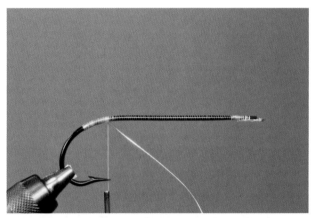

5 Attach the fine oval silver tinsel for the tip immediately above the barb. Advance the thread five wide wraps forward to get it out of the way. Make five wraps of the tinsel spiraling forward with each wrap tightly touching the previous. Don't overlap—one single layer is all you want—and do not allow any gaps between wraps. Unwrap the five wide thread wraps until back at the end of the finished wraps of the tinsel. Tie off the tinsel securely with several tight wraps of thread spiraling forward. Trim off the excess.

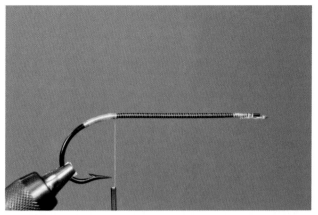

6 Advance the thread in a smooth layer to a position where the thread hangs down even with the hook point. Use a burnisher to smooth out and flatten the thread wraps if in doubt.

Unless your hands are very clean with smooth fingers to handle the silk floss, you may want to use silk gloves to provide a clean smooth surface to handle the delicate floss. Attach a single strand of white silk floss with three tight wraps of thread. Make five open wraps of thread to the eye to move the thread and bobbin out of your way. Stroke the floss a few times to straighten and even the fibers. Wrap a single smooth layer of the floss back to the tinsel, then reverse direction, wrapping back up the bend to where the floss was tied in above the point. Once there, unwrap the five turns of thread over the shank and two more tie-down wraps, then tie off the end of the floss tightly and end up above the point again. Trim the excess floss, and you are now ready to tie in the tail.

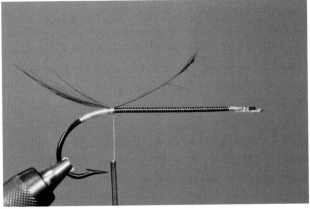

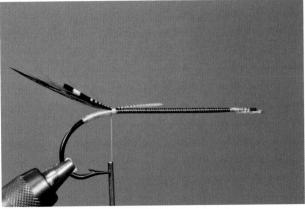

7 Select a single black-dyed golden pheasant crest feather. Length and curvature depend on your fly style preference. A short, tightly curved tail will give a more traditional Old World look to the fly. It will require a high wing and tightly curved topping to match the tail's shape. A longer, less curved crest will result in a longer, shallower wing with a "sleeker," more streamlined appearance. Use a feather of size and quality as one that could be used as a topping. Smaller feathers just don't have the "body," curvature, or fiber length to match with a crest used for a topping. Strip fibers off the rachis to the tie-in point. Make a couple of tight wraps while holding the crest in position on top of the hook, then release to see how it sits. Untie and retie in as needed until properly set.

9 Cut out a section of a black-barred wood duck flank feather, hold above the tail, and measure for length. The tips should extend back to the midpoint of the golden pheasant crest tail. Tie in securely.

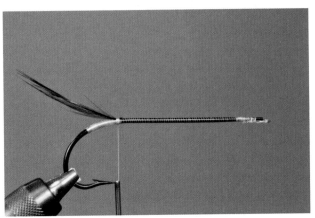

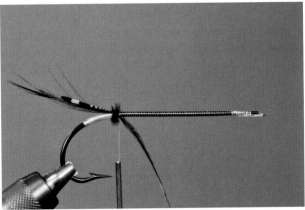

8 Once set correctly, make a couple more tight wraps to lock it in place. Trim off the excess.

10 Trim off the excess of the black-barred wood duck flank fibers. Tie in a single strand of black ostrich herl. The herl has a slant to the fibers off of the core rachis. Ideally the herl is tied in so when wrapped, the fibers slant back toward the hook bend. Advance the tying thread slightly and make four to six wraps spiraling toward the hook eye. Keep wraps close together with no gap between or overlap. Tie off and trim the excess herl.

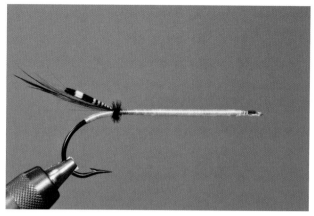

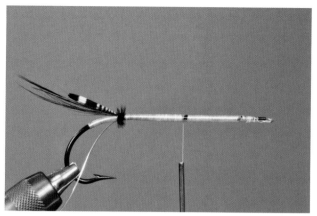

11 Construct the underbody. The purpose of the underbody is to provide a smooth tapering up to the ends of the gut loop which is attached underneath the hook shank. Attach a long single or paired strands of smooth, flat white floss at the front of the hook shank behind the gut loop ends on the underside of the hook. Make smooth, even wraps with the floss back to the rear of the body, then start wrapping back to the front. Stop at the ends of the gut loop and start wrapping toward the back again but this time stop about one-fifth of the body length away from the rear of the body. Repeat as needed, each time stopping farther away from the rear of the body. When built up sufficiently to match the diameter of the shank and gut eye ends, wrap forward to the end of the body. DO NOT GO TOO FAR FORWARD!!! Leave about one-fifth of the shank and eye uncovered to use for the winging and throat. Tie off the floss at the front of the body and add a couple of half-hitch knots to secure the thread temporarily. Cut the thread off. Use a burnisher to smooth out the underbody. Reattach the tying thread at the rear of the body. See the aforementioned DVD for detailed steps for this process.

12 Use a body divider (get mine *free* at my website, www.modernclassicsflytying.com) and mark off the position of the end of the body near the eye; then divide the body into two equal sections, marking off the location of the butt that will divide the body sections.

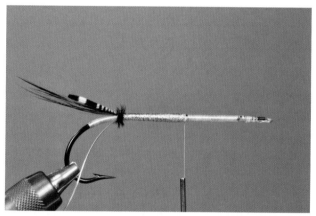

13 Attach the medium oval silver tinsel at the butt. Advance the tying thread in a smooth single layer to the first mark. Attach the flat embossed silver tinsel and wrap evenly back to the rear butt, then reverse direction, wrap back up to the thread position, and tie off. Keep tight, even wraps with no gaps or overlap.

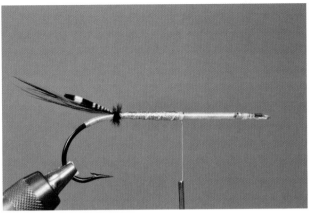

14 Wrap the rib forward in five even turns and tie off on the bottom of the end of the body section.

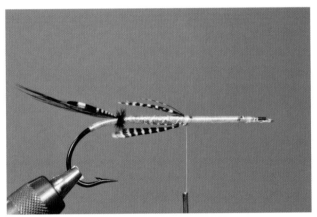

15 Select two matched black francolin black-barred flank feathers for the veilings. Place back-to-back and position above the front of the body section just created. Tips should extend back to right above or slightly beyond the ostrich herl butt. Where they will be tied in, trim the fibers off the rachis on both sides. This creates a flat area that helps orient the feathers horizontally, which is how you want to tie them in. Secure the first feather flat above the end of the body section and extending back to the ostrich herl butt. Tie in tightly. Repeat and tie in the other veiling feather on the bottom flat. Trim the excess on both feathers.

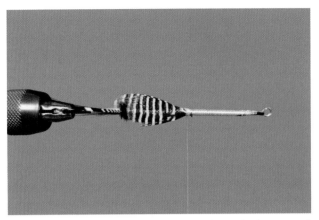

16 Top view of the veilings positioned above and below the rear half of the body and extending back to the ostrich herl butt.

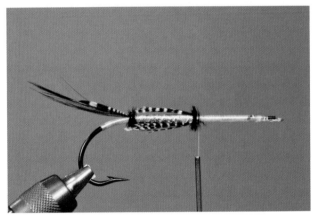

17 Tie in a single strand of black ostrich herl. The herl has a slant to the fibers off of the core rachis. Ideally the herl is tied in so when wrapped, the fibers slant back toward the hook bend. Advance the tying thread slightly and make four to six wraps spiraling toward the hook eye. Keep wraps close together with no gap between or overlap. Tie off and trim the excess herl.

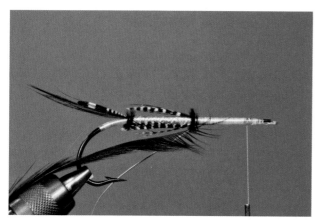

18 Tie in the black rooster saddle hackle feather by the tip end. Size the fiber length to be one and a half the gap of the hook (distance from the shank down to the point) at the start of the tip of the feather. Also attach the flat silver tinsel and oval silver tinsel at the ostrich herl butt.

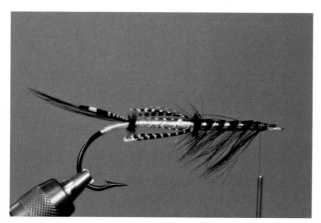

19 Advance the tying thread in a single smooth layer to the front mark at the end of the body. Tie in a single strand of black silk floss. Wrap the floss evenly and smoothly back to the ostrich herl joint just created and back up. Tie off tightly and trim the excess. Wrap the flat silver tinsel for five turns and tie off tightly. Wrap the oval silver tinsel along the back edge of the flat tinsel with no gap or overlap and tie off tightly. Fold and wrap the hackle tightly behind the oval silver tinsel. Tie off tightly and trim all excess from the tinsel and hackle. Fold the hackle down the sides to get all fibers lying at or below the hook to provide a clear area above the body to tie the wings in.

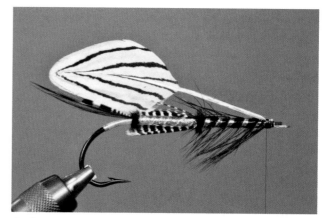

20 Select a matched pair of silver pheasant body or wing covert feathers. Place back-to-back with the tips even and measure for length. The tips should extend back to the end of the tail and sit inside the tail's curve. Strip fibers off of both sides of the feather about halfway up. You need to strip this far up in order for the feather to lie flat and tuck into the curve of the tail. If fibers were left on the feather farther down, they would cause the feather to "stand up" and lift away from the tail. Additional feathers will cover the stripped sections as you proceed. Tie in carefully and check often to be sure the feathers stay aligned, fit in the tail correctly, sit on edge vertically, and are not crooked or lying off to one side or the other. They should be vertical and centered directly over the top of the hook shank.

21 Select a matched pair of Crawford Kalij pheasant body feathers. Place this pair back-to-back outside of the first pair and measure for length. The tips should extend about a third of the overall wing length back from the first pair, leaving the tip of the first pair clearly visible underneath. Strip fibers off of both sides of the feather about halfway up. Tie in securely and make sure the feathers are flat up against the first pair and are vertical. They should lie against the first pair and help press them together. If needed, untie and pinch the inside of the rachis to help curve the outer pair in against the first pair.

22 Repeat the last process with a third matched pair of Lewis's pheasant body feathers. Place this pair back-to-back outside of the second pair and measure for length. The tips should extend about a third of the overall wing length back from the second pair, leaving the tip of the second pair clearly visible underneath. Strip fibers off of both sides of the feather about halfway up. Tie in securely and make sure the feathers are flat up against the first pair and are vertical. They should lie against the first pair and help press them together. If needed, untie and pinch the

inside of the rachis to help curve the outer pair in against the first pair.

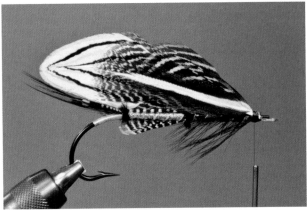

23 Select a matched pair of vulturine guinea body feathers. You want a longer pair with a vivid white center stripe and long enough to extend back to the rear butt at the tail. Place back-to-back with the tips matched and position so they will extend back to the rear ostrich herl butt. Trim them slightly longer than needed, and trim off a few fibers on each side of the rachis to ensure they will lie flat when tied in on the side of the wing. Tie in tightly and trim the excess.

24 Select a larger Lewis's pheasant body feather. Tie in at the front of the body and make several wraps for the throat. Pull the fibers from the top and sides and fold down to lie neatly under the hook. Make a few wraps of thread as needed to hold them in place underneath.

25 Select two matching Mearn's quail spotted body feathers for the cheeks, ideally six or more spots. Place back-to-back and measure for length. The tips should extend back to nearly the middle of the body. Where they will be tied in, trim several fibers from both sides of the rachis. Tie in one on each side of the vulturine guinea, following the angle up the wing. Tie in tightly and trim the excess.

26 Select a long, full, black-dyed golden pheasant crest feather for the topping. Lay it over the top of the wing and measure for length. The tip should meet the tip of the tail, and the curvature should match the curve of the wing. The center portion of the topping may need to be "straightened" a bit to match the shape of the wing. If needed, *gently* stroke the top edge of the topping with your fingernail. This will take out some of the curvature. Go slowly and little by little until it matches the upper edge curvature when you hold the crest over or beside the top edge of the wing. Strip off excess fibers beyond the tie-in point. Use a small pair of flat-nose smooth-jaw pliers to flatten the rachis at the tie-in point. Hold the top of the wing tightly and make several wraps to tie in the topping. Lift it up a bit to be sure it is aligned with the top edge of the wing and doesn't twist or curve away. If it does, untie and retie until it sits correctly on its own. Trim off the excess.

Select two long matching Lady Amherst's center tail fibers for the horns. Measure for length: The tips should extend to the end of the wing. Tie in angling up above the wing so the tips match well above the wing's upper edge. Secure the fibers tightly. Tie off and trim the excess.

Form the head of the fly and tie the thread off by either using several half hitches or, my preferred method, whip finishing. Trim the thread, cement the head, and you are finished!

OCELLATION

The name is a play on words based on the source of the underwing—the ocellated turkey. This turkey has a brilliantly colored body, flank, and starting tail feathers with a mix of powder blue and rusty orange tips. Add Indian crow for veilings on the body and Palawan peacock pheasant for cheeks, and you have a fly with magic colors that both anglers and fish find attractive.

Hook: Blind eye black salmon fly—style and size of your choice

Thread: BlackTip: Fine oval silver twist

Tag: Yellow silk floss

Tail: Golden pheasant crest and Indian crow

Butt: Black ostrich herl

Body: Two equal sections: First half is light orange floss veiled above and below with Indian crow and butted with black ostrich herl. Second is light blue floss.

Rib: Fine flat copper over rear half. Flat and oval silver tinsel over front half.

Hackle: Light blue (often termed "silver doctor" blue) Sebright rooster neck hackle over front half of body

Underwing: Matched pair of bronze ocellated turkey wing coverts extending to just inside the tip of the tail. Outside of which is a matched pair orange-and-blue-tipped ocellated turkey body feathers, one-third shorter than the prior pair. Outside of which is another matched pair orange-and-blue-tipped ocellated turkey body feathers, one-third shorter than the prior pair.

Wing: Married strands of kori (speckled) bustard; yellow-, orange-, and blue-dyed turkey tail; and brown mottled turkey tail

Throat: Light rusty orange hen saddle

Shoulder: Palawan peacock pheasant body feathers

Sides: Jungle cock

Cheeks: Indian crow

Topping: Golden pheasant crest

Horns: Blue-and-gold macaw

Head: Black

Tying the Ocellation

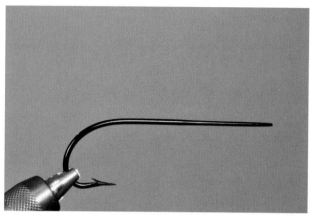

1 Create a liner to place between the hook wire and the vise jaws. I apply a single strip of Scotch tape to a 3-by-5-inch note card edge, then cut out a small rectangle about ½ by ¼ inch. Fold it over lengthwise with the tape on the inside. Taper the folded tip edges to match the jaw size and taper. Fold this piece around the hook bend where it will be placed in the vise jaws and move into place.

Secure the hook tightly in the vise with the hook shank level. Having the hook shank as level as possible is very important. The starting positions for material placement as well as overall proportions are based on where the tying thread hangs down from the hook. The positions of the thread as "even with the barb" or "even with the point" are starting positions for tags, tips, and the butt and/or body of the fly. If the hook shank is not level, the position indicated will not be correct. If the hook shank is drooping excessively, the tag and body positions will be too far back. Same if the hook shank is tilted up too much—the tag and body will be too short. Likewise, be sure the hook is held securely so good, tight thread wraps and material positioning can be accomplished without the hook working loose.

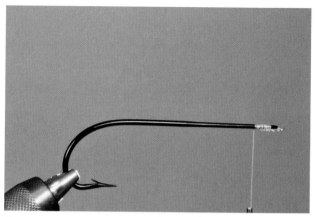

2 Attach the tying thread back from the end of the shank or eye. Be sure the wraps are tight and the thread end is secured well as a starting point for the entire fly. Create a single layer of wraps as a base for attaching the gut eye. Make sure to stay far enough back from the end of the shank tip. The tip of the shank on a blind-eye hook should be exposed ever so slightly and show over the gut loop eye.

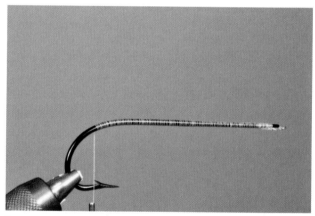

3 Secure the gut eye by folding it over and laying both "legs" under the shank and wrapping over them tightly. As genuine silkworm gut material is both hard to find and expensive, modern tiers use only a small length to form the eye. Traditional flies that were actually used for fishing had strands extending back for the full shank length, well secured to provide a strong and durable connection for hooking and landing the large Atlantic salmon of old. Create a smooth layer of thread all the way back on the shank to the starting point of the tag or tip. The underbody needs to be as smooth as possible; whatever the underbody shows as rough or inconsistent spots

will often show through the body wrapped over it. I can always improve my underbody work and never seem to get it as consistent or smooth as I'd like it to be—stick with it and practice often.

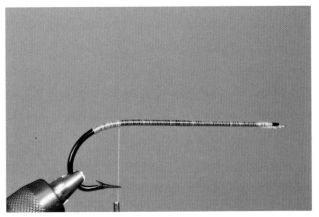

4 Attach the fine oval silver tinsel for the tip immediately above the barb. Advance the thread five wide wraps forward to get it out of the way. Make five wraps of the tinsel spiraling forward with each wrap tightly touching the previous. Don't overlap—one single layer is all you want—and do not allow any gaps between wraps. Unwrap the five wide thread wraps until back at the end of the finished wraps of the tinsel. Tie off the tinsel securely with several tight wraps of thread spiraling forward. Trim off the excess. Advance the thread in a smooth layer to a position where the thread hangs down even with the hook point. Use a burnisher to smooth out and flatten the thread wraps if in doubt.

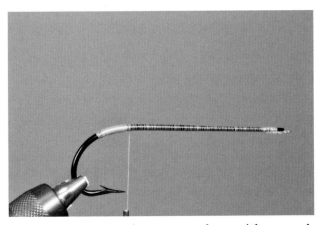

5 Unless your hands are very clean with smooth fingers to handle the silk floss, you may want to use silk gloves to provide a clean smooth surface to handle the delicate floss. Attach a single strand of yellow silk floss with three tight wraps of thread.

Make five open wraps of thread to the eye to move the thread and bobbin out of your way. Stroke the floss a few times to straighten and even the fibers. Wrap a single smooth layer of the floss back to the tinsel, then reverse direction, wrapping back up the bend to where the floss was tied in above the point. Once there, unwrap the five turns of thread over the shank and two more tie-down wraps, then tie off the end of the floss tightly and end up above the point again. Trim the excess floss, and you are now ready to tie in the tail.

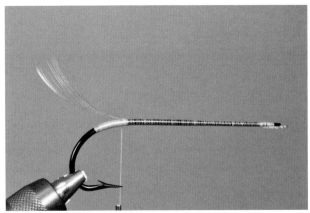

6 Select a single, full golden pheasant crest feather for the tail. The tip should preferably have a red cast to it. Length and curvature depend on your fly style preference. A short, tightly curved tail will give a more traditional Old World look to the fly. It will require a high wing and tightly curved topping to match the tail's shape. A longer, less curved crest will result in a longer, shallower wing with a "sleeker," more streamlined appearance. Use a feather of size and quality as one that could be used as a topping. Smaller feathers just don't have the "body," curvature, or fiber length to match with a crest used for a topping. Strip fibers off the rachis to the tie-in point. Make a couple of tight wraps while holding the crest in position on top of the hook, then release to see how it sits. Untie and retie in as needed until properly set. Once set correctly, make a couple more tight wraps to lock it in place. Trim off the excess.

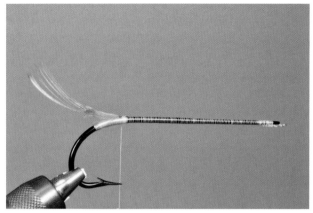

7 Select a single Indian crow breast feather and measure for length. The tip should reach back close to halfway up the golden pheasant crest tail. Prepare it by trimming off fiber closely on both sides of the rachis at the tie-in point. Tie the feather in with the shiny, or good, side up. This ensures the feather shows the best color on top and helps press down the golden pheasant crest beneath to keep a sleeker profile. Tie in securely and trim off the excess.

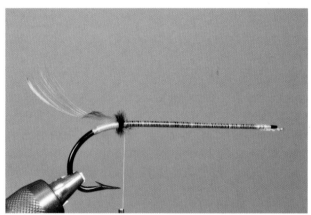

8 Tie in a single strand of black ostrich herl. The herl has a slant to the fibers off of the core rachis. Ideally the herl is tied in so when wrapped, the fibers slant back toward the hook bend. Advance the tying thread slightly and make four to six wraps spiraling toward the hook eye. Keep wraps close together with no gap between or overlap. Tie off and trim the excess herl.

9 Construct the underbody. The purpose of the underbody is to provide a smooth tapering up to the ends of the gut loop which is attached underneath the hook shank. Attach a long single or paired strands of smooth, flat white floss at the front of the hook shank behind the gut loop ends on the underside of the hook. Make smooth, even wraps with the floss back to the rear of the body, then start wrapping back to the front. Stop at the ends of the gut loop and start wrapping toward the back again but this time stop about one-fifth of the body length away from the rear of the body. Repeat as needed, each time stopping farther away from the rear of the body. When built up sufficiently to match the diameter of the shank and gut eye ends, wrap forward to the end of the body. DO NOT GO TOO FAR FORWARD!!! Leave about one-fifth of the shank and eye uncovered to use for the winging and throat. Tie off the floss at the front of the body and add a couple of half-hitch knots to secure the thread temporarily. Cut the thread off. Use a burnisher to smooth out the underbody. Reattach the tying thread at the rear of the body. See the aforementioned DVD for detailed steps for this process.

Use a body divider (get mine *free* at my website, www.modernclassicsflytying.com) and mark off the position of the end of the body near the eye; then divide the body into two equal sections, marking off the location of the butt that will divide the body sections.

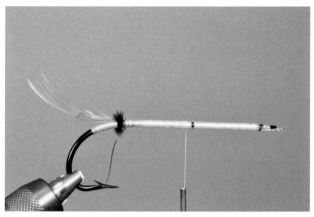

10 Attach the fine flat copper tinsel at the butt. Advance the tying thread in a smooth single layer to the first mark.

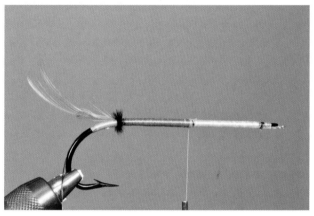

11 Attach the orange silk floss and wrap evenly back to the rear butt, then reverse direction, wrap back up to the thread position, and tie off. Keep tight, even wraps with no gaps or overlap.

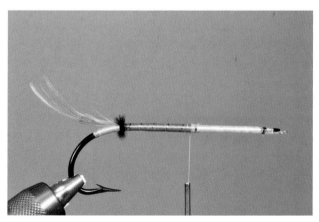

12 Wrap the rib forward in five even turns and tie off on the bottom of the end of the body section.

13 Select two matched Indian crow breast feathers for the veilings. Place back-to-back and position above the front of the body section just created. Tips should extend back to right above or slightly beyond the ostrich herl butt. Where they will be tied in, trim the fibers off the rachis on both sides. This creates a flat area that helps orient the feathers horizontally, which is how you want to tie them in. Secure the first feather flat above the end of the body section and extending back to the ostrich herl butt. Tie in tightly. Repeat and tie in the other veiling feather on the bottom flat as well. Trim the excess on both feathers.

14 Tie in a single strand of black ostrich herl. The herl has a slant to the fibers off of the core rachis. Ideally the herl is tied in so when wrapped, the fibers slant back toward the hook bend. Advance the tying thread slightly and make four to six wraps spiraling toward the hook eye. Keep the wraps close together with no gap between or overlap. Tie off and trim the excess herl.

15 Tie in the light blue Sebright rooster neck hackle feather by the tip end. Size the fiber length to be about one and a half the gap of the hook (distance from the shank down to the point) at the start of the tip of the feather. Also attach the flat silver tinsel and oval silver tinsel at the ostrich herl butt.

16 Advance the tying thread in a single smooth layer to the front mark at the end of the body. Tie in a single strand of light blue silk floss. Wrap the floss evenly and smoothly back to the ostrich herl joint just created and back up. Tie off tightly and trim the excess.

17 Wrap the flat silver tinsel for five turns and tie off tightly. Wrap the oval silver tinsel along the back edge of the flat tinsel, making sure there is no gap or overlap, and tie off tightly. Fold and wrap the hackle tightly behind the oval silver tinsel. Tie off tightly and trim all excess from the tinsel and hackle.

18 Fold the hackle down along the sides to get all fibers lying at or below the hook to provide a clear area above the body to tie the wings in.

19 Select a matched pair of bronze-colored ocellated turkey wing covert feathers for the first part of the underwing. Place back-to-back with the tips even and measure for length to extend to just inside the tip of the tail. Strip fibers off of both sides of the feather about halfway up. You need to strip this far up in order for the feather to lie flat and tuck into the curve of the tail. If fibers were left on the feather farther down, they would cause the feather to "stand up" and lift away from the tail. Additional feathers will cover the stripped sections as you proceed. Tie in carefully and check often to be sure the feathers stay aligned, fit in the tail correctly, sit on edge vertically, and are not crooked or lying off to one side or the other. They should be vertical and centered directly over the top of the hook shank.

20 Select a matched pair of blue-and-orange-tipped ocellated turkey body feathers. Place this pair back-to-back outside of the first pair and measure for length. The tips should extend about a third of the overall wing length back from the first pair, leaving the tip of the first pair clearly visible underneath. Strip fibers off of both sides of the feather about halfway up. Tie in securely and

make sure the feathers are flat up against the first pair and are vertical. They should lie against the first pair and help press them together. If needed, untie and pinch the inside of the rachis to help curve the outer pair in against the first pair.

21 Repeat the last process with a third matched pair of blue-and-orange-tipped ocellated turkey body feathers. Place this pair back-to-back outside of the second pair and measure for length. The tips should extend about a third of the overall wing length back from the second pair, leaving the tip of the second pair clearly visible underneath. Strip fibers off of both sides of the feather about halfway up. Tie in securely and make sure the feathers are flat up against the first pair and are vertical. They should lie against the first pair and help press them together. If needed, untie and pinch the inside of the rachis to help curve the outer pair in against the first pair.

22 Build the married-fiber main wing. Techniques for this process are illustrated in chapter 2, "Anatomy of a Feather and a Fly," which shows how feather strips from different birds can be joined or "married" together, and in detail in the excellent DVD by Michael Radencich titled *Tying the Classic Salmon Fly.* Tie in securely with the tips extending back to the inside tip of the tail. Add a drop of cement once set properly and allow to dry, then carefully trim off the excess.

23 Select, tie in, and wrap a light rusty orange hen chicken hackle. Tie off and fold all fibers below the hook. Make a wrap or two of thread if needed to secure in place. Select a matched pair of Palawan peacock pheasant body feathers for the shoulders. Place back-to-back with the tips matched. Position so they will extend back about one-quarter of the main wing length. Trim off a few fibers on each side of the rachis to ensure they will lie flat when tied in on the side of the wing. Tie in tightly against the wing and trim the excess.

24 Select a matching pair of jungle cock neck feathers for the sides. Place back-to-back and measure for length. The tips should extend back to the tip of the Palawan peacock pheasant shoulders. Trim off fibers on both sides of the rachis where they will be tied in. Tie one on each side tightly and trim off the excess.

25 Select two matching Indian crow breast feathers for the cheeks. Place back-to-back and measure for length. The tips should extend back to the middle of the jungle cock sides. Where they will be tied in, trim several fibers from both sides of the rachis. Tie in one on each side, following the angle up the wing of the sides beneath them. Tie in tightly and trim the excess.

26 Select a long, full golden pheasant crest feather for the topping. Preferably the tip has a reddish cast. Lay it over the top of the wing and measure for length. The tip should meet the tip of the tail, and the curvature should match the curve of the wing. The center portion of the topping may need to be "straightened" a bit to match the shape of the wing. If needed, *gently* stroke the top edge of the topping with your fingernail. This will take out some of the curvature. Go slowly and little by little until it matches the upper edge curvature when you hold the crest over or beside the top edge of the wing. Strip off excess fibers beyond the tie-in point. Use a small pair of flat-nose smooth-jaw pliers to flatten the rachis at the tie-in point. Hold the top of the wing tightly and make several wraps to tie in the topping. Lift it up a bit to be sure it is aligned with the top edge of the wing and doesn't twist or curve away. If it does, untie and retie until it sits correctly on its own. Trim off the excess.

27 Select two long matching blue-and-gold macaw center tail fibers. Measure for length: The tips should extend to the end of the wing. Tie in angling up above the wing so the tips match well above the wing's upper edge. Secure the fibers tightly. Tie off and trim the excess. Form the head of the fly and tie the thread off by either using several half hitches or, my preferred method, whip finishing. Trim the thread, cement the head, and you are finished!

SPOTTED TIGER

Combining satyr tragopan and Temminck's tragopan pheasant feathers in the wing gives a rich, deep color with the unique bordered spots on both birds' feathers. Add a hoopoe crest feather for a spot in the tail, Andean cock of the rock for shoulders, and jungle cock for the final orange cast, and you have a fly that is reminiscent of a tiger's color with spots instead of stripes for catching an angler and hopefully a fish or two as well.

Hook: Blind eye black salmon fly—style and size of your choice

Thread: Black

Tip: Fine oval gold tinsel

Tag: Yellow silk floss

Tail: Temminck's tragopan pheasant crest feather with a matched pair of hoopoe spotted crest feathers back-to-back and set vertically

Butt: Black ostrich herl

Body: Two equal sections: First is flat gold tinsel butted with black ostrich herl. Second is a rusty orange dubbing mix consisting of 50 percent orange, 25 percent brown, and 25 percent golden tan seal's fur.

Rib: Oval gold over rear half; flat gold and oval gold over front half

Hackle: Orange-dyed Sebright rooster neck hackle

Wing: Matched pair of Temminck's tragopan pheasant covert feathers extending back to just inside the tip of the tail. Outside of which is a matched pair of satyr tragopan pheasant body feathers one-quarter shorter than the prior pair. Outside of which is a matched pair of Temminck's tragopan pheasant body feathers one-quarter shorter than the prior pair. Outside of which is a final matched pair of satyr tragopan pheasant body feathers one-quarter shorter than the prior pair.

Throat: Light rusty orange hen saddle

Shoulders: Andean cock of the rock set high to complete the curve of the upper edge of the wing

Sides: Jungle cock

Cheeks: Satyr tragopan pheasant body feathers
with the round spot centered on the orange tip
of the jungle cock feather beneath it

Topping: Golden pheasant crest

Horns: African crowned crane crest feathers

Head: Black

Tying the Spotted Tiger

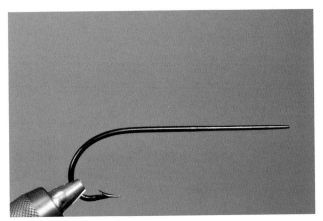

1 Create a liner to place between the hook wire and the vise jaws. I apply a single strip of Scotch tape to a 3-by-5-inch note card edge, then cut out a small rectangle about ½ by ¼ inch. Fold it over lengthwise with the tape on the inside. Taper the folded tip edges to match the jaw size and taper. Fold this piece around the hook bend where it will be placed in the vise jaws and move into place.

Secure the hook tightly in the vise with the hook shank level. Having the hook shank as level as possible is very important. The starting positions for material placement as well as overall proportions are based on where the tying thread hangs down from the hook. The positions of the thread as "even with the barb" or "even with the point" are starting positions for tags, tips, and the butt and/ or body of the fly. If the hook shank is not level, the position indicated will not be correct. If the hook shank is drooping excessively, the tag and body positions will be too far back. Same if the hook shank is tilted up too much—the tag and body will be too short. Likewise, be sure the hook is held securely so good, tight thread wraps and material positioning can be accomplished without the hook working loose.

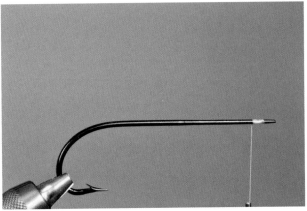

2 Attach the tying thread back from the end of the shank or eye. Be sure the wraps are tight and the thread end is secured well as a starting point for the entire fly. Create a single layer of wraps as a base for attaching the gut eye. Make sure to stay far enough back from the end of the shank tip. The tip of the shank on a blind-eye hook should be exposed ever so slightly and show over the gut loop eye.

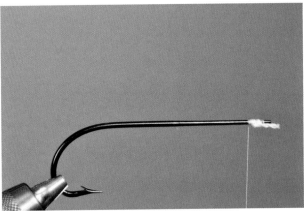

3 Secure the gut eye by folding it over and laying both "legs" under the shank and wrapping over them tightly. As genuine silkworm gut material is both hard to find and expensive, modern tiers use only a small length to form the eye. Traditional flies that were actually used for fishing had strands extending back for the full shank length, well secured to provide a strong and durable connection for hooking and landing the large Atlantic salmon of old.

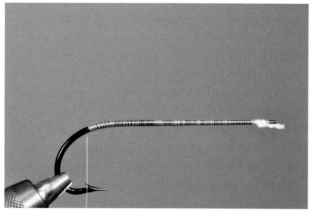

4 Create a smooth layer of thread all the way back on the shank to the starting point of the tag or tip. The underbody needs to be as smooth as possible; whatever the underbody shows as rough or inconsistent spots will often show through the body wrapped over it. I can always improve my underbody work and never seem to get it as consistent or smooth as I'd like it to be—stick with it and practice often.

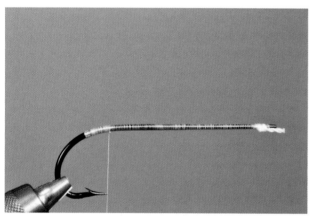

5 Attach the fine oval gold tinsel for the tip immediately above the barb. Advance the thread five wide wraps forward to get it out of the way. Make five wraps of the tinsel spiraling forward with each wrap tightly touching the previous. Don't overlap—one single layer is all you want—and do not allow any gaps between wraps. Unwrap the five wide thread wraps until back at the end of the finished wraps of the tinsel. Tie off the tinsel securely with several tight wraps of thread spiraling forward. Trim off the excess. Advance the thread in a smooth layer to a position where the thread hangs down even with the hook point. Use a burnisher to smooth out and flatten the thread wraps if in doubt.

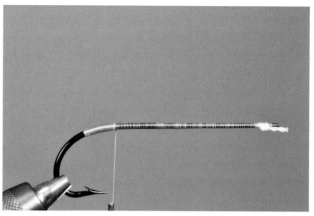

6 Unless your hands are very clean with smooth fingers to handle the silk floss, you may want to use silk gloves to provide a clean smooth surface to handle the delicate floss. Attach a single strand of yellow silk floss with three tight wraps of thread. Make five open wraps of thread to the eye to move the thread and bobbin out of your way. Stroke the floss a few times to straighten and even the fibers. Wrap a single smooth layer of the floss back to the tinsel, then reverse direction, wrapping back up the bend to where the floss was tied in above the point. Once there, unwrap the five turns of thread over the shank and two more tie-down wraps, then tie off the end of the floss tightly and end up above the point again. Trim the excess floss, and you are now ready to tie in the tail.

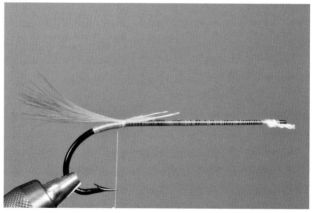

7 Select a single Temminck's tragopan pheasant crest for the tail. Length and curvature depend on your fly style preference. A short, tightly curved tail will give a more traditional Old World look to the fly. It will require a high wing and tightly curved topping to match the tail's shape. A longer, less curved crest will result in a longer, shallower wing with a "sleeker," more streamlined appearance. Use a feather of size and quality as one that

could be used as a topping. Smaller feathers just don't have the "body," curvature, or fiber length to match with a crest used for a topping. Strip fibers off the rachis to the tie-in point. Make a couple of tight wraps while holding the crest in position on top of the hook, then release to see how it sits. Untie and retie in as needed until properly set. Once set correctly, make a couple more tight wraps to lock it in place. Trim off the excess.

8 Select a matched pair of hoopoe spotted crest feathers. Place them back-to-back and measure for length. The tip should reach back close to half-way up the Temminck's tragopan pheasant crest tail. Prepare the pair by stripping off the fibers on both sides of the rachis at the tie-in point. This creates a flat area on the rachis to help orient the feathers vertically when tied in. Tie the feathers in securely and trim off the excess.

9 Tie in a single strand of black ostrich herl. The herl has a slant to the fibers off of the core rachis. Ideally the herl is tied in so when wrapped, the fibers slant back toward the hook bend. Advance the tying thread slightly and make four to six wraps spiraling toward the hook eye.

Keep wraps close together with no gap between or overlap. Tie off and trim the excess herl.

10 Construct the underbody. The purpose of the underbody is to provide a smooth tapering up to the ends of the gut loop which is attached underneath the hook shank. Attach a long single or paired strands of smooth, flat white floss at the front of the hook shank behind the gut loop ends on the underside of the hook. Make smooth, even wraps with the floss back to the rear of the body, then start wrapping back to the front. Stop at the ends of the gut loop and start wrapping toward the back again but this time stop about one-fifth of the body length away from the rear of the body. Repeat as needed, each time stopping farther away from the rear of the body. When built up sufficiently to match the diameter of the shank and gut eye ends, wrap forward to the end of the body. DO NOT GO TOO FAR FORWARD!!! Leave about one-fifth of the shank and eye uncovered to use for the winging and throat. Tie off the floss at the front of the body and add a couple of half-hitch knots to secure the thread temporarily. Cut the thread off. Use a burnisher to smooth out the underbody. Reattach the tying thread at the rear of the body. See the aforementioned DVD for detailed steps for this process.

11 Use a body divider (get mine *free* at my website, www.modernclassicsflytying.com) and mark off the position of the end of the body near the eye; then divide the body into two equal sections, marking off the location of the butt that will divide the body sections. Attach the oval gold tinsel at the butt. Advance the tying thread in a smooth single layer to the first mark.

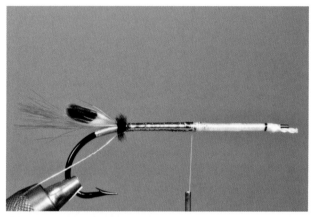

12 Attach the flat gold tinsel and wrap evenly back to the rear butt, then reverse direction, wrap back up to the thread position, and tie off. Keep tight, even wraps with no gaps or overlap.

13 Wrap the rib forward in five even turns and tie off on the bottom of the end of the body section.

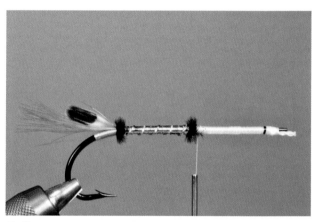

14 Tie in a single strand of black ostrich herl. The herl has a slant to the fibers off of the core rachis. Ideally the herl is tied in so when wrapped, the fibers slant back toward the hook bend. Advance the tying thread slightly and make four to six wraps spiraling toward the hook eye. Keep the wraps close together with no gap between or overlap. Tie off and trim the excess herl.

15 Tie in the orange Sebright rooster neck hackle feather by the tip end. Size the fiber length to be about one and a half the gap of the hook (distance from the shank down to the point) at the start of the tip of the feather. Also attach the flat gold tinsel and oval gold tinsel at the ostrich herl butt.

16 Mix the dubbing per the pattern listing. Apply a thin layer to the thread and dub the body to the mark at the front end of the body.

17 Wrap the flat gold tinsel for five turns. Tie off tightly.

18 Wrap the oval gold tinsel behind and along the back edge of the flat tinsel, making sure there is no gap or overlap. Tie off tightly.

19 Fold the feather and wrap snugly behind the oval gold tinsel to the front of the body. Tie off securely and trim the excess. Fold the hackle down along the sides to get all fibers lying at or below the hook to provide a clear area above the body to tie the wings in.

20 Select a matched pair of Temminck's tragopan pheasant covert feathers for the first part of the wing. Place back-to-back with the tips even and measure for length to go back to just inside the tip of the tail. Strip fibers off of both sides of the feather about halfway up. You need to strip this far up in order for the feather to lie flat and tuck into the curve of the tail. If fibers were left on the feather farther down, they would cause the feather to "stand up" and lift away from the tail. Additional feathers will cover the stripped sections as you proceed. Tie in carefully and check often to be sure the feathers stay aligned, fit in the tail correctly, sit on edge vertically, and are not crooked or lying off to one side or the other. They should be vertical and centered directly over the top of the hook shank.

21 Select a matched pair of satyr tragopan pheasant body feathers. Place this pair back-to-back outside of the first pair and measure for length. The tips should extend about a quarter of the overall wing length back from the first pair, leaving the tip of the first pair clearly visible underneath. Strip fibers off of both sides of the feather about halfway up. Tie in securely and make sure

the feathers are flat up against the first pair and are vertical. They should lie against the first pair and help press them together. If needed, untie and pinch the inside of the rachis to help curve the outer pair in against the first pair.

22 Repeat the last process with a third matched pair of Temminck's tragopan pheasant body feathers. Place this pair back-to-back outside of the second pair and measure for length. The tips should extend about half of the overall wing length, leaving the tips of the second pair clearly visible underneath. Strip fibers off of both sides of the feather about halfway up. Tie in securely and make sure the feathers are flat up against the first pair and are vertical. They should lie against the first pair and help press them together. If needed, untie and pinch the inside of the rachis to help curve the outer pair in against the first pair.

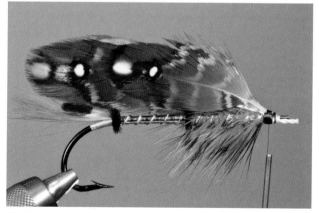

23 Select a final matched pair of satyr tragopan pheasant body feathers. Place this pair back-to-back outside of the last pair and measure for length. The tips should extend about a quarter of the overall wing length, leaving the tip of the first pair clearly visible underneath. Trim fibers off of both sides of the feather about halfway up. Tie in securely and make sure the feathers are flat up against the first pair and are vertical. They should lie against the first pair and help press them together. If needed, untie and pinch the inside of the rachis to help curve the outer pair in against the first pair.

24 Select, tie in, and wrap a light rusty orange hen chicken hackle. Tie off and fold all fibers below the hook. Make a wrap or two of thread if needed to secure in place.

25 Select a matched pair of Andean cock of the rock body feathers for the shoulders. Place back-to-back with the tips matched. Position so they will extend back about one-quarter of the main wing length and angle upwards to complete the front taper of the upper wing edge. Trim off a few fibers on each side of the rachis to ensure they will lie flat when tied in on the side of the wing. Tie in tightly against the wing and trim the excess.

26 Select a long, full golden pheasant crest feather for the topping. Preferably the tip has a reddish cast. Lay it over the top of the wing and measure for length. The tip should meet the tip of the tail, and the curvature should match the curve of the wing. The center portion of the topping may need to be "straightened" a bit to match the shape of the wing. If needed, *gently* stroke the top edge of the topping with your fingernail. This will take out some of the curvature. Go slowly and little by little until it matches the upper edge curvature when you hold the crest over or beside the top edge of the wing. Strip off excess fibers beyond the tie-in point. Use a small pair of flat-nose smooth-jaw pliers to flatten the rachis at the tie-in point. Hold the top of the wing tightly and make several wraps to tie in the topping. Lift it up a bit to be sure it is aligned with the top edge of the wing and doesn't twist or curve away. If it does, untie and retie until it sits correctly on its own. Trim off the excess.

27 Select a matching pair of jungle cock neck feathers for the sides. Place back-to-back and measure for length. The tips should extend back to the tip of the shoulders. Trim off fibers on both sides of the rachis where they will be tied in. Tie one on each side tightly and trim off the excess.

29 Select two long matching African crowned crane crest feathers for the horns. Measure for length: The tips should extend to the end of the wing. Tie in angling up above the wing so the tips match well above the wing's upper edge. Secure the fibers tightly. Tie off and trim the excess.

28 Select two matching satyr tragopan pheasant breast feathers for the cheeks. Place back-to-back and measure for length. The tips should extend back to the tips of the jungle cock sides, and the single spot should be centered on the orange tip of the jungle cock feathers. Trim several fibers from both sides of the rachis where they will be tied in. Tie in one on each side tightly and trim the excess.

30 Form the head of the fly and tie the thread off by either using several half hitches or, my preferred method, whip finishing. Trim the thread, cement the head, and you are finished!

SWINHOE'S SPLENDOR

This is my favorite of the flies I created with the amazing crescent of bright electric blue on the dark cobalt blue Swinhoe's pheasant body feathers. Add the striking straw-necked ibis feathers, and you have a stunning blend of nature's fantastic work. With the addition of fairy bluebird and bright blue-dyed Sebright hackle with its unique black-barred tips, this fly pays homage to the splendor of the Swinhoe's pheasant.

Hook: Blind eye black salmon fly—style and size of your choice

Thread: BlackTip: Fine oval silver tinsel

Tag: Yellow silk floss

Tail: Golden pheasant crest and fairy bluebird

Butt: Black ostrich herl

Body: Royal blue silk floss

Rib: Flat silver tinsel with oval silver tinsel tight behind

Hackle: Sebright rooster neck feather dyed silver doctor blue from second turn of ribbing

Wing: Matched pair of straw-necked ibis extending to just inside the tip of the tail. Outside of which are three pairs of Swinhoe's pheasant body feathers spaced equally and occupying the middle third of the overall wing length. Final third is another matched pair of straw-necked ibis.

Throat: Guinea fowl dyed silver doctor blue

Sides: Jungle cock

Cheeks: Fairy bluebird

Topping: Golden pheasant crest

Horns: Blue-and-gold macaw

Head: Black

Tying the Swinhoe's Splendor

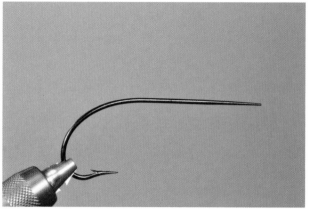

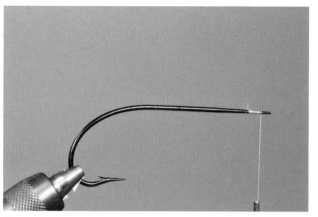

1 Create a liner to place between the hook wire and the vise jaws. I apply a single strip of Scotch tape to a 3-by-5-inch note card edge, then cut out a small rectangle about ½ by ¼ inch. Fold it over lengthwise with the tape on the inside. Taper the folded tip edges to match the jaw size and taper. Fold this piece around the hook bend where it will be placed in the vise jaws and move into place.

Secure the hook tightly in the vise with the hook shank level. Having the hook shank as level as possible is very important. The starting positions for material placement as well as overall proportions are based on where the tying thread hangs down from the hook. The positions of the thread as "even with the barb" or "even with the point" are starting positions for tags, tips, and the butt and/or body of the fly. If the hook shank is not level, the position indicated will not be correct. If the hook shank is drooping excessively, the tag and body positions will be too far back. Same if the hook shank is tilted up too much—the tag and body will be too short. Likewise, be sure the hook is held securely so good, tight thread wraps and material positioning can be accomplished without the hook working loose.

2 Attach the tying thread back from the end of the shank or eye. Be sure the wraps are tight and the thread end is secured well as a starting point for the entire fly. Create a single layer of wraps as a base for attaching the gut eye. Make sure to stay far enough back from the end of the shank tip. The tip of the shank on a blind-eye hook should be exposed ever so slightly and show over the gut loop eye.

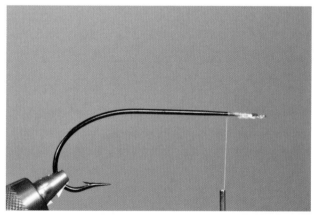

3 Secure the gut eye by folding it over and laying both "legs" under the shank and wrapping over them tightly. As genuine silkworm gut material is both hard to find and expensive, modern tiers use only a small length to form the eye. Traditional flies that were actually used for fishing had strands extending back for the full shank length, well secured to provide a strong and durable connection for hooking and landing the large Atlantic salmon of old.

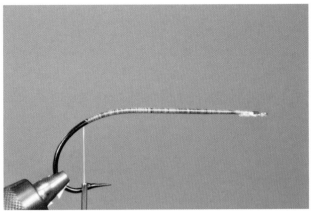

4 Create a smooth layer of thread all the way back on the shank to the starting point of the tag or tip. The underbody needs to be as smooth as possible; whatever the underbody shows as rough or inconsistent spots will often show through the body wrapped over it. I can always improve my underbody work and never seem to get it as consistent or smooth as I'd like it to be—stick with it and practice often.

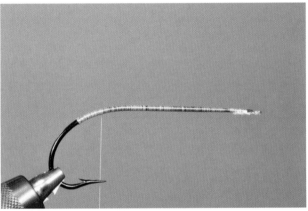

5 Attach the fine oval silver tinsel for the tip immediately above the barb. Advance the thread five wide wraps forward to get it out of the way. Make five wraps of the tinsel spiraling forward with each wrap tightly touching the previous. Don't overlap—one single layer is all you want—and do not allow any gaps between wraps. Unwrap the five wide thread wraps until back at the end of the finished wraps of the tinsel. Tie off the tinsel securely with several tight wraps of thread spiraling forward. Trim off the excess. Advance the thread in a smooth layer to a position where the thread hangs down even with the hook point. Use a burnisher to smooth out and flatten the thread wraps if in doubt.

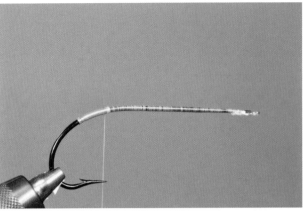

6 Unless your hands are very clean with smooth fingers to handle the silk floss, you may want to use silk gloves to provide a clean smooth surface to handle the delicate floss. Attach a single strand of yellow silk floss with three tight wraps of thread. Make five open wraps of thread to the eye to move the thread and bobbin out of your way. Stroke the floss a few times to straighten and even the fibers. Wrap a single smooth layer of the floss back to the tinsel, then reverse direction, wrapping back up the bend to where the floss was tied in above the point. Once there, unwrap the five turns of thread over the shank and two more tie-down wraps, then tie off the end of the floss tightly and end up above the point again. Trim the excess floss, and you are now ready to tie in the tail.

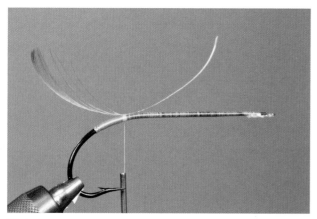

7 Select a single golden pheasant crest for the tail. Ideally it has a reddish cast to the tip Length and curvature depend on your fly style preference. A short, tightly curved tail will give a more traditional Old World look to the fly. It will require a high wing and tightly curved topping to match the tail's shape. A longer, less curved crest will result in a longer, shallower wing with a "sleeker," more streamlined appearance. Use a feather of size and quality as one that could be used as a topping. Smaller feathers just don't have the "body," curvature, or fiber length to match with a crest used for a topping. Strip fibers off the rachis to the tie-in point. Make a couple of tight wraps while holding the crest in position on top of the hook, then release to see how it sits. Untie and retie in as needed until properly set. Once set correctly, made a couple more tight wraps to lock it in place. Trim off the excess.

8 Select a single fairy bluebird body feather and measure for length. The tip should reach back close to halfway up the golden pheasant crest tail. Prepare the feather by trimming some of the fibers on both sides of the rachis at the tie-in point. This creates a flat area across the feather to help orient the feather horizontally when tied in. Tie in securely flat on top of the golden pheasant tail with the good, or shiny, side up. This makes the best appearance and helps press the golden pheasant crest feather down for a sleeker appearance. Trim off the excess.

9 Tie in a single strand of black ostrich herl. The herl has a slant to the fibers off of the core rachis. Ideally the herl is tied in so when wrapped, the fibers slant back toward the hook bend. Advance the tying thread slightly and make four to six wraps spiraling toward the hook eye. Keep wraps close together with no gap between or overlap. Tie off and trim the excess herl.

10 Construct the underbody. The purpose of the underbody is to provide a smooth tapering up to the ends of the gut loop which is attached underneath the hook shank. Attach a long single or paired strands of smooth, flat white floss at the front of the hook shank behind the gut loop ends on the underside of the hook. Make smooth, even wraps with the floss back to the rear of the body, then start wrapping back to the front. Stop at the ends of the gut loop and start wrapping toward the back again but this time stop about one-fifth of the body length away from the rear of the body. Repeat as needed, each time stopping farther away from the rear of the body. When built up sufficiently to match the diameter of the shank and gut eye ends, wrap forward to the end of the body. DO NOT GO TOO FAR FORWARD!!! Leave about one-fifth of the shank and eye uncovered to use for the winging and throat. Tie off the floss at the front of the body and add a couple of half-hitch knots to secure the thread temporarily. Cut the thread off. Use a burnisher to smooth out the underbody. Reattach the tying thread at the rear of the body. See the aforementioned DVD for detailed steps for this process.

11 Use a body divider (get mine *free* at my website, www.modernclassicsflytying.com) and mark off the position of the end of the body near the eye; then divide the body into five equal sections representing the position of the ribbing wraps. Attach the oval silver and flat silver tinsel underneath the hook at the ostrich herl butt. Advance the tying thread in a smooth single layer to the first mark.

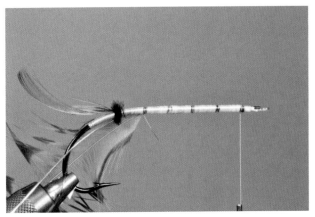

12 Attach the Sebright hackle underneath the hook at the point of the start of the second wrap of the ribbing. By tradition the ribbing starts and ends underneath the hook and consists of five even wraps up to the end of the body. Advance the thread up to the end of the body in smooth, even wraps.

13 Attach a single strand of royal blue silk floss for the body. Wrap evenly back to the rear butt, working carefully around the hackle as you go. Once at the butt, reverse direction, wrap back up to the thread position, and tie off. Keep tight, even wraps with no gaps or overlap. Use a burnisher to smooth the body if needed.

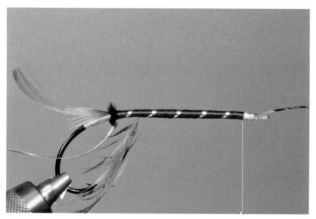

14 Wrap the flat silver rib forward in five even turns. Tie off on the bottom of the end of the body section.

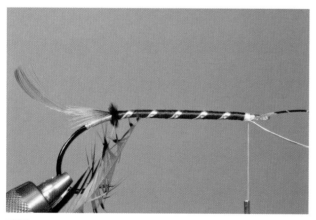

15 Wrap the oval silver tinsel snugly behind the flat to the front of the body. Tie off underneath and trim the excess.

16 Fold the feather and wrap snugly behind the oval silver tinsel to the front of the body. Tie off securely and trim the excess. Fold the hackle down along the sides to get all fibers lying at or below the hook to provide a clear area above the body to tie the wings in.

17 Select a matched pair of straw-necked ibis covert feathers for the first part of the wing. Place back-to-back with the tips even and measure for length to extend to just inside the tip of the tail. Strip fibers off of both sides of the feather about halfway up. You need to strip this far up in order for the feather to lie flat and tuck into the curve of the tail. If fibers were left on the feather farther down, they would cause the feather to "stand up" and lift away from the tail. Additional feathers will cover the stripped sections as you proceed. Tie in carefully and check often to be sure the feathers stay aligned, fit in the tail correctly, sit on edge vertically, and are not crooked or lying off to one side or the other. They should be vertical and centered directly over the top of the hook shank.

18 Select a matched pair of Swinhoe's pheasant body feathers. Place this pair back-to-back outside of the first pair and measure for length. The tips should extend back to about two-thirds of the overall wing length, leaving the tip of the first pair clearly visible underneath. Strip fibers off of both sides of the feather about halfway up. Tie in securely and make sure the feathers are flat up against the first pair and are vertical. They should lie against the first pair and help press them together. If needed, untie and pinch the inside of the rachis to help curve the outer pair in against the first pair.

19 Select another matched pair of Swinhoe's pheasant body feathers. Place this pair back-to-back outside of the last pair and measure for length. The tips should extend back to about halfway of the overall wing length, leaving the tip of the last pair clearly visible underneath. Strip fibers off of both sides of the feather about halfway up. Tie in securely and make sure the feathers are flat up against the last pair and are vertical. They should lie against the last pair and help press them together. If needed, untie and pinch

the inside of the rachis to help curve the outer pair in against the last pair.

20 Select a third and final matched pair of Swinhoe's pheasant body feathers. Place this pair back-to-back outside of the last pair and measure for length. The tips should extend back to about one-third of the overall wing length, leaving the tip of the last pair clearly visible underneath. Strip fibers off of both sides of the feather about halfway up. Tie in securely and make sure the feathers are flat up against the last pair and are vertical. They should lie against the last pair and help press them together. If needed, untie and pinch the inside of the rachis to help curve the outer pair in against the last pair.

21 Select another matched pair of straw-necked ibis body feathers for the final part of the wing. Place back-to-back with the tips even and measure for length. The tips should extend back to a point where they match the length of the first pair of straw-necked ibis feathers tied in and bookend the Swinhoe's feathers evenly. Where they will be tied in, trim fibers off of both sides of the rachis and tie one in per side flat and pressing against the feathers underneath. The entire wing should be thin and as if a single pair of feathers were tied in on each side. Trim the excess from all feathers and wrap a few extra-tight turns of thread to lock them in place.

22 Tie in a guinea fowl feather dyed silver doctor blue for the throat. Wrap several turns and tie off. Pull the fibers down and underneath the hook, sweeping back toward the point. Make a few wraps of thread over the hackle if needed to secure the fibers in place.

23 Select a matched pair of jungle cock neck feathers for the sides. Place back-to-back with the tips matched. Position so they will extend back about one-quarter of the main wing length and angle upwards to lie centered within the wing. Trim off a few fibers on each side of the rachis to ensure they will lie flat when tied in on the side of the wing. Tie in tightly against the wing and trim the excess.

24 Select a matched pair of fairy bluebird body feathers for the cheeks. These should extend back to about halfway on the sides. Trim some fibers off both sides of the rachis at the tie-in point. Tie in tightly on the outside of the jungle cock feathers and trim the excess.

25 Select a long, full golden pheasant crest feather for the topping. Preferably the tip has a reddish cast. Lay it over the top of the wing and measure for length. The tip should meet the tip of the tail, and the curvature should match the curve of the wing. The center portion of the topping may need to be "straightened" a bit to match the shape of the wing. If needed, *gently* stroke the top edge of the topping with your fingernail. This will take out some of the curvature. Go slowly and little by little until it matches the upper edge curvature when you hold the crest over or beside the top edge of the wing. Strip off excess fibers beyond the tie-in point. Use a small pair of flat-nose smooth-jaw pliers to flatten the rachis at the tie-in point. Hold the top of the wing tightly and make several wraps to tie in the topping. Lift it up a bit to be sure it is aligned with the top edge of the wing and doesn't twist or curve away. If it does, untie and retie until it sits correctly on its own. Trim off the excess.

26 Select two long matching blue-and-gold macaw center tail fibers for the horns. Measure for length: The tips should extend to the end of the wing. Tie in angling up above the wing so the tips match well above the wing's upper edge. Secure the fibers tightly. Tie off and trim the excess.

27 Form the head of the fly and tie the thread off by either using several half hitches or, my preferred method, whip finishing. Trim the thread, cement the head, and you are finished!

WHITE-WINGED AKROYD

Dating back to the 19th century, the White-Winged Akroyd was named for Charles Akroyd. This fly is a classic favorite of the Aberdeenshire Dee, a river in Scotland that gave birth to a whole style of fly: the "Dee" fly. Dee flies are typically tied on very long-shank hooks to provide larger silhouettes and heavier flies to get deep and in front of Atlantic salmon in the roiling currents of swollen winter and spring-level rivers. It has caught fish for dukes and earls, the royal family of Great Britain, army officers, and gentlemen fishing the Dee and many other waters around the world.

Characteristic of the Dee style of fly is a long, flowing hackle to provide great movement in the swirling currents. Fished swimming across or against the current on an arcing swing, the Dee-style fly is an attractive and visible fly in any water condition. Another characteristic of this style are the flat swept-style wings that provide minimal resistance to sinking or swimming and a color contrast or complement to the overall color scheme.

Starting with the body, the White-Winged Akroyd utilizes golden pheasant crest for the tail. As in many flies, the golden pheasant crest

provides a glistening, translucent burst of color at the rear of the fly. Next is a vivid yellow hackle wrapped over the rear half of the body. The pulsing fibers provide a bright spot of color to go with the tail and make the fly highly visible against dark backgrounds or peat-stained river flows.

Hook: Blind eye black salmon fly—style and size of your choice

Thread: Black

Tag: Flat silver tinsel

Tail: Golden pheasant crest and tippet strands

Body: Rear half: light orange seal's fur. Front half: black floss.

Rib: Fine oval silver over rear half. Flat silver tinsel and medium oval silver tinsel over front half.

Hackle: Yellow over rear half of body. Black heron (substitute rhea or blue eared pheasant dyed black) over front half.

Throat: Teal

Wings: Divided white turkey tail strips tied in flat in the traditional "Dee" style

Cheeks: Jungle cock tied in drooping style under body

Head: Black

Tying the White-Winged Akroyd

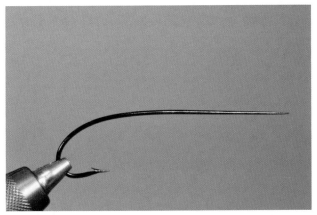

1 Create a liner to place between the hook wire and the vise jaws. I apply a single strip of Scotch tape to a 3-by-5-inch note card edge, then cut out a small rectangle about ½ by ¼ inch. Fold it over lengthwise with the tape on the inside. Taper the folded tip edges to match the jaw size and taper. Fold this piece around the hook bend where it will be placed in the vise jaws and move into place.

Secure the hook tightly in the vise with the hook shank level. Having the hook shank as level as possible is very important. The starting positions for material placement as well as overall proportions are based on where the tying thread hangs down from the hook. The positions of the thread as "even with the barb" or "even with the point" are starting positions for tags, tips, and the butt and/or body of the fly. If the hook shank is not level, the position indicated will not be correct. If the hook shank is drooping excessively, the tag and body positions will be too far back. Same if the hook shank is tilted up too much—the tag and body will be too short. Likewise, be sure the hook is held securely so good, tight thread wraps and material positioning can be accomplished without the hook working loose.

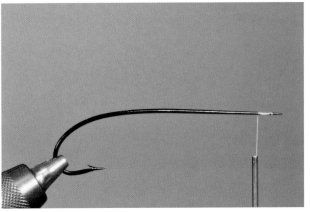

2 Attach the tying thread back from the end of the shank or eye. Be sure the wraps are tight and the thread end is secured well as a starting point for the entire fly. Create a single layer of wraps as a base for attaching the gut eye. Make sure to stay far enough back from the end of the shank tip. The tip of the shank on a blind-eye hook should be exposed ever so slightly and show over the gut loop eye.

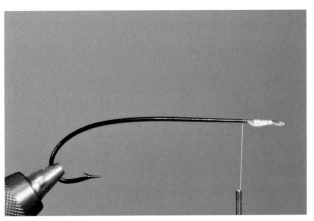

3 Secure the gut eye by folding it over and laying both "legs" under the shank and wrapping over them tightly. As genuine silkworm gut material is both hard to find and expensive, modern tiers use only a small length to form the eye. Traditional flies that were actually used for fishing had strands extending back for the full shank length, well secured to provide a strong and durable connection for hooking and landing the large Atlantic salmon of old.

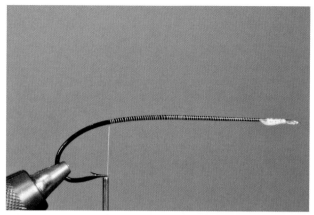

4 Create a smooth layer of thread all the way back on the shank to the starting point of the tag above the point in this case. The underbody needs to be as smooth as possible; whatever the underbody shows as rough or inconsistent spots will often show through the body wrapped over it. I can always improve my underbody work and never seem to get it as consistent or smooth as I'd like it to be—stick with it and practice often.

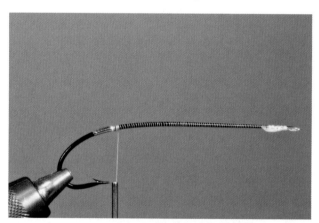

5 Attach the flat silver tinsel for the tip immediately above the point. Advance the thread five wide wraps forward to get it out of the way. Wrap the tinsel spiraling backwards with each wrap tightly touching the previous. Don't overlap—one single layer is all you want—and do not allow any gaps between wraps. Once above the barb, reverse direction and wrap back up to the starting position above the point. Unwrap the five wide thread wraps until back above the point at the end of the finished wraps of the tinsel. Tie off the tinsel securely with several tight wraps of thread spiraling forward. Trim off the excess.

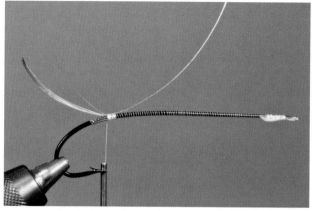

6 Select a single golden pheasant crest for the tail. Ideally it has a reddish cast to the tip. Length and curvature depend on your fly style preference. A short, tightly curved tail will give a more traditional Old World look to the fly. A longer, less curved crest will result in a longer, shallower wing with a "sleeker," more streamlined appearance. Use a feather of size and quality as one that could be used as a topping. Smaller feathers just don't have the "body," curvature, or fiber length to match with a crest used for a topping. Strip fibers off the rachis to the tie-in point. Make a couple of tight wraps while holding the crest in position on top of the hook, then release to see how it sits. Untie and retie in as needed until properly set. Once set correctly, make a couple more tight wraps to lock it in place.

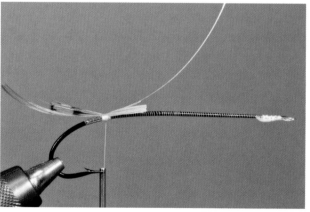

7 Select a golden pheasant tippet feather with good orange coloring and vivid black barring. Strip several fibers from one side and even the tips. Position above with the tips reaching back to the middle of the golden pheasant crest feather. Tie in tightly on top.

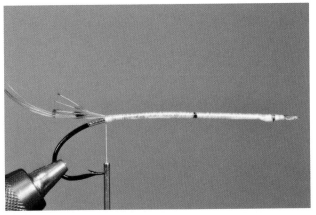

8 Construct the underbody. The purpose of the underbody is to provide a smooth tapering up to the ends of the gut loop which is attached underneath the hook shank. Attach a long single or paired strands of smooth, flat white floss at the front of the hook shank behind the gut loop ends on the underside of the hook. Make smooth, even wraps with the floss back to the rear of the body, then start wrapping back to the front. Stop at the ends of the gut loop and start wrapping toward the back again but this time stop about one-fifth of the body length away from the rear of the body. Repeat as needed, each time stopping farther away from the rear of the body. When built up sufficiently to match the diameter of the shank and gut eye ends, wrap forward to the end of the body. DO NOT GO TOO FAR FORWARD!!! Leave about one-fifth of the shank and eye uncovered to use for the winging and throat. Tie off the floss at the front of the body and add a couple of half-hitch knots to secure the thread temporarily. Cut the thread off. Use a burnisher to smooth out the underbody. Reattach the tying thread at the rear of the body. See the aforementioned DVD for detailed steps for this process.

9 Use a body divider (get mine *free* at my website, www.modernclassicsflytying.com) and mark off the position of the end of the body near the eye; then divide the body into two equal sections. Attach the fine oval silver tinsel for the ribbing on the underside of the shank.

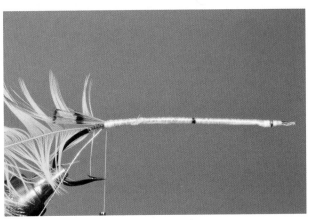

10 Secure the tip of the yellow hackle on the underside of the shank.

11 Dub the rear half of the body with the light orange seal's fur (Angora goat or any other good Euro-Seal are good substitutes).

12 Wrap the ribbing over the rear half of the body. By tradition the ribbing starts and ends underneath the hook and consists of five even wraps up to the end of the body section. Tie the ribbing off securely.

13 Fold and wrap the hackle snugly behind the ribbing. Tie off securely and trim the excess from both rib and hackle.

14 Attach the oval silver tinsel underneath the shank.

15 Attach the flat silver tinsel underneath the shank.

16 Attach the hackle by the tip underneath the shank. Advance the thread in even smooth wraps to the front end of the body mark.

17 Unless your hands are very clean with smooth fingers to handle the silk floss, you may want to use silk gloves to provide a clean smooth surface to handle the delicate floss. Attach a single strand of black silk floss. Stroke the floss a few times to straighten and even the fibers. Wrap a single smooth layer of the floss back to the midpoint of the body, then reverse direction, wrapping back up the shank to where the floss was tied in. Once there, tie off the end of the floss tightly. Trim the excess floss.

18 Wrap the flat silver rib forward in five even turns. Tie off on the bottom of the end of the body section.

19 Wrap the oval silver tinsel snugly behind the flat to the front of the body. Tie off underneath and trim the excess.

20 Fold the feather and wrap snugly behind the oval silver tinsel to the front of the body. Tie off securely and trim the excess.

21 Fold the hackle down along the sides to get all fibers lying at or below the hook to provide a clear area above the body to tie the wings in. Select a teal flank feather for the throat. Tie in, wrap four or five turns, tie off tightly, and trim the excess. Pull the fibers down the sides to collect into the lower part of the hook as the throat. Make a few wraps over fibers as needed to secure them in place.

22 Select two matching strips of white goose, swan, or turkey tail—both should be around half the hook gap (distance from the shank down to the point) in width. The tips should extend back to the end of the body and are tied in the "Dee" style—flat on top of the body and spreading slightly out to the sides. These are often easiest to tie in one side at a time. I'll often reverse the thread. Tie it off with a half hitch or two, then start wrapping backwards to tie in the far wing. Once tied in, tie off the thread and start wrapping again in the normal manner. Try a variety of techniques and see what works best for you. Once secured, trim off the excess closely.

23 View from above of the top of the completed wings. They swim well in the water and provide a good silhouette from below for the fish to see.

25 Form the head of the fly and tie the thread off by either using several half hitches or, my preferred method, whip finishing. Trim the thread, cement the head, and you are finished!

24 Select a matched pair of jungle cock neck feathers for the sides. Place back-to-back with the tips matched. Position so they will extend back to about the midpoint of the body and "droop" (angle downwards) underneath the hook at around a 30-degree angle. Trim off a few fibers on each side of the rachis to ensure they will lie flat when tied in on the side of the wing. Tie in tightly against the side of the hook, usually one at a time. Check for position—they should sit vertically and angle down correctly. Reposition and untie/retie as needed. Trim off the excess.

Substitute
Feathers

One of the biggest hurdles to overcome in starting to tie classic salmon flies is finding the right materials for the fly you wish to construct. Like when building fine homes or furniture, the end result depends on the quality of the materials you use. Poor-quality wood makes it nearly impossible to end up with a quality home or piece of furniture. Likewise in fly tying, poor materials—be it the wrong type, texture, size, or color—can't be overcome or fixed to get the correct result.

Many materials used in classic salmon flies are unique. Among the hardest to find are good, long-fibered wing or tail quills to make the "married" main wings used in many patterns. Luckily there are now great alternatives, and in some cases the substitutes are *better* than the originals, with more vivid markings and better fiber length allowing much larger flies to be made.

Resources for genuine and substitute classic salmon fly tying materials include:

AO Feathers, www.aofeathers.com
Castle Arms, www.castlearms.com
Deschutes Angler, www.deschutesangler.com
Featherfreak.com, www.featherfreak.com
FeathersMc, www.feathersmc.com
River City Fly Shop, www.rivercityflyshop.com
Waters West, www.waterswest.com

One of the best sources is Featherfreak.com, a unique sourcing network for legal, non-impactful exotic materials developed by Doug Millsap. If you really want to try tying a fly with genuine cotinga, cock of the rock, argus, or jungle cock, he may well have it. And even better, he bought the business Jens Pilgaard had developed catering to classic salmon fly tiers called Fugl & Fjer Fluebinding, which translates to "Bird & Feather Fly Tying." Jens developed unique techniques for dyeing turkey tails to match many exotic quills. Kori bustard and florican bustard were primary focuses, but they also included many unique and original color mixes. Doug has taken it to a new level with unique color combinations called Dragon Tail, Jurassic Tail, Majic Tail, and Phoenix Tail, among many others. You will also find a great selection of natural and dyed feathers of unusual birds, including dyed argus body feathers, and many more unique materials.

When thinking about substitutes, it is interesting to register that in the old days, gallina dyed blue was used as a jay substitute when longer fibers were required. Also cotinga, something that was never in great supply, was often replaced with kingfisher. Substitutes are a part of classic salmon fly tying, and with the constantly increasing price levels for rare materials, as well as a rapid decrease in availability, it is obvious that the next logical progression in classic fly tying is the development, discovery, and use of proper and credible substitutes.

There are two ways to substitute a feather. We can find natural feathers that are a close-enough match, or we can take a completely different material and process it to our need. When looking for a natural substitute, it is most responsible to obtain materials from birds that aren't on the endangered species list. A popular example is that dyed argus wing is often recommended as a golden pheasant tail substitute, but the argus is one of the rarest of species right now, while the golden pheasant is being bred by the thousands.

Robert Verkerk, founder of Classic Fly Tying Net (www.classicflytying.net), has compiled a list of materials on his website. He has included information about the materials and common or potential substitutes as far as they are known, along with pictures when available. He is continuously working on this list in the hope that someday it will be complete.

I would like to thank Robert for allowing me to combine substitute materials I have found with his wonderful list. Be sure to visit his site for more excellent content. Here is my list combined with his:

African Emerald Cuckoo

Java Green peacock body and flank feathers
White peacock back feathers dyed a brilliant green

African Gray Crowned Crane

Dun saddle hackle is a fair substitute for the gray neck hackles. For the crests, stripped cree or grizzly rooster neck hackles dyed tan, the darker the barring the better.

Argus Pheasant

Argus feathers are nearly impossible to substitute. The white spots on the black tail feathers are difficult to mimic.Closest thing is dyed black bustard substitute from Featherfreak.com. Color some spots with a red permanent marker.

Asian Kingfisher

Ringneck pheasant white neck feathers dyed bright electric blue
Electric blue hen neck hackle, larger with longer fibers

Banded Gymnogene

Also known as the African harrier hawk, the banded gymnogene has distinctive black-and-white-barred leg and breast feathers used for hackling and throats on classic salmon patterns. Mini grizzly marabou with vivid barring makes a good substitute for fishing use. Larger black francolin flank feathers can fill in on medium to smaller flies.

Banksian Red-Tailed Black Cockatoo

Both male and female red-tailed black cockatoos have tail feathers once used in classic patterns. A good substitute is Lady Amherst pheasant tail, died red/orange. Blend about 80 percent orange and 20 percent scarlet to get a Banksian shade. You can also add sections with yellow and orange. Another is white turkey tail died scarlet, black stripes added with a non-acid textile marker.

Barred Rail

In *The Salmon Fly*, George M. Kelson writes: "But, to my mind, the best black and white speckled hackle is taken from a Rail (*Hypotænidia torquata*), which is a native of the Philippine Islands." We use the double speckled feathers from the back of the gallina for this same purpose.

Kelson goes on to describe the pattern for the Green Queen. The throat calls for "Bittern dyed yellow—the white speckled feather." This is an error in the book, and Kelson intended for a rail feather, dyed yellow, to be used instead.

Bittern

Many variations, but basically all have the same patterns and coloration. Subsitutes include:
- Hen saddle mottled brown and tan
- Mottled hen pheasant flank and covert feathers

Blue Eared Pheasant

Considered a substitute for gray heron, it has some substitutes as well:
- Gray rooster neck, largest and webbiest hackles
- Gray marabou, sparse fibers with a thin stem (great for fishing use)
- "Burned" mini gray ostrich plumes; see the gray heron listing for the technique.

Bustard

There are many different bustard subspecies, and not a single one isn't protected. When a classic pattern calls for bustard, it always means the speckled feathers. "Dark" ideally means Indian black bustard or Ludwig's bustard. Any of the other dark species qualify too, or even dark-toned kori. "Light" means one of the lighter species: light Arabian bustard (some of it can be darker than kori), houbara bustard, or light-phase kori. Only use the barred European florican feathers if a pattern calls for English bustard, great bustard, or florican.

With the above in mind, let's divide this section into three groups: light, dark, and florican.

Light Bustard

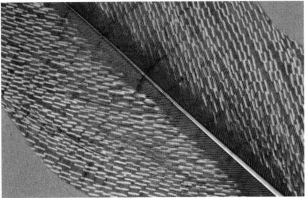

It is a common belief—or rather, an assumption—that the sand-colored Arabian bustard and houbara bustard feathers are the only appropriate "light bustard" feathers. People don't realize that kori is a "light" bustard species as well, especially the lighter-phase feathers. Arabian bustard has thus far failed to breed in farming programs, unlike kori, which is therefore readily and legally available.

Substitute feathers for light bustard:
- Dyed white turkey tail substitute from Featherfreak.com
- Light mottled turkey tail
- Peacock wing feathers
- Peahen saddle feathers

Dark Bustard

Florican (Great) Bustard

The only true "dark" bustard feathers come from the Ludwig's bustard and the Indian florican bustard. Both species are extremely rare.

Substitute feathers for dark bustard:

Dyed white turkey tail substitute from Featherfreak.com

Very mature male capercaillie center tail feathers are near black with near white speckles. They are almost identical to "dark bustard" and qualify as a perfect and unprotected substitute.

Argus pheasant tail feathers are black with white spots. A little rearranging of the fibers provides an excellent substitute, especially for fishing flies.

Kori feathers come in different shades of brown, lighter and darker. For flies that call for both light and dark bustard, a good solution is to combine different shades of kori feathers.

Also commonly referred to as European florican. In *The Salmon Fly*, George Kelson mentions that the feathers of the great bustard are inferior. However, the illustrations in the journal *Land and Water*, where there is reference to the florican, clearly show the barred European bird's feathers. The feathers description is "Florican, Light, and Dark Bustard," three different materials. T. E. Pryce-Tannatt was extremely fond of great bustard, and used it in most of his versions of classic patterns.

Substitute feathers for florican (great) bustard:

Dyed white turkey tail substitute from Featherfreak.com

Peacock wing quills with black markings similar to great bustard

Lady Amherst pheasant center or side tails dyed tan

Cinnamon turkey or capercaillie tails, bleached for a short time, then bleach applied in stripes

Cock of the Rock

Umbrella cockatoo body feathers have a very similar profile. The easiest way to make a realistic sub is to use hen hackles and blend hot orange and yellow until you have the desired nuance. Other substitutes are dyed CDC (cul de canard) or white guinea fowl body feathers, dyed hot orange.

Cotinga (Blue Chatterer)

Cotinga has a unique appearance and a tricky color to imitate. The combination of shape, size, texture, and color is one of a kind. For classic salmon flies, it is most often utilized in cheeks, so smaller feathers suffice. Some good substitutes include kingfisher neck, back, and rump feathers. Robert Verkerk has a tutorial for a realistic and easy substitute; go to www.classicflytying.net to see it. Other good substitutes are:

> Ringneck pheasant white neck feathers dyed
> > bright electric blue
> European starling undertail coverts dyed blue
> Turquoise tanager
> Spangled tanager
> Swallow-tailed tanager

Fairy Bluebird

Hen saddle dyed bright electric blue is a very close match, even for the lapwing. Several parrot species have wing and tail coverts that make a decent substitute. Rosella parrots have wing coverts that are close. These will work as cheeks on, for example, the Gitana.

Golden Bird of Paradise

The golden bird of paradise was called the black-faced golden bowerbird at the time when the bowerbird was still classified as a bird of paradise. Somewhere early in the 20th century, it was classified as an independent species. George M. Kelson describes these feathers in *The Salmon Fly*, and the Silver Ardea pattern calls for these feathers in the tail. However, Kelson had his species confused. When the remainder of his personal tying kit was discovered a few years back, it was in fact the flamed bowerbird that he had in stock. For the Silver Ardea, three of the orange feathers were used to create the tail.

The best way to substitute these is probably with an Am-gold topping.

Golden Eagle

For the eagle series, we need the marabou hackles from under the belly, between the legs. The larger feathers of the marabou turkey near the tail have similar fibers. The rachis is a little tougher to work with, but on the fly the difference is not noticeable.

Golden Pheasant

Sometimes it's tough to get feathers with long enough fibers and/or fibers that will marry well. Many are thin and don't have enough barbules. The golden pheasant tail dyed turkey substitute from Featherfreak.com will allow you to tie 8/0-plus-size hooks and marry very well.

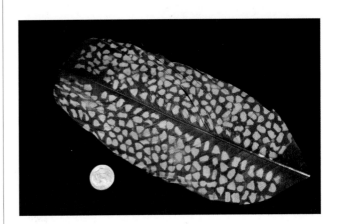

Gray Heron

> Blue eared pheasant rump feathers
> Rhea feather tips, natural and dyed
> Whiting Spey hackle; chicken feathers that
>   look like heron
> "Burned" mini ostrich for larger hooks

Here are the steps:

You need a feather with a thin rachis to be able to wrap after treating it, or you'll have to split it before being able to wrap without breaking.

In a well-ventilated room (the bathroom with the fan on is good) or outdoors, use a medium-size (8 by 13 inch or so) plastic container and pour in a mix of 50 percent liquid laundry bleach and 50 percent water.

Drop the feathers (I usually treat about six at a time) into this concoction and agitate them with a plastic fork or similar. This is to be sure all surfaces are saturated and an even reaction over all of the fibers will occur.

Watch as the barbules are literally burned off. Go a bit longer than you may think you need—be sure the barbs are bare to simulate the sleek heron feather.

When ready, pull the feathers out and rinse them *thoroughly* in warm water. Soak them in the sink and swish them around to ensure all signs of the bleach are rinsed off.

The bleach often discolors and stiffens the fibers and rachis. Restore the color to your liking. I use Rit dye often for this, as it is inexpensive and does a reasonable job. One trick is to use hot enough water—just at boiling. Add the dye, mix thoroughly, and then let sit and cool well. Then add white vinegar as an agent to help the dye "bite" into the fibers more aggressively.

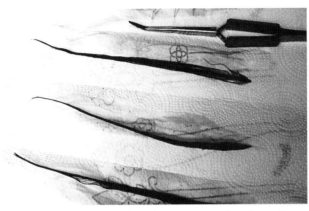

To revitalize the feathers' texture and soften them for use, soak overnight in a mix of 75 percent water and 25 percent glycerin. This will soften the stem and help prevent splitting when wrapping tightly around the hook.

The end result lends itself well to a large hook, 4/0 and up, and even long shanks, and gives a good impression of heron.

Gray Junglefowl (Jungle Cock)

Trimmed spotted guinea fowl feather with the tip spot colored golden orange is a good jungle cock substitute.

Greater Bird of Paradise

Use emu dyed a pale light yellow for the long, delicate, and beautiful flank display feathers.

Hoopoe

Specifically for the unique crest feathers on the head, substitute almond with black-tip ringneck pheasant body feathers burned to shape. Two well-soaked Popsicle sticks back-to-back with the feather between works well for a burner—for a while. These feathers give nearly the right size (a bit big) and shape.

Impeyan (Himalayan Monal) Pheasant

The Impeyan is successfully breeding in captivity, and these channels provide a legal supply of feathers on a regular basis. A substitute for the crest feathers, however, is a greenish-tint natural black rooster saddle or schlappen hackle. Strip the fibers on both sides of the stem up to the tip, then carefully trim the tip into an oval shape.

For the neck feathers, the center tails of the European magpie have a green/copper hue that is similar to that of the neck feathers of the Impeyan. With a custom wing burner or even a pair of scissors, the tip of each tail feather can be cut into the typical triangular shape of the Impeyan neck feathers that are used for the Bronze Pirate.

Jay, Eurasian or Blue

Guinea fowl dyed blue
Hen grizzly neck hackle dyed blue

Macaw, Blue-and-Gold

Single strands of yellow- and blue-dyed white
turkey tail married together
Hybrid macaw center tail

Macaw, Scarlet

White turkey tail dyed scarlet
Hybrid macaw center tail

Magnificent Riflebird

Green sunbird
Small dark green feathers from the throat of
the Impeyan pheasant

Malayan Crested Fireback Pheasant

A good substitute for the "fireback" feathers
is bright rusty-orange-dyed hen saddle. For the
crimson and blue body feathers, Swinhoe's pheasant flank feathers.

Nicobar Pigeon

Black East India duck
Green peacock shoulder feathers (thin and
narrow are best)

Ocellated Turkey

A light-colored, heavily speckled/mottled oak
turkey wing quill can be substituted for ocellated
turkey.

Palawan Peacock Pheasant

Hen neck and/or saddle dyed teal blue, tips
burned round or tapered
Impeyan greenish blue body feathers
Ringneck pheasant white neck feathers dyed a
rich teal greenish blue

Peacock

For the chocolate and tan mottled secondary
wings, use a very light speckled turkey tail dyed
tan. Excellent for large hooks.

Peacock Pheasants

So unique, they are tough to substitute.

Try my "feather sandwich" tool and substitute
technique for both peacock and western tragopan
pheasant feathers.

Caution: The following steps require the use of
hand and power tools, and all risk and liability is
with you, the reader. I provide the steps I used to
make the following tool—it is your responsibility
to exercise care and proper safety procedures if
you choose to follow these instructions. Neither
the author nor the publisher is to be held liable
for any accidents that occur during or after the
construction or use of the tool.

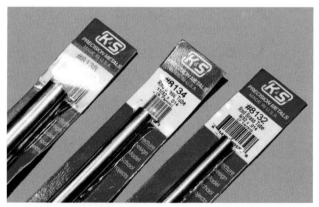

Go to a hobby store or online and get some thin-
wall brass tubing. This will become the tool to cut
the feathers with. Diameter varies—determine
what sizes you need to match the size of the peacock pheasant eye spot. I am using sizes from ¼
to ⅜ inch.

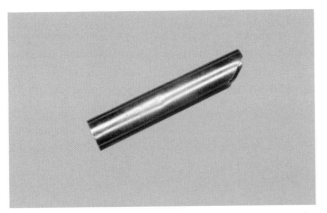

Cut a 3-inch or so piece of the brass tubing in the size you want to use for the eye spot. Wrap the piece with masking tape. Place securely in a ⅜-inch drill chuck and tighten snugly. Use the drill to spin the tubing and file or sand the edge down as fine and sharp as possible. You want to create a sharp cutting edge on both ends of the tubing. I started with a small file and finished with fine sandpaper. When one end is done, flip it over and repeat the process. When both ends are sharpened, use a fine-toothed hacksaw to cut a 45-degree angle from the outside edge of the tubing down to the center of one end. This will create a convex half-round to cut the end of the eye with. The other end will cut out a matching half-round opening in the hen back feather.

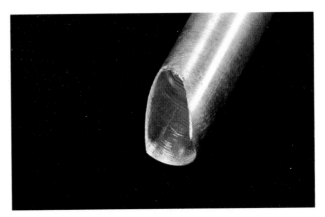

Close-up of sharpened half-round end

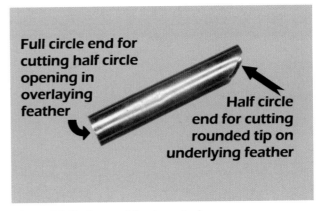

Full circle end for cutting half circle opening in overlaying feather

Half circle end for cutting rounded tip on underlying feather

View of fully formed tool ready for use

Close-up of sharpened fully round end

Use Whiting Brahma hen neck or back (or any light speckled/mottled hen hackle) for the main feather.

Use a natural black or dyed natural black schlappen or saddle hackle—you want a feather that is very webby to hold shape and to capture the richness of color in the peacock pheasant eye spot.

Select both feathers so they have a similar size at the tips and for good color.

Use the tool as follows:

1. Using the full round end of the tubing, cut out a half-circle from the tip of the hen back feather to look as shown here.

2. Use the half-round end of the tool to cut the tip of the underlying natural black schlappen feather to a matching round tip. Trim the fibers off the sides well down the feather so it will lie flat when tied in underneath the hen back feather.

3. Lay the hen back over the top of the schlappen, and you now have your substitute peacock pheasant feather.

Red Kite

The red kite is also known as the gled. Its cinnamon-colored center tail feather is the one traditionally used in flies. Red kite tail feathers are easily recognized due to the gray stripes. Yet, for the winging of classic Spey and Dee flies, sections without the gray were preferred.

Red slate turkey tail feathers make for a perfect, legal, and responsible substitute. Impeyan monal tail feathers are an exact match, but lack in fiber length.

Red-Ruffed Fruitcrow (Indian Crow)

Red-ruffed fruitcrow breast feathers are the prized feathers for classic flies, used for everything from tailing through butts, bodies, hackling, wings, veilings, sides, and cheeks. Traditionally, *Pyroderus scutatus granadensis* were the only feathers used. They have an obvious crimp at their tips, making them wave in a manner that was desirable to the tiers of old. The other four subspecies look similar, but all of them lack this crimp. *Granadensis* has a gorgeous orange color with bright red tips and an obvious crimp. This crimp is best visible from the side. The other subspecies vary a bit in color, depending on where the bird came from and what it was feeding on. Generally, *scutatus* and *orenosensis* are the closest match. *Masoni* and *occidentalis* have more of a brown hue instead of the orange.

Later, Hardy flies used red weaver as a substitute. It is a lovely, natural substitute, especially on flies that are smaller than 1/0. It has a similar translucence and a very bright orange to red color. In *Fly tying for Salmon* by Eric Taverner, the red-breasted thrush is recommended. I am not sure which bird this is, nor do I know what the feathers look like.

Substitutes for breast feathers from the red-ruffed fruitcrow (Indian crow):

Red weaver

White neck feathers from a ringneck pheasant dyed orange and tip-dyed red

Ringneck pheasant hen, buff-colored body feathers

Hen neck

Golden pheasant crest feathers from the side of the head/neck

Bleached and dyed coot

Temminck's or satyr tragopan neck feathers

Substitute nape feathers for the Black Prince:

Ringneck pheasant neck feathers dyed black

Black crow

Magpie

Upper breast feathers from the Impeyan pheasant

Hen saddle or neck dyed black

Resplendent Quetzal

Wing coverts from the resplendent quetzal make for the best "back-to-back" feathers, while the tail coverts from the golden-headed quetzal make for the best hackles.

Substitute suggestions include emu feathers, dyed emerald green and then cut into that typical quetzal covert shape. Java green peahen tails over dyed chartreuse green is a scintillating green quetzal sub. The fiber length is longer than the real thing, but when false-hackled at body joints (on flies like the Ondine), you can hardly tell the difference.

Satyr Tragopan Pheasant

The Temminck's tragopan has similar feathers, though not identical.

Scarlet Ibis

The applicable feathers from the scarlet ibis have a structure to them that is strongly reminiscent of swan. Good substitutes are:

Goose shoulder dyed scarlet

White turkey tail dyed scarlet

Scarlet macaw hybrid body and/or tail feathers

Swan

Goose shoulder can be substituted for swan.

Teal

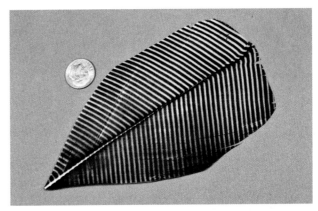

Teal flank dyed turkey tail from Featherfreak .com (marries better and is much longer than the original)

Prominently barred mallard flank

Pintail

Toucan

Some of the many species are the ariel toucan, channel-billed toucan, black-necked aracari, green aracari, sulfur-breasted toucan, toco toucan, common toucan, white-throated toucan, saffron toucan, chestnut eared aracari, and red-breasted toucan. The golden yellow breast feathers are the prize sought for classic flies as veilings, cheeks, and more.

Substitute for toucan include:
Swan neck feathers dyed golden yellow (by far the most realistic sub)
Flat golden pheasant crest found between crests and tippets
Dyed magpie
Yellow weaver
Yellow-breasted pigeon
Yellow oriole
Soft CDC (cul de canard) dyed pale golden yellow

Twelve-Wired Bird of Paradise

The neck feathers from the ocellated turkey have a similar green ruff, though the shape isn't a match. A possible substitute is golden or Lady Amherst pheasant tippets dyed black. They are darker on the tips but have a similar shape and are available in larger sizes.

Western Tragopan Pheasant

It is the spotted breast feathers that Traherne's Black Argus calls for. The yellow throat "crests" are used in the tail of the 2nd Ghost Fly. Substitutes include Temminck's tragopan spotted breast feathers, painted with black Pantone or textile markers or in the original brown-red color. Or try my "feather sandwich" substitute made from cut schlappen and hen saddle feathers.

Caution: The following steps require the use of hand and power tools, and all risk and liability is with you, the reader. I provide the steps I used to make the following tool—it is your responsibility to exercise care and proper safety procedures if you choose to follow these instructions. Neither the author nor the publisher is to be held liable for any accidents that occur during or after the construction or use of the tool.

Go to a hobby store or online and get some thin-wall brass tubing. This will become the tool to cut the feathers with. Diameter varies—determine what sizes you need to match the size of the spots for the feathers you are imitating. I am using sizes from ¼ to ⅜ inch.

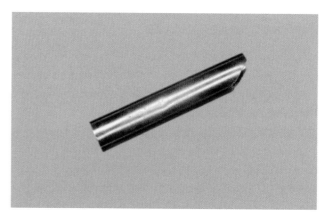

Cut a 3-inch or so piece of the brass tubing in the size you want to use for the eye spot. Wrap the piece with masking tape. Place securely in a ⅜-inch drill chuck and tighten snugly. Use the drill to spin the tubing and file or sand the edge down as fine and sharp as possible. You want to create a sharp cutting edge on both ends of the tubing. I started with a small file and finished with fine sandpaper. When one end is done, flip it over and repeat the process. When both ends are sharpened, use a fine-toothed hacksaw to cut a 45-degree angle from the outside edge of the tubing down to the center of one end. This will create a convex half-round to cut the end of the eye with. The other end will cut out a matching half-round opening in the hen back feather.

Close-up of sharpened fully round end

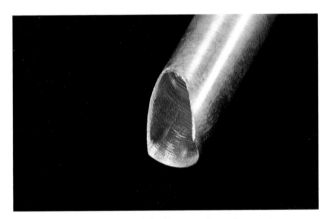

Close-up of sharpened half-round end

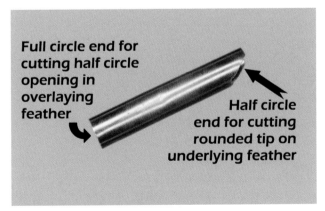

Full circle end for cutting half circle opening in overlaying feather

Half circle end for cutting rounded tip on underlying feather

View of fully formed tool ready for use

For a western tragopan pheasant substitute "feather sandwich" for the Black Argus fly, you need black-dyed schlappen feathers.

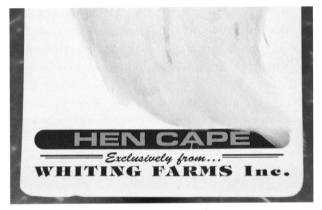

And a natural white hen neck—a full cape is best to have a good variety of feathers from both sides to choose from.

One side of the Black Argus fly's wing needs four schlappen and three white hen feathers. Select all feathers so they have a similar size at the tips and good color. Set aside one of the black schlappen feathers for the base feather.

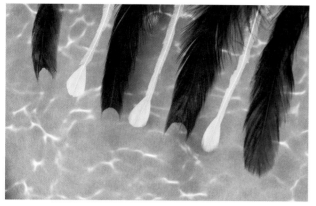

Use the tool as follows:
1. Using the full round end of the tubing, cut out a half-circle from the tip of the overlying black schlappen feather to look as shown here.
2. Use the half-round end of the tool to cut the tip of the underlying white hen feather to a matching round tip. Trim the fibers off the sides well down the feather so it will lie flat when tied in underneath the hen back feather.

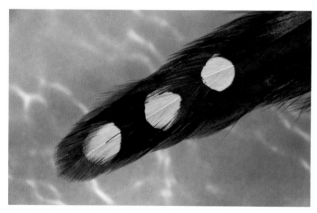

Lay the first hen back feather over the top of the uncut schlappen; then a cut schlappen over the hen feather, then another hen feather, another schlappen, the last hen feather, and the last schlappen. You now have your substitute wing for the Black Argus. Repeat the process for the other side.

The end result: a substitute wing set on top and genuine western tragopan feather wing on the Black Argus. This substitute wing is so cheap and easy to make that you can tie up a few to carry in your box and even throw one at a hungry salmon or steelhead once in a while!

Wood Duck

It is nearly impossible to find a substitute for the wood duck's black-barred flank feathers, but fortunately the real material is readily available. One possible sub is a well marked mallard flank colored on the tip with a black permanent marker in a wide bar across the width.

Many other birds and feathers are used in classic salmon and other flies. If you get stuck, let us know and we'll try to help. Reach Robert Verkerk at www.classicflytying.net, which has a link to his Facebook page. Reach me at info@modernclassicsflytying.com.

About the Photography

Photographing the birds, feathers, and flies for this book was both a challenge and a treat. Let's start out with the fact that I am not a professional photographer. I enjoy photography and have learned quite a bit from others and plain old trial and error—just like tying flies. That said, I am glad to share what I've found and the setups used in case you'd like to try your hand at it as well.

Here is what I used for the photos in the book:
  Camera: Nikon D5200 DSLR
  Lens: Tamron AF18-270mm f/3.5-6.3 Di II VC PZD AF lens for Nikon
  Filter: Circular polarizer
  Lighting: Daylight temperature (4600K) LED lights

Additional items:
  Extension tubes
  32GB SDHC memory card
  Cable shutter release
  Tripod
  Kodak 18% grayscale white balance card

Setup is pretty straightforward. Two lights at about a 45-degree angle on both sides of the vise and hook. The camera is set up on the tripod with the cable shutter release. A background (I used light blue poster board) is suspended/supported a good distance; I had it about 3 feet behind the subject. You need a light on the background or it is too dark, overexposing the subject. With a light on the background, exposure is even and you also avoid harsh contrast between it and the subject.

It took quite a bit of experimentation with both camera setup and lighting to find a combination to get the results I hoped for. I was on a fairly tight budget—so going out and just buying the best Nikon macro lenses at $2,000-plus each wasn't an option.

I first tried the inexpensive screw-on close-up filters you can get. Results were fair at best, as they had a lot of distortion as you moved out of the

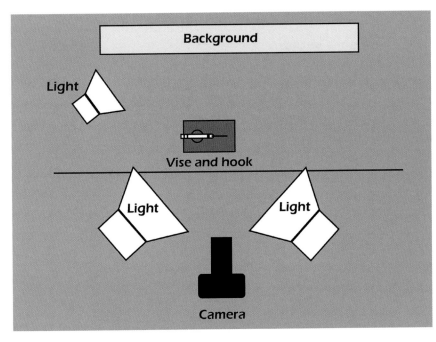

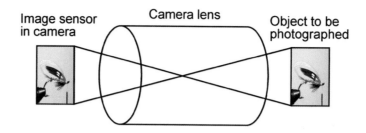

Image sensor in camera
Camera lens
Object to be photographed

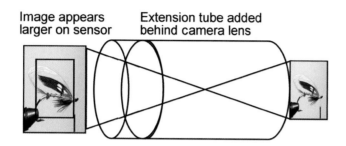

Image appears larger on sensor
Extension tube added behind camera lens

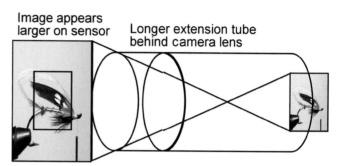

Image appears larger on sensor
Longer extension tube behind camera lens

center toward the edges. Perhaps acceptable if I cropped it about 50 percent, but not a process I wanted to spend time having to go through for hundreds of photos. As the old saying goes, you get what you pay for.

I found the solution when I started looking at what others have used over the years: extension tubes. They were the answer to getting sharp, full-image-clarity close-ups of the feathers and flies without any distortion. Simple to use and they got the results I was after. You insert an extension tube between the camera body and your lens. This moves the image away from the sensor, resulting in a magnified portion of the center of the normal image hitting the sensor.

Here's how they work:

For rich color saturation and to reduce glare, I always use a circular polarizer filter. Rotate it to cut glare and achieve vivid colors. Also doubles as a good lens protector.

To get good depth of field and detail, I set the ISO to 100 and the aperture (f stop) to f32 or as small as possible. This combination achieves the best quality but requires long exposures from 2 to 15 seconds. For this, the camera must be mounted on a solid tripod and a cable shutter release used. Even with a cable release, you must stay perfectly still after releasing the shutter—any movement or vibration can cause a blurry image with those long exposures.

Light is always important. I used several light sources, primarily two LED light fixtures. LED bulbs produce bright, cool, nearly daylight-color white light and are a great innovation. Always measure the light temperature to get "white" whites. I used an 18% gray card and measured the white balance frequently as I took images throughout the day. The camera has an option to set the white balance to preset levels, but I find these never work as well as when I measure the light temperature through the lens. Study your camera's user's guide and learn how to use this option—it will save hours trying to correct things after the shot is done.

For personal use, even the simplest camera can get good results. Get a small tabletop tripod and use the camera's timer to release the shutter without having to touch the camera. Learn the camera's settings, and set the white balance and force the lowest ISO and aperture setting in a manual mode. Some cell phones now have amazing quality and get great images. Give them a try!

Organizations to Support

There are lots of organizations that you can join to support the birds and fish we enjoy and appreciate. Pick your favorite and give when and what you can to help. Here are some of my personal favorites to help support the amazing birds and the fish we chase with the flies we make not only to survive but also thrive in today's world.

Audubon Society of Portland

Founded in 1903, the Audubon Society of Portland was one of the first in the nation and has been a steward of nature protection and appreciation for more than a century. Audubon Society of Portland is devoted to the conservation of Oregon's last remaining wild places and the birds and animals that call them home.

I've been fortunate in that I live close by, so I have visited the Care Center and have been able to photograph some of the birds they have helped to rehabilitate and sometimes release back into the wild. Those that can't be released have a safe home and provide a rare close-up glimpse of their beauty and why they are so special. The web address is http://audubonportland.org.

Kori Bustard Program (Kori SSP)

Kori bustards are large, strictly terrestrial birds. They are birds of wide, open grasslands and lightly wooded savannah. The distribution of the kori is becoming fragmented, and overall, the species is declining in numbers. Local extinctions have been recorded. Given the continual habitat destruction from agriculture and development, hunting pressure, and a slow reproduction rate, kori bustards do not face a promising future in the wild. Zoos are now breeding kori bustards and studying them to learn more about how to save them in the wild.

A favorite feather of classic salmon fly tiers, kori bustard has a beautiful, finely speckled and striped brown-and-tan pattern. The flight feathers are large, and feather sections are used alone or often as part of a married wing.

Donate directly to the Kori SSP (Species Survival Plan) at Zoo Atlanta by using the PayPal option on their website. You can make a one-time or monthly donation—it is entirely up to you. Just know it is going to a good cause. The web address is www.koribustardssp.org.

Native Fish Society

Just as the wild birds we admire are in need, so are the wild fish we go in search of with our fancy fur-and-feather-adorned flies. The Native Fish Society's mission statement is simple and powerful: "Guided by the best available science, Native Fish Society advocates for the recovery of wild, native fish and promotes the stewardship of the habitats that sustain them."

Please join the Native Fish Society today and help restore, maintain, and grow wild fish populations. Their web address is http://nativefishsociety.org.

Recommended Reading and Viewing

Delacour, J. *The Pheasants of the World*. 2nd ed. Hindhead, UK: World Pheasant Association and Spur Publications, 1977.

Game Birds & Water Fowl. www.gbwf.org.

Howman, K. *Pheasants of the World: Their Breeding and Management*. Surrey, BC: Hancock House Publishers, 1991.

Johnsgard, P. A. *The Pheasants of the World: Biology and Natural History*. 2nd ed. Washington, DC: Smithsonian Press, 1999.

Kelson, George M. *The Salmon Fly*. London: Wyman & Sons, 1895.

Madge, S., and P. McGowan. *Pheasants, Partridges, and Grouse*. Princeton, NJ: Princeton University Press, 2002.

Robson, C. *Birds of Thailand*. Princeton, NJ: Princeton University Press, 2002.

Taverner, Eric. *Fly Tying for Salmon*. London: Seeley Service London, 1942.

Wayne, P. *A Guide to the Pheasants of the World*. Butter Market, Ipswich, UK: W. S. Cowell, 1969.

Wikipedia. www.en.wikipedia.org.

I recommend the following books and DVDs from Stackpole to learn basic to advanced techniques for tying flies of all types, but especially the classic salmon fly. They cover in detail the many steps involved and also are a great resource for pattern listings and tips and tricks that everyone can use to improve their fly-tying techniques.

Nolte, Marvin. *Basic Fly Tying DVD: All the Skills and Tools You Need to Get Started* (photographs by Michael D. Radencich). Mechanicsburg, PA: Stackpole Books, 2002.

Radencich, Michael D. *Classic Salmon Fly Materials: The Reference to All Materials Used in Constructing Classic Salmon Flies from Start to Finish*. Mechanicsburg, PA: Stackpole Books, 2006.

———. *Classic Salmon Fly Patterns: Over 1,700 Patterns from the Golden Age of Tying*. Mechanicsburg, PA: Stackpole Books, 2012.

———. *Twenty Salmon Flies: Tying Techniques for Mastering the Classic Patterns*. Mechanicsburg, PA: Stackpole Books, 2009.

———. *Tying the Classic Salmon Fly—DVD*. Mechanicsburg, PA: Stackpole Books, 2009.

———, ed. *Tying the Classic Salmon Fly: A Modern Approach to Traditional Techniques*. Mechanicsburg, PA: Stackpole Books, 1997.

Rounds, Jon, ed. *Basic Fly Tying: All the Skills and Tools You Need to Get Started* (contributions by Wayne Luallen; photographs by Michael D. Radencich; illustrated by John McKim). Mechanicsburg, PA: Stackpole Books, 2002.

Veverka, Bob. *Spey Flies & How to Tie Them*. Mechanicsburg, PA: Stackpole Books, 2015.

Index